The Young Actor's Book of Improvisation

DRAMATIC SITUATIONS FROM
SHAKESPEARE TO SPIELBERG

AGES 12–16

Sandra Caruso

with

Susan Kosoff

HEINEMANN
Portsmouth, NH

Heinemann
A division of Reed Elsevier Inc.
361 Hanover Street
Portsmouth, NH 03801-3912
Offices and agents throughout the world

Several of Lowell Swortzell's plays are the basis of improvisations in this book.

Library of Congress Cataloging-in-Publication Data
Caruso, Sandra.
 The young actor's book of improvisation : Dramatic situations from Shakespeare to Spielberg, plays, and films : ages 12–16 / Sandra Caruso with Susan Kosoff.
  p. cm.
 Includes bibliographical references and index.
 Summary: A sourcebook of techniques designed to develop improvisational skills in young actors.
 ISBN 0-325-00049-2 (alk. paper)
 1. Improvisation (Acting)–Juvenile literature. [1. Plays–Improvisation. 2. Acting–Technique.] I. Kosoff, Susan, 1943– .
 II. Title.
PN2071.I5C273   1998
792'.028–dc21   97–
46817

                                                           CIP
                                                           AC

Editor: Lisa A. Barnett
Cover design: Barbara Werden
Manufacturing: Courtney Ordway

Printed in the United States of America on acid-free paper
02 01 00 99 98   DA   1 2 3 4 5 6 7 8 9

Improvisation vanishes, which makes it unique—
a kiss, a sunset, a dance, a joke—
none will ever return in quite the same way.
Each happens only once in the history of the universe.
                                        Stephen Nachmanovitch

To my sweet husband, Dee Caruso
My dear parents, Tom and Helen Maley
My wonderfully bizarre brother, Tim, his wife, Eileen,
    and my special niece, Chloe
My sister-in-law, Dorothy James
and all my dogs, past and present

                                        Sandra Caruso

To my Eliot Street family
Amanda, Andi, Sue
and—of course—Emily, who is love
                            Susan Kosoff

CONTENTS

Foreword by Lowell Swortzell   vii
Acknowledgments   xi
Introduction   xiii
A User's Guide   xix

1. Climactic Moment/Discovery   1
2. Confrontation/Conflict   43
3. Fantasy   71
4. Relationship   81
5. Solo Moment   123
6. Special Problems: Physical/Psychological   159
7. Subtext   183
8. Unusual Circumstances   209

Bibliography   231
Index   251

FOREWORD

THE MANY MEANINGS OF IMPROVISATION

Remember that moment in *Alice's Adventures in Wonderland* when the March Hare admonishes Alice to say what she means? "I do," she hastily replies, but, after pausing, adds, "at least I mean what I say—that's the same thing, you know" (Carroll 1965, 68–69).

But is it? The Mad Hatter doesn't seem to think so: "Not the same thing a bit. Why, you might just as well say that 'I see what I eat' is the same thing as 'I eat what I see'" (Carroll 1965, 174). And he does have a point, doesn't he? Words can mean many things, and we may mean many different things even as we speak them. But we can't be like Humpty Dumpty, who scornfully tells Alice that when he uses a word it means exactly what he chooses it to mean, neither more nor less. Well, we all know what happened to him!

Actors, perhaps better than anyone else, recognize the importance of knowing the meanings of words. They first must find the significance of every line of dialogue and then determine how to make that meaning clear in the ways they speak, move, and gesture. Often they go well beyond this stage to *become* the meaning, as they actually display a sense of fear, hope, or whatever emotional state they may be playing. Pinocchio, after his long and sometimes painful discovery of the meaning of truth, eventually becomes a real boy, the personification of honesty and the very meaning of his character.

Improvisation is an actor's most effective tool for discovering the exact meanings of their character's words and behavior. It allows actors to respond in as many different actions as they need to find the one that seems to them the most correct for the moment, for the scene, and for the play. And no matter how experienced they may be or how many awards they may have won, most performers depend on improvisation to develop each new role and each new situation they play on stage or on film. It is at the heart of their craft and essential to yours as well, whether you are taking acting classes, preparing to appear in a play, or just reading a script at home for the fun of it.

But what is it, exactly? The word *improvisation* contains different meanings and offers several possible challenges to readers of this book. One definition, according to my dictionary, is the "invention" or "composition" of something from available materials; in other words, it means to make something out of the things around us. In the case of acting, this "something" is a character made from two kinds of available materials: a story or situation (the script or idea) and ourselves (the performers). The challenge for actors is to bring these two together and make them one. And that, as you are about to discover in the many opportunities that await you here, is what you do when you follow the process of response and reaction that is the essence of improvisation.

My dictionary goes on to say that *improvisation* also may mean "to foresee" or "to provide." To be sure, when we improvise we are doing both of these at the same time: we are foreseeing a conclusion for the scene by responding to some basic questions. What are the situations in which the characters find themselves? What can they do to work their way out of or through these circumstances? How can they gain what they want in life? Or from each other? What will happen if they do? What will happen if they don't? By reacting to these questions, we discover the motivation of our characters and the behavior that defines their identity; this exploration through action provides the meaning of what they say and do.

Another dictionary agrees that *improvisation* signifies to utter or to perform *extempore*, impromptu, or on the spur of the moment. This definition includes a valuable phrase we should keep in mind as we use this book. When we improvise, it says, we "provide for the occasion." I can't think of a better motto for a class or workshop in improvisation, because that is exactly what we do each time we perform. Through our actions we provide the occasion by defining it, by making it happen, and by seeming to experience it. Once our character speaks with our voice, moves with our movement, and takes on aspects of our personality, it and the occasion begin to merge and to belong to us.

Another definition says that *improvisation* also means to recite or to make something offhand or to perform spontaneously. But beware, for then the dictionary adds two words that are dangerous to actors: *without preparation*. This thought makes me madder than the Mad Hatter, for I firmly believe that this is not the same thing, not a bit! In improvisation there *must be* preparation! However quick and spontaneous actors may seem to be, their words and actions come from their knowledge of situations and from their intuition to pursue appropriate directions in developing them. Preparation for improvisation is *exactly* what this book is all about, offering the background information and basic ingredients you need to act out the lives of your characters. Read each selection carefully and you will be prepared to respond—ready to improvise!

One also can see the word *improve* lurking inside the word *improvise,* and that is yet another challenge lurking inside the pages of this book. It gives us the opportunity to take these characters and stories and find solutions that in some cases may be quite different from those in the original sources. Part of the fun in improvising a scene is going back to see the actual outcomes in the plays, novels, and films from which they are taken. Comparing our solution with those of others can be enlightening, especially when they prove to be quite different. And it's always a nice feeling when we think our personal solution improves on the original, as sometimes happens.

By improvising, you may seize the exciting situations and dynamic characters you meet here and go anywhere you want with them, make them say and do what you think they should, and have them become your friends or, better still, part of yourself.

Yes, these are a lot of meanings for one little word to contain, I agree. But be prepared to detect many more as you proceed through these pages. For improvisation, by its very nature, keeps acquiring new life and finding new meanings to stimulate our imaginations and to energize our creative reflexes. It's a word so alive that it refuses to stand still or to stay quiet for very long, and it's waiting here for you to tell it what to do next!

So put it to work now and discover where improvisation can take you and where your responses can deliver it. You soon will recognize that you are acting better, and with deeper meaning, than ever before.

Happy improvising!

LOWELL SWORTZELL
New York University

ACKNOWLEDGMENTS

My thanks to all my acting teachers—Sanford Meisner, Lee Strasberg, Uta Hagen, Charles Conrad, Jeff Corey, Estelle Harman, Howard Storm, Charles Nelson Reily, Michael Shurtleff, and Milton Katselas—as well as to my inspiring colleagues and students in the School of Theater, Film and Television at UCLA. For suggesting material, special thanks to Deirdre Grace Callanan, high school English teacher; Christine Coker, UCLA student; Orlin Corey, Anchorage Press; Maggie Nolan Donovan, teacher; Ursula Ferro, Child Development Consultant; Hanay Geiogamah, faculty, Playwriting and Native American Studies, School of Theater, Film and Television, UCLA; Krista Harrison, high school student; Pat Harter, professor, School of Theater, Film and Television, UCLA; Ina Levin, Editorial Project Manager, Teacher Creative Materials; Michael Levin, high school English teacher; Dr. Susan Popkin Mach, Adolescent and Young Adult Literature, UCLA; Helen Maley, Associate Professor, Early Childhood Education, Wheelock College; Gay Nelson, Children's Librarian, West Tisbury Library, Martha's Vineyard, Massachusetts; Beverly Robinson, professor, School of Theater, Film and Television, UCLA; Lowell Swortzell, professor, Educational Theater, New York University; Edit Villarreal, Vice Chair, School of Theater, Film and Television, UCLA, faculty, playwriting and Chicano studies; Laura Wessel, Anchorage Press. Thanks to Cella, Florence Street Elementary School, and Peter Lecouras, Fremont High School in Los Angeles, for allowing me to test some of the improvisations in their classrooms. Thanks to Adam de la Pena for assistance in film research on the web.

SANDRA CARUSO

Thank you to Betty Bobp, who urged me, in her inimitable fashion, to work with Sandra Caruso on this book, and to Sandra for her gracious invitation to join her on the project. Heartfelt thanks to Marjorie and Harald Bakken, Martha Bakken, Debbie Grozen Bieri, Maggie and Edward

Donovan, Kay Arden Elliott, Priscilla Fales and Liz Moore, Laura and Michael Garand, Jesse and Bee, Jeffrey Kosoff, Melissa and Alan Miller, Barbara Phillips, Hanna Schneider, Betsy and Ray Schoen, Jane Staab, and the Wheelock Family Theatre for helping me get from there to here, and to Becky Thompson, my north star in the journey.

SUSAN KOSOFF

We extend our sincere gratitude to Vicky Bijur, our literary agent; Kay Arden Elliott, our editorial coordinator and researcher; and Arthur Leigh, our editor.

INTRODUCTION

Improvisation is at the heart of human experience. It is the wellspring of many forms of artistic expression. Creative work, by definition, demands the invention of multiple solutions to problems with whatever resources are available. The creative process is inherently spiritual, it is "about us, about the deep self, the composer in all of us, about originality, meaning not that which is all new, but that which is fully and originally ourselves" (Nachmanovitch 1990).

Improvisation in theater, as in no other artistic endeavor except jazz, has particular purposes, distinctive functions. It serves as a tool and as a technique, as an approach to performance and production as well as a stand-alone theatrical genre. Improvisation can be traced historically from the earliest dramatic rituals to the initial telling of *The Odyssey,* on to sixteenth-century Commedia dell'Arte troupes (which used familiar plots and stock characters), through to stand-up comics and nightclub performers (who use situations and characters to entertain an audience—something with which users of this book need not concern themselves), Chicago's Second City, Broadway's *Godspell,* Joseph Chaikin's Open Theatre, and the Group Theatre of the 1930s (which arrived at performance scripts through improvisation), and to the mid-1990s' Blue Man Group.

Despite the widespread use of improvisation, it was not until the publication of Caruso and Clemens' *The Actor's Book of Improvisation: Dramatic Situations for the Teacher and Actor* (1992) that there was a single, comprehensive source of material on which to base improvisations. That book, a thoughtfully crafted response to a long-standing need experienced by acting teachers and students in professional training and higher education arenas, is the template for *The Young Actor's Book of Improvisation.*

As its title suggests, this book is intended to respond to the same need for a single sourcebook, this time for students between the ages of twelve and sixteen, and for the teachers who work with them. In the author's notes for her play, *In a Room Somewhere,* playwright Suzan Zeder writes, "This play is aimed at the child within the adult and the adult within the child who exists in all of us" (Zeder 1988, vii). In that sense, this book is intended both for young people and adults. In formal, full-fledged productions, whenever possible, it is best to cast children as children and adults as adults. Author Sandra Caruso directed a most successful production of *The Prime of Miss Jean Brodie,* in which the roles of the faculty in the play were performed by school faculty, while the roles of the students were performed by student actors.

Many of the situations in this book are from plays successfully mounted, with casts of multiracial, multiethnic, able-bodied and physically challenged young people and adults at Boston's Wheelock Family Theatre, of which author Susan Kosoff is a founder and the producer. Wheelock enjoys a national reputation as a venue that produces multicultural and intergenerational theater. At Wheelock, the title role in *Charlotte's Web* was played by an African American woman, while Wilbur was played by an Asian man; a Latina woman played the title role in *Peter Pan;* an Asian girl played Dorothy in *The Wizard of Oz;* and a Latino man played Sammy in *The Dark at the Top of the Stairs.* This casting practice is based on the premise that, in order for theater to be relevant today, casts should reflect the diversity represented in the larger society. Equally significant is the way in which the understanding of a character, even the interpretation of a play, is enhanced, for actors and audience members alike, by challenging the traditional approach to casting.

Some of the situations in this book are included precisely because the characters are strictly defined by their race, age, sex, culture, or class. This allows actors to explore and to play characters who are like and different from themselves. For example, *Escape From Slavery: The Autobiography of Frederick Douglass,* provides several solo moments, because they allow all students, regardless of their race, the opportunity to experience the realities of a young boy's life as a slave. By contrast, some of the situations, such as *Swimmy* or *The Wind in the Willows,* are included because they are *not* specific about race, age, sex, culture, or class, thereby allowing students and teachers the opportunity to experience and appreciate the difference that casting choices can have on plays and players.

The Young Actor's Book of Improvisation addresses a broad age range of young people, from childhood to mid-adolescence. Many creative drama books are directed toward elementary-school-aged children. The difference in the intended audience reflects an inherent difference in purpose. In conventional informal drama, creative drama, and theater games, there is a strong emphasis on the creative process, with an explicit commitment to play for play's sake. The technique used in this book makes rigorous demands on students by structuring situations that require that they work in greater depth than is usually required by theater games. Although the focus remains on the actors' development as opposed to audience response, the technique helps young people make the transition to the serious study of acting.

Young people—those who have completed several sessions of creative drama or, depending on their ages, have taken a few classes in the basic techniques of acting, as well as those who have begun scene-study work or performed in full productions—need the process outlined here to further their growth, for it is a developmentally appropriate next step. Improvisation is presented as a disciplined method for learning the craft of acting, as opposed to a laissez-faire activity.

Improvisation, as an acting technique, refers to the method actors use to create their own dialogue and actions in imaginary circumstances. These imaginary circumstances may be created by the actors themselves or may be provided by an acting coach or director. Using this technique, an actor surrenders to the excitement of not knowing what is coming next. One may know what *might* happen, but no one knows what *will* happen. Improvisation pushes people to become comfortable with surprise (Nachmanovitch 1990).

Many drama teachers, as well as theater directors, use improvisation as a tool to help actors make situations more immediate and more real for themselves. Sandra Caruso uses background improvisations extensively in her acting classes at UCLA to help students fill in their characters' lives. For example, if a scene is about a spouse asking for a divorce, students improvise the couple's first meeting, the marriage proposal, the birth of their first child, and the incidents that led to the failure of the marriage. Theater directors also use improvisation when actors, who have been rehearsing or performing a play for a long period, get stale and stop listening to each other. Improvisation can force them to listen again; they do not know what is coming next.

As Stephen Nachmanovitch noted in *Free Play:* "Martha Graham described this as 'a vitality, a life force, an energy, a quickening that is translated through you into action, and because there is only one of you . . . this expression is unique. And if you block it, it will never exist through any other medium and will be lost'" (1990, 25).

We have given structure to these improvisations, because, as Nachmanovitch says, "structure ignites spontaneity" (1990). We have provided some form to keep the improvisations from wandering off course. Picasso confined his palette, in his "blue period," to the color blue, and this opened a whole new vista for him. Actors will ultimately be working in a tight structure dictated by lines, blocking, objects, sets, lights, and a director. These improvisations provide some boundaries in terms of the characters, place, background information, and situation.

Within this external structure, the actors can play. Since everything is held together by structure, the imagination is free.

Successful exploration demands that there be some concrete element to focus and clarify what the actor is doing. Strasberg pointed out that,

> When you tell a pianist, "Improvise," he immediately asks, "What do you want me to improvise on?" He knows so many things he can do that he finds it difficult to limit himself to one thing. When you say, "Chopin," he then takes a phrase from Chopin and improvises. Improvisation is very difficult to do without a theme. There must be something given as a problem. (Strasberg 1965, 277)

Improvisation is used to achieve a deeper understanding of physical actions and conflict. Actors are active, not passive; they move from the external to the internal, from the physical—how characters reveal themselves through body movement and vocal expression—to the psychological—why characters behave as they do. Improvising the material before approaching the text motivates students to investigate the original source upon which the improvisation is based. Even reluctant readers will want to read the original source material, because they already have some familiarity with it or have the impetus to learn about it. On the other hand, improvising the material *after* approaching the text can enrich students' understanding.

Improvisation, as suggested for use here, is rooted in the method of "active analysis" developed by Stanislavski late in his life and still in use in Moscow's theater training studios. When the actors are rehearsing a play, they begin acting even before they know the words of the script. They are able to get to the heart of their work by using an improvisational approach. This approach is the cornerstone of this book.

James Thomas brings attention to Michael Chekhov's phrase, "the psychology of the improvising actor," as an apt description of the need for characters to come naturally from within. Chekhov believes that improvisation helps actors begin to think, feel, and even speak like their characters before they fully understand a text intellectually. As long as the process is not forced and is trusted to work, the right combination of actor and character eventually emerges. The actors need the words of the text and want to use them.

> Expressing the play in their own words, finding the essence of the play through physical action, developing the logic of the play to its correct conclusion—seems to make the play arrive out of the imaginations of the actors themselves and not from memorization and repetition of the lines. The actors reach the

kind of deep understanding of the text, improvisationally, that is often unsuccessfully tried in standard rehearsals using intellectual analysis alone. This is what Stanislavski meant when he said that characterization should emerge unconsciously from the actors. (Thomas 1993)

Young people are as open and able to work in this manner as are adult actors.

This book provides a bridge from informal drama and theater games to formal drama using established text. Working with the structured improvisations found here will allow young people to approach an actual working text with increasing insight and sensitivity. When actors—of any age—are asked to create their own situations for improvisation, there is a tendency for the themes that are generated to be repeated with great regularity. By providing situations that are not defined by or limited to actors' personal experiences, they are challenged to expand the limits of their imagination; indeed, they come to understand that they can play any character in any situation.

These improvisations are divided into chapters by specific categories. Each category consists of a group of situations that allow particular acting problems to be addressed. This format is, to a large extent, a matter of organizational convenience; the categories are somewhat arbitrary. All of the situations in the book can be used to work on a number of acting problems outside of the specific category to which they have been assigned. Furthermore, some elements of drama, such as relationships and subtext, are present in all situations, regardless of the designation assigned.

Many of the situations in *The Young Actor's Book of Improvisation* have been field-tested with young people between the ages of twelve and sixteen in regular and special education classrooms in school and theater settings, in order to identify weaknesses or problems in the material. The data gathered as a result of this research have been analyzed and included as comments, which accompany each improvisation. These comments are meant as guidelines for use by student and teacher. The intent is to enlarge what can happen in a scene rather than to limit or predetermine the outcome. For instance, young actors may laugh during situations that make them emotionally uncomfortable. Nervous laughter is not unusual when people hear shocking news, such as the death of a loved one. Let the laughter play itself out, as long as it is the truth of the moment. If the students are not ready to deal with the situation, let it go; they still will have had an acting experience. Further, the actors might imagine or remember a pet animal that has died, to make treading this territory feel less threatening.

Sometimes, the outcome of an improvisation will run contrary to the original source material. It is important to remember that even though the source for a given situation is either tragic or comic, the resulting improvisation does not need to fall into that category. The same scene can be acted successfully from different perspectives. In fact, it is an instructive and sometimes provocative process to approach the same material from different standpoints. It is in this same spirit that time periods, as well as the sex, age, race, culture, or class of a character, can be changed to add different dimensions to the scene, to inject humor, or to reflect reality.

The purpose of the background information provided for each improvisation is to increase the actors' understanding of the characters they are playing. It is not meant as exposition for the actors. Too much explanatory dialogue is deadly; it dissipates any real tension or excitement in a scene, causing the improvisation to seem artificial and lifeless. Teachers must help students guard against their inclination to talk too much, to explain too much, to "tell the story." When teachers find specific background information crucial to an understanding of a particular scene, it is best to give the information to the actors at the beginning of the improvisation.

The notion that "less is more" is often critical in acting. To illustrate this point, Caruso uses the example of an actor, playing a mother, who says to her daughter, "Your father and I have been divorced for twelve years and are planning a reunion." Logically, the daughter would know how long her parents have been divorced: the mother would not have to give her daughter this information. As a sign in Sanford Meisner's office read, "An ounce of behavior is worth a pound of words."

Finally, the effective use of this book requires that every situation be treated with respect by actor and coach. Students need to internalize and personalize the information provided. Teachers need to trust that it has been assimilated. Both must be willing to let the improvisation happen and to believe that the characters will develop in an organic process. Neither teacher nor student should assume the role of director but, rather, should allow the acting to be spontaneous, so that the process will lead to interesting terrains in sometimes unexpected territories.

It is our hope that *The Young Actor's Book of Improvisation* will challenge students and teachers to take risks, to try new ways of being and acting that will lead to an ever-increasing understanding of themselves and others, as well as of the world in which they live.

A User's Guide

Source: The original source—novel, short story, film, poem, play—from which the situation is taken. ("Film by" signifies that the film was directed and written by the same person.) There are many sources that have multiple situations. These situations are numbered chronologically in the index by source title.

Characters: The number and gender of the characters, their names, their relationship to each other, and miscellaneous identifying information. In many improvisations, the gender of the characters is not necessarily germane to the exercise; an improvisation for two males may, in some cases, be done by two females. (Occasionally, when a character's name is not considered intrinsic to the exercise, it is not given.)

Place: The specific locale in which the situation occurs. If relevant, the time period in which the scene takes place is also given.

Background: Story information necessary for the actors' understanding of their characters and the situation, leading to the point at which the improvisation is to begin. In some instances, there will be more than one improvisation from the same source, but they will be placed in different chapters. All such scenes are listed in the index. For further background information, actors are encouraged to read all improvisations from the same source.

Situation: Details of the specific situation on which the improvisation is based. This is where it all comes together.

Comments: Notes and tips to the actors and teachers—helpful hints, as well as warnings of possible pitfalls inherent in the material. This section often contains supplemental background information that may further enhance the actors' understanding of story and character.

Situations within chapters are organized alphabetically. A list at the start of each chapter classifies the situations according to number and gender in the following manner:

one male, one female

two females

two males

ensemble (any situation with more than two characters)

A number of the improvisations in this book have been supplied by students from Sandra Caruso's acting classes at the UCLA School of Theater, Film and Television. Teachers are encouraged to have their students write their own improvisations. In addition, for a complete listing of the sources used in the text, readers may refer to the bibliography at the back of this book.

1

Climactic Moment/ Discovery

Every scene is filled with realizations or insights that characters will discover for the first time. This chapter contains situations in which the characters make especially significant discoveries, which may be about themselves or the other characters. Discoveries about another character may be: he loves me, he hates me, he's lying to me, he's scared, and so on. Discoveries about oneself might be: I love him, I hate him, I'm scared, I'm in charge, and so on. Old or new secrets may be revealed. If the actor constantly makes new discoveries in these situations, the improvisations will never be dull, but will always be exciting. In *Audition*, Michael Shurtleff discusses that in the play, *Whose Afraid of Virginia Woolf*, the scenes between Martha and George "would be boring and tiresome if the actors did not find what is new, what is different, what is particularly at stake in the scene. Acting is a whole series of discoveries. . . . Ask yourself: What is new?" (1978, 58–59).

These realizations, or insights, are the "aha" moments in life—the very kind of discoveries that are life-changing. Usually these heightened moments occur at the climax of a play, film, or novel, or at a climactic moment in a character's life. Although characters experience important changes throughout a dramatic work, it is the specific time at which these changes happen or a realization occurs that is considered a climactic moment.

CLIMACTIC MOMENT/DISCOVERY SITUATIONS

One male, one female

Awakenings

The Boiler Room

The Catcher in the Rye

Changes of Heart (Double in Constancy)

"Desiree's Baby"

The Diary of Anne Frank

The First Kiss

First Possession

God Would Be Rich

Journey Home

The Kentucky Cycle—Part One

The Language of Flowers

A Little Princess

The Mambo Kings

The Odyssey

The Pickwick Papers

Pink Cookies

Rebecca

The Rest of My Life

Waterland

Two females

Aunt Gail

Bedside Care

The Children's Hour

Little Women

Parenthood

The Prime of Miss Jean Brodie

The Story

Two males

Great Expectations

Inventing the Abbotts

The Mambo Kings

The Odyssey

Ensemble
The Colonel and His Son
Fools Rush In
The Grapes of Wrath
Jane Eyre
"Manila House"
The Matsuyama Mirror
The Moon by Night
Newcomer
Nightjohn

Source: *Aunt Gail* (an original improvisation, based on an actual event, written by UCLA student Sam Sunde)

Characters
Two females: Caroline, a nineteen-year-old student; her thought-to-be aunt Gail, in her early fifties

Place
The visitor's room of a jail in Northern California

Background
Caroline grew up in a seemingly normal, relatively happy home. She had no reason to believe that her mother was not her true birth-mother, that her father was not her true birth-father, and that her sisters were not her sisters by birth. Members of her extended family, such as her unmarried aunt, Gail, have had problems with drug and alcohol abuse, but this knowledge has not tempered Caroline's affections for them to any extent. Caroline has had no reason to believe that appearance is not reality, although she has always wondered why there are no baby pictures of her in the family photograph album.

Situation
Caroline has come to visit Aunt Gail, who is in jail for drug dealing. For the first time, Gail reveals that she is Caroline's true mother. It is a complete shock to Caroline. She doesn't know how to react.

Comments
To be truly surprised at the truth that has been revealed, Caroline needs to have complete faith in the life she has been living. She might begin to

piece together certain clues that make sense now, but her initial reaction is one of shock and confusion. All of a sudden she has learned that her life has been one big lie. The actors should make specific choices about the nature of their previous—and future—relationship. Caroline must contend with the realization that her Aunt Gail is not the image of the mother she would have chosen for herself.

Source: *Awakenings,* a film by Penny Marshall based on the book by Dr. Oliver Sacks, screenplay by Steve Zaillian

Characters
One male, one female: Leonard, aged forty-one; a visitor, in her late twenties or early thirties

Place
The cafeteria of a hospital

Background
Leonard contracted encephalitis when he was eleven years old, leaving him in a coma-like state for thirty years. Dr. Sayers has recently been hired by the hospital in which Leonard is a patient to work in its chronic diseases ward. He has discovered that a new, "miracle" drug used to treat Parkinson's disease, L-Dopa, revived Leonard and other patients.

    Leonard had been conscious for only a few days when he noticed a woman who had come to the hospital to visit her father, who had had a stroke. Leonard escaped from his ward, where he was still under observation, and followed her to the cafeteria. Because he has been virtually unconscious for thirty years, he is now something of a babe in the woods.

Situation
Leonard and the woman sit at the same table. At this point, she does not know that he is a patient and not a normal, healthy man. These people know nothing about each other. The young woman is concerned about her father; she doesn't know if he is conscious of her presence when she visits him. Leonard is attracted to the young woman, but he doesn't really know what to do about it.

Comments
The actors need to let this relationship emerge. It is fraught with discoveries. The young woman is also attracted to Leonard, but he is certainly dif-

ferent from other men she has met. The actor playing Leonard needs to remember that he is not retarded or mentally disturbed. However, the fact that he has not spoken for thirty years would have an effect on his speech.

This situation is based on an actual case, conducted in 1969 by Dr. Oliver Sacks. His patients revived for a short time and then, when the drug failed, they regressed to an unconscious state, in which they remain to the present day.

See index for other improvisations from this source.

Source: *Bedside Care* (an original improvisation written by UCLA student Laura Wales)

Characters
Two females: Mimi, in her late teens; Jack's girlfriend, a young woman approximately Mimi's age; Jack, in his early twenties

Place
A hospital room

Background
Mimi and Jack had been dating for over a year when each of them left home for different colleges. Although they agreed that it would be difficult to consider themselves a couple, they were still very much in love. They spent all their school breaks together at home. On Saint Valentine's Day of their first year apart, Jack's sister called Mimi to say that Jack had been in an accident at school and was in the hospital.

Situation
Mimi enters Jack's hospital room to find him in much worse shape than she had imagined. There are monitors and I.V. equipment all around, and Jack is not awake. A girl sitting at his bedside introduces herself as Jack's girlfriend. Mimi is left stunned both by the seriousness of Jack's condition and by the presence of this girl, about whom she knows nothing.

Comments
The hospital room and Jack must be clearly imagined by the actor playing Mimi. Bear in mind that Mimi is unsure of the extent of Jack's injuries; the fear that he might not survive makes her realize just how much she loves him. Jack and Mimi's past relationship must also be quite clear to the actor. Remember, too, that the last time Mimi saw Jack they were still a couple. Barely two months have gone by and, while she and Jack have

spoken together, he has told Mimi nothing about another girl. The mixed feelings of anger and love should surface. The scene can be played with an actor representing Jack.

This situation has been written from Mimi's point of view; Jack's other girlfriend is nameless. However, the actor in this role must decide whether she has any previous knowledge of Mimi and what her relationship is with Jack.

Source: *The Boiler Room,* a play by Reuben Gonzalez in *Nuestro New York: An Anthology of Puerto Rican Plays,* edited by John V. Antush

Characters
One male, one female: Doug, in his twenties; Olga Acosta, his mother-in-law

Place
The boiler room in a New York City apartment building

Background
Mrs. Acosta lives in a boiler room with her son, Anthony. They are immigrants from Puerto Rico. Although her husband is dead, Mrs. Acosta tells everyone that he is away so that she can keep her job as superintendent of the building. Olivia, her daughter, will be moving into one of the apartments with her husband, Doug. Mrs. Acosta has hopes of moving in with them and getting out of the boiler room. Olivia has told her mother that Doug is a rich lawyer and that they have just returned from Paris.

Situation
Doug has been living with a terrible secret, and he can't take it any longer. He confesses to Mrs. Acosta that he is not a rich lawyer and that he and Olivia have not just returned from Paris. In fact, he was laid off from his job as a law clerk, and he and Olivia have been living out of the back of his car for the past two months. He tells Mrs. Acosta that he is leaving Olivia, who does not really care much about him now that she knows he has no money.

Comments
This is a huge disappointment for Mrs. Acosta; she was depending on Doug to be her savior. She believed completely what her daughter had said about him. The boiler room is an important element of this scene—it is the title of the play—and it creates an atmosphere around the characters.

Source: *The Catcher in the Rye,* a novel by J.D. Salinger (improvisation written by UCLA theater student Nikolai Kinsky)

Characters
One male, one female: Holden Caulfield, seventeen years old; Sunny, a young prostitute

Place
A seedy hotel room in New York City

Background
One week before Christmas break, Holden was expelled from boarding school for "not asserting himself." He decided not to tell his parents about what happened until vacation; this is not the first time he has been kicked out of school. Holden has some money saved and is staying in a hotel room for a few nights. To while away his days until Christmas, he has been calling and visiting various people from his past.

Situation
At this moment, Sunny has just walked into Holden's room. The elevator man (her pimp) sent her up to Holden. Holden has been pacing frantically in his room and trying to prepare himself for her arrival, but when she finally arrives, he is turned off by her matter-of-fact attitude. He also feels sorry for her. Much to her surprise, he asks if it is okay if they just talk.

Comments
Holden is a virgin, but he does not want the prostitute to know (although she can tell). The actor should keep in mind that Holden is extremely cynical. At the same time, he is likely the most sensitive client the prostitute has ever had. Sunny may discover something about herself as well.

Source: *Changes of Heart (Double Inconstancy),* a play by Pierre Carlet de Chamblain de Marivaux, translated and adapted by Stephen Wadsworth

Characters
One male, one female: The prince, posing as a guardsman; Silvia, a young woman

Place
The drawing room of the prince's palace in France; the eighteenth century

Background
Silvia, a young subject of the prince, is betrothed to Harlequin; they have
known each other since childhood. Meanwhile, unbeknownst to Silvia, the
prince has fallen in love with her. He has confided in Flaminia, a member of
the royal household, and she has promised to help him win Silvia's affections.
Flaminia has contrived a scheme whereby the prince poses as a guardsman;
the idea is that without the trappings of his royalty he will be able to stand
on his own merits and woo Silvia as an ordinary man. The scheme has been
a success, and Silvia has fallen in love with the guardsman. And in the midst
of her machinations, Flaminia herself has fallen in love with Harlequin.

In a seemingly selfless gesture, Flaminia has offered to marry Harlequin
so that Silvia will be free to marry the guardsman. Although she loves the
guardsman, Silvia believes that she must honor her commitment to Harlequin. She has gone to meet the guardsman in a state of painful confusion.

Situation
The guardsman professes his love for Silvia, but, when he sees how it up-
sets her, he offers to depart. She begs him not to leave but says that she
can never marry him because she has pledged herself to another man. She
explains that only the prince's command could release her from her obli-
gation to Harlequin. Eventually the prince reveals his true identity. He
rejoices that Silvia loves him for himself and not for his position.

Comments
In the play, this situation is divided into two different scenes. There is
much subtext here for the guardsman, who must listen while Silvia slan-
ders the prince. In telling Silvia who he really is, he runs a risk: she may
feel manipulated and tricked, and he may lose her. The actor playing the
prince must realize the depth of his love for Silvia and the revolutionary
quality of his attachment to her. Despite the decadence and frivolity of the
French court, it was unheard of for a monarch to wed a commoner.

The appeal of opposites is also at work here. Silvia is a simple country
girl, and the prince is charmed by her honesty and lack of sophistication.

See index for other improvisations from this source.

Source: *The Children's Hour,* a play by Lillian Hellman (improvisation written by UCLA student Tess Masters)

Characters
Two females: Martha Dobie; Karen Wright—best friends, both are
twenty-eight years old

Place

The living room of their quarters at the Wright-Dobie School for Girls; about ten miles from Lancet, Massachusetts; 1934

Background

Martha and Karen saved money for years and were finally able to open the Wright-Dobie School for Girls in a converted farmhouse. They developed a warm, informal environment of study, where the students were like family. Karen recently became engaged to Joe Cardin, the town doctor and cousin of Mary Tilford, an unpleasant Wright-Dobie student much given to lying and trouble-making. Martha had always been jealous of Karen's relationship with Joe; her feelings for Karen go beyond "a healthy natural friendship." One day, Martha's aunt confronted her about these feelings. Two students overheard the conversation and told the story to Mary. Mary repeated it to her grandmother, with embellishments. Scandalized, Mary's grandmother told the other parents, who immediately withdrew their daughters from the school.

Martha and Karen filed a slander case against the town, but they lost. They became outcasts. Karen realized that Joe, who had supported her throughout the trial, had doubts about her relationship with Martha. Unable to live with his uncertainty, she ended their engagement.

Situation

Karen and Martha have not been out of the house in eight days. Karen has just broken up with Joe, and he is gone. At first, Martha tries to find out what has happened with Joe; she then confesses her love for Karen, who refuses to accept the truth of the confession. Devastated and filled with self-loathing, Martha leaves the room and shoots herself.

Comments

The actors playing Karen and Martha must realize that their whole world has been destroyed—they are in debt, they cannot go out of the house because the whole town regards them as freaks, and they now feel uncomfortable around each other. Although Martha is confused about the nature of her love for Karen, she feels impelled to make a full confession. Karen does not want to hear that Martha is in love with her; she is decidedly not in love with Martha. But, she cares for Martha and must find a gentle way to put distance between them. Despite Karen's efforts to be kind, Martha is on an inevitable path of self-destruction. She has risked—and lost—everything. The actors must be aware of the attitude toward homosexuality in the 1930s.

Source: *The Colonel and His Son,* an incident from the life of a colonel in the United States Army

Characters
Ensemble; Three males, one female: A colonel in the United States Army; the colonel's son; the son's lover; the colonel's second wife

Place
A hotel balcony in Washington, D.C.; 1993

Background
This event took place during the period when President Clinton was addressing the issue of allowing gays to serve in the military. United States Senator Sam Nunn had requested that the colonel, a strong opponent of the policy, testify before the Armed Services Commission. He is scheduled to appear before the commission in several days. His wife has asked him to spend a weekend with her in a hotel; she has something important to tell him.

Situation
They have just had dinner and are sitting outside on the balcony of the hotel when the colonel's wife tells him that his son is gay. Since childhood, the son has had a close male friend, and this friend has now become his lover. Clearly, this news stirs a profound inner turmoil. The colonel loves his son, but not his son's sexual orientation. With this new knowledge, he must also decide how he is to confront the commission.

Part Two: This improvisation can continue with the confrontation between the colonel and his son, at which the son's lover was, in reality, also present.

Comments
The actors must take the moral positions of their characters regarding homosexuality, disregarding their own personal positions, should they conflict. While the colonel is strong in his beliefs, this discovery about his own son may—or may not—alter his convictions. The actors must explore a range of emotions in this situation: love, anger, hurt, embarrassment, disgust.

Source: "Desiree's Baby," a short story by Kate Chopin in *The Awakening and Selected Stories,* edited by Sandra M. Gilbert

Characters
One female, one male: Desiree, a young white woman; Armand, her husband, also white

Place
The couple's home in New Orleans; just before the Civil War

Background
A happily married couple, Desiree and Armand became parents three months ago.

Situation
One day, Desiree is gazing at the baby. She realizes that it is black. Armand enters, and she asks him how this can be. He replies, "It means that the child is not white; it means that you are not white." This explanation is bewildering to Desiree. As far as she knows, she is white. Armand tells her to take the baby and leave.

Comments
The period in which this story takes place is most important; at that time and in that culture "black blood" in one's family was considered by whites to be a disgrace. Only slaves were black, and they were unquestionably inferior. Armand is quick to assume that the black blood came from Desiree's family, but it turns out that it was from Armand's family.

    The actor playing Armand must realize that he still loves Desiree and the baby. However, a black child is unacceptable in his world, and he must banish all tender feelings from his heart as he has banished his wife and child from his home. Desiree is confused and deeply wounded. She loves her husband and her baby, but Armand's behavior toward her is cruel and inhumane.

See index for other improvisations from this source.

Source: *The Diary of Anne Frank,* a dramatization by Frances Goodrich and Albert Hackett of the book *Anne Frank: Diary of a Young Girl*

Characters
One female, one male: Anne Frank, a thirteen-year-old girl; Peter Van Daan, a sixteen-year-old boy

Place
Amsterdam, Holland; 1943

Background
With the help of friends, the Frank family and the Van Daan family have gone into hiding to escape the persecution of the Nazis and the horrors

of the concentration camps. Anne Frank and Peter Van Daan had never met each other before their families started living together. They attended the same school, but they were very different kinds of people—Anne was an extrovert, and Peter was self-conscious and shy.

Situation
The families have been in hiding now for a year and a half. Frustrated with the living situation, Anne has just exploded at her mother. She runs into her bedroom, slams the door, and throws a book across the room. Peter follows Anne into her room with a piece of cake that she left behind. He wants to express his support of her outburst. They begin to form a connection with one another based on their alienation from their parents.

Comments
Anne and Peter both feel misunderstood by their parents and yearn for a friend, someone who will understand and empathize. This is the first time that they really communicate, and this is the first time it has ever occurred to them that they could be friends and confidants. The scene is charged with the anticipation of what may evolve between them. The actor playing Anne should determine what caused the fight between Anne and Mrs. Frank.

See index for other improvisations from this source.

Source: *The First Kiss* (an original improvisation written by UCLA student Anel Lopez)

Characters
One male, one female: George; Adrianne—both are college students

Place
The cab of Adrianne's parked truck

Background
Adrianne and George began working together at a children's summer camp three weeks ago and have grown very fond of each other. Neither one is aware of the other's attraction, but they had a long telephone conversation last night, which left them both with a flare of hope. In fact, Adrianne was sufficiently encouraged to ask George out on a date. Tonight, they had dinner at a small Italian restaurant, where they sat out on the patio while the sun died down and the summer heat subsided. Later they went to a movie, where they didn't kiss or hold hands but just kind of snuggled—leaving them with more hope. Now, Adrianne is about to

drop George off at his apartment. Before they part, there is a long pause in the cab of Adrianne's truck.

Situation
Adrianne knows that she has fallen for George, but she wants him to make the first move. George has fallen for Adrianne and wants to kiss her, but he is overcome with shyness and hesitancy. There is something cosmic and natural about this tension. After a period of inner debate, they confess their feelings for each other and share one long, soft kiss.

Comments
The situation that occurs in Adrianne's cab is completely innocent, pure, and passionate. They don't make out or grope each other. George and Adrianne simply let their instincts and emotions loose and in the process experience the beginning of a wonderful love.

Source: *First Possession* (an original improvisation written by UCLA student Kim Vernon)

Characters
One male, one female: Mat; Renee, his girlfriend—both are in their late teens

Place
Mat's bedroom; mid-morning

Background
Mat and Renee have been seeing each other for three years. Six months ago, Mat cheated on Renee but he has kept this a secret from her. Mat and Renee have a mutual friend, David, with whom Mat grew up. David is a sweet and generous guy, but he has been dabbling in petty theft. He is often on hand to comfort Renee after she and Mat have disagreements. Mat has always suspected that Renee has deeper feelings for David than she will admit. Neither of them had seen David for five months when they ran into him last night, New Year's Eve. The festivities ended with an argument between Mat and Renee.

Situation
It is New Year's Day. Mat and Renee are watching television when a news flash interrupts the program. A fight, apparently gang related, had broken out at the place where they celebrated New Year's Eve. David was

stabbed in the neck with a broken beer bottle. He died on the way to the hospital.

Comments
The actors must not only contend with the immediate aftermath of this horrific event, but they must also consider the effect that it will have on their relationship. The actor playing Renee may realize for the first time how much she cared for David. She must also be sensitive to Mat, who is torn between two emotions: jealousy and grief.

Source: *Fools Rush In*, a screenplay by Katherine Reback, story by Joan Taylor and Katherine Reback

Characters
Ensemble; Two males, two females: Alex Whitman, white; Isabelle Whitman, Mexican American; Mr. and Mrs. Whitman, Alex's parents

Place
Alex's home in Las Vegas, Nevada

Background
Isabelle and Alex had a one-night stand. She became pregnant, and he married her. Alex rented a home in Las Vegas near his job; he is working as a civil engineer on a casino construction project.
    Alex's family is very conservative. Because they would not be able to accept his marriage to a Mexican girl, he has not told them about Isabelle. His parents are away on a trip.

Situation
Alex's parents have unexpectedly returned from their trip, arriving at Alex's house with no warning. They encounter Isabelle and mistake her for the maid. Isabelle realizes that Alex has not told them about his marriage; they have to be enlightened.

Comments
This is a shock to Isabelle. Even though the initial encounter between Isabelle and Alex was a one-night stand, the two love each other deeply. Isabelle, however, now doubts Alex's love, believing that their marriage cannot work because of their cultural differences.
    The news will also have an impact on Alex's parents. They are victims of their own prejudices and live in their own protected world. The actors playing Mr. and Mrs. Whitman need to be able to view Alex's mar-

riage from his parents' narrow perspective. (N.B.: Isabelle comes from a loving family, but her parents also disapprove of this marriage.)

Source: *God Would Be Rich,* a play by Helen Maley based on a true story

Characters
One female, one male: Verinda Brown; Father Sublime—both are African American

Place
Father Sublime's office, Sayville, Long Island; 1936

Background
It has been several months since Verinda and Thomas Brown joined Father Sublime's church. The male and female members of the congregation are housed separately and not allowed to communicate with one another. Verinda has given all of her possessions to Father Sublime and continues to hand over her wages, which she earns by cleaning houses.

Verinda's husband, Thomas, has been given the nickname, Mr. Universe. He has been serving the minister for no charge; he also gave Father Sublime all of his brand new suits. Thomas asked the minister to give him a little money so that he could buy himself a suit, because he felt ashamed of what he was wearing. Father Sublime refused his request.

Situation
Verinda has come to give her wages to Father Sublime. He reprimands her for talking to Mr. Universe and forbids her to speak with him or even to look at him again. Verinda replies that she treats him as a brother, like any other member of the congregation. Father Sublime insists that she obey his instruction not to communicate with Mr. Universe.

Verinda gives Father Sublime seventy-five dollars, money that she earned from house cleaning. She has to get back to work. As she is about to depart, rummaging through her purse, she realizes that she forgot to set aside two nickels for subway fare. She holds out her hand for two nickels; Father Sublime ignores her.

Comments
This scene is a turning point for Verinda. She comprehends for the first time what kind of a man Father Sublime really is. Conversation may follow his refusal to give her subway fare, or he may leave and the scene may become a solo moment for her. Any confrontation with him would, at this

point, entail some danger, because Father Sublime is powerful. This is a major discovery for Verinda—her god has fallen in her esteem. It is a great disappointment to find that this man, whom she worshipped, is a charlatan. This incident is what initiates her escape (with her husband, Mr. Universe) from Father Sublime.

The character of Father Sublime is based on a real man, Father Divine, who became very powerful in the nineteen thirties.

See index for other improvisations from this source.

Source: *The Grapes of Wrath,* a play adapted by Frank Galati from the novel by John Steinbeck

Characters
Ensemble; Two females, two males: Ma Joad; Rose of Sharon, her daughter; a starving man; his son

Place
An abandoned barn near a boxcar camp in California; the early twentieth century

Background
Impoverished by the Great Depression, the Joads lost their Oklahoma farm. They loaded all their belongings on an old truck and set off for California, hoping to start a new life. Their journey west was filled with one hostile encounter after another as they struggled to endure against harsh odds. Their last hopes were dashed when they arrived in California only to find that the people and times there were as desperate as those the Joads had left behind. The Joads ended up living beside a stream in a boxcar camp, which consisted of two rooms of six boxcars with their wheels removed. Two families lived in one car—a family at each end.

Situation
A terrible thunder and lightning storm begins as Rose of Sharon goes into labor. The Joads wait until she gives birth (the baby is stillborn) to seek refuge from the flooding in a nearby barn. In the barn, they encounter a man and his son. Ma Joad borrows a comforter so that Rose of Sharon can get out of her wet clothes. It soon becomes apparent that the man is starving to death and must have some nourishment. Ma looks at Rose of Sharon, who nods in understanding and agreement. Ma and the boy leave. Rose of Sharon moves to the man and, with quiet dignity, offers him her breast.

Comments
At first, the man is reluctant to accept this gift of life, but he really has no choice. Rose must still be in great physical and emotional pain from her recent ordeal. The actors playing Rose of Sharon and the man she saves must strike a balance between the absolute sincerity and simplicity of her life-saving act and its symbolic significance. They must feel the final moment of the play—Rose of Sharon's act—as testimony to the essential goodness and strength of the human spirit. This improvisation should be reserved for mature actors.

Source: *Great Expectations,* a novel by Charles Dickens

Characters
Two males: Magwitch, a convict; Pip, a twenty-year-old

Place
Pip's new apartment, London; the early nineteenth century

Background
When Pip was a boy living on the English marshes, he gave food and an iron file to Magwitch, an escaped convict, who was still in shackles. Magwitch was later recaptured and exiled to New South Wales, Australia, where he worked for many years. He never forgot Pip's kindness and vowed to help Pip become what Magwitch could never be—a gentleman. Eventually, the ex-convict amassed enough money to begin sending allotments to Pip. Because the money came to him through a lawyer, Pip never knew that Magwitch was his mysterious benefactor.

In fact, Pip believes that the money has been coming from his employer, a wealthy and eccentric old lady named Miss Havisham. Pip has fallen in love with Estella, Miss Havisham's adopted daughter, and assumes that the old woman has secretly been providing the funds so that he and Estella can marry. Pip has become a gentleman, but he has also become a snob.

Situation
Pip is reading a book in his new quarters when he hears footsteps on the stairs below. A rough-looking man appears at the door. Pip does not recognize him until he produces an iron file. Pip then realizes that this is the convict, Magwitch, whom he had saved. The two are reunited after all these years. Magwitch tells Pip that he has never forgotten his help. Pip replies that, as a gentleman, he cannot renew this old acquaintance. Gradually, as Magwitch reveals knowledge of the way Pip has spent his money, Pip realizes who his real benefactor has been.

Comments

That Pip's great expectations are supported by a convict—a person un-mentionable in society—is a great blow. All of Pip's hopes for Estella melt before his eyes, as do his pretensions to high society. Initially, he finds the convict repugnant. Magwitch, however, has devoted his life to making Pip a gentleman, and he loves Pip like a son.

So many rich details precede this climactic moment, that it would be beneficial for the actors to read *Great Expectations* before attempting the improvisation. (There are many great situations in the novel that also lend themselves to improvisation.) It is essential that the actors have an understanding of the class distinctions in English society in the early nine-teenth century and of what it meant at that time to be a "gentleman." In today's terms, Pip's situation could be compared to a young man meet-ing his real father for the first time, expecting a distinguished and digni-fied gentleman, but encountering a criminal instead.

Source: *Inventing the Abbotts,* a film by Pat O'Connor based on the short story by Sue Miller, screenplay by Ken Hixon (improvisation written by UCLA student Milo Ventimiglia)

Characters

Two males: Jacey, twenty-two years old; Doug, nineteen years old

Place

Jacey's apartment

Background

Jacey and Doug grew up in a small town and were raised by their mother; their father died before Doug was born. The Abbotts, their wealthy neighbors, have three daughters; much to the chagrin of Mr. Abbott, Jacey has been involved with the two eldest. Pamela, the young-est daughter, dated Doug in high school, but he never betrayed the ex-tent of his considerable feelings for her. Doug and Jacey are now attending Penn State, while Pamela is at Bryn Mawr. Unbeknownst to Doug, Jacey has become involved with Pamela, but he is basically just using her for sex.

Situation

Doug is hanging out at Jacey's apartment when Pamela arrives, slightly drunk. Doug believes that she is looking for him, but she walks right past him and directly into Jacey's arms.

Comments
The actors playing Doug and Jacey must keep in mind that they are brothers. No matter how angry they are, they could never inflict serious physical harm on each other. But it is also important to remember that the brothers have always been competitive and that Jacey consistently seems to win. Doug envies Jacey, but he has always looked up to him, too. This situation signals a profound change in their relationship.

Source: *Jane Eyre,* a novel by Charlotte Brontë

Characters
Ensemble; One female, three males: Jane Eyre; Edward Rochester; Richard Mason, Rochester's brother-in-law; a clergyman

Place
A wedding chapel in the English countryside; the early nineteenth century

Background
Jane Eyre came to the Rochester mansion as a governess to Adele, Mr. Rochester's daughter. In time, he and Jane fell in love. Although Mr. Rochester was to marry Mary Ingram, a woman of his own social status, he proposed to Jane when he realized that he was in love with her.

What Mr. Rochester hasn't told Jane is that his fifteen-year marriage to Adele's mother has never been dissolved. Mrs. Rochester suffers from schizophrenia, a family dysfunction through three generations. When he married her, Mr. Rochester was unaware of the family history of mental illness. For the past fifteen years, Mrs. Rochester has lived in a remote part of the mansion, watched over by nurses and guards.

Situation
This is Jane and Rochester's wedding day. The clergyman is in the midst of the wedding ceremony when the door bursts open. Enter Richard Mason, a lawyer, demanding that the ceremony be stopped. Mason exclaims that his sister is married to Mr. Rochester and that he has a copy of their marriage certificate with him. Mr. Rochester finally confesses to Jane that Mason's sister *is* his wife, referring to her as "the mysterious lunatic."

Comments
For Jane, this comes as a complete shock; she is very much in love with Rochester and excited about her wedding. There she is in a beautiful wedding gown, experiencing the happiest moment of her life, and it is shattered in a second by this astonishing news. Rochester, too, is devastated;

he thought he had finally found happiness. Richard Mason is simply trying to protect his sister, although she is clearly unable to live a normal life
as Rochester's wife.

It is suggested that, following this situation, the actors improvise
an additional improvisation from *Jane Eyre* in the chapter, Special Problems, in which Rochester brings Jane to meet his wife, "the mysterious
lunatic."

See index for other improvisations from this source.

Source: *Journey Home,* a novel by Yoshiko Uchida

Characters
One male, one female: Ken Sakane, in his late teens; Yuki Sakane, twelve
years old

Place
The Sakane family's new home in Berkeley, California; after World War II

Background
The Sakanes have moved into their new home after two years in an intern-
ment camp. The young Japanese American men in the camps were asked
to enlist in the war against the Japanese, and Ken Sakane was one of these
men. He is now being sent home due to a shrapnel injury that disabled
his leg. Ken is haunted by the memory of his friend, Jim, who threw himself on a live grenade to save the rest of the company. He feels guilty that
he is alive and Jim is dead. Meanwhile, Yuki assumes that Ken is still the
same boy who left to go to war for his country two years ago.

Situation
Ken arrives in a taxi, on crutches but still in uniform. He is thin, and
his skin is pale. He has become a somewhat somber young man. Yuki
is beside herself with the excitement of seeing Ken again. But, she
finds that she must adjust to a very different person than the brother
she expected.

Comments
Ken went to war to prove that the interned Japanese Americans were as
patriotic as any other Americans. He didn't want Yuki to be ashamed of
being Japanese. Later on in the novel, Ken reveals his feelings of guilt
about the death of his friend, Jim, to his Uncle Oka, but, in this scene

with Yuki, they may or may not be expressed. The actors may choose to improvise the scene between Uncle Oka and Ken as well.

Source: *The Kentucky Cycle—Part One,* a play by Robert Schenkkan

Characters
One male, one female: Patrick Rowen, in his late teens; Morning Star Rowen, his mother

Place
The front yard of the Rowen house in eastern Kentucky; 1792

Background
When Michael Rowen needed a wife, he kidnapped a Cherokee woman. Although Morning Star bore Michael a son, Patrick, she has never forgiven Michael for separating her from her Cherokee heritage. Patrick, now a teen-ager, has worked very hard to help his father maintain their homestead in the wilderness.

Situation
Morning Star tells Patrick that his father hates him because he is half Cherokee. She also says that Michael has another son in Saint Louis to whom he will leave everything that he has.

Comments
This is an unexpected blow to Patrick, who worships his father. His anger over the news is so powerful that, in the play, it drives him to kill his father. Patrick doesn't know that Morning Star has invented this story to drive him to avenge her resentment. The actor playing Patrick, however, should hear this news and allow it to affect him with no idea of what it may eventually lead him to do.

See index for other improvisations from this source.

Source: *The Language of Flowers,* a free adaptation by Edit Villarreal of William Shakespeare's *Romeo and Juliet*

Characters
One male, one female: Romeo Martinez, fifteen years old; Julieta Bosquet, fourteen years old

Place
Julieta's bedroom

Background
Romeo and Julieta met and fell in love at a party at Julieta's house. Numerous difficulties surround their romance, including a difference in class between their families, Julieta's engagement to another man, Romeo's involvement in a street gang, and his status as an illegal alien. However, with the help of Julieta's maid, Maria, the lovers are married secretly by a New Age priest, Father Lawrence.

Meanwhile, Julieta's cousin, Tommy, killed Romeo's best friend, Benny, in a gang fight, and Romeo killed Tommy in his anger and grief over Benny's death. So, while the Bosquet family is grieving over Tommy's death, they are making elaborate preparations for Julieta's wedding in a few days. Because of the killing, Romeo is being deported to Mexico. Father Lawrence and Maria collaborate in arranging a meeting between Julieta and Romeo.

Situation
This is the first time Romeo and Julieta have seen each other since Tommy's death. Although Julieta loves Romeo, she is distraught over the loss of her cousin, and Romeo is full of remorse over the bloody act he has committed. They don't know if they will ever see each other again. If Romeo stays in the United States, he is faced with a long jail term or a life with Julieta on the run. If Julieta goes with Romeo to Mexico, she may never see her father again.

Comments
There is danger present. Romeo is on enemy turf and must not be found there. While the taboo nature of this relationship adds to its excitement, it also creates enormous problems. Romeo and Julieta are in a very difficult situation. Julieta must deal with her feelings about a husband who has killed a family member; they must both consider the hardships of a life on the run. Julieta is very young and used to a comfortable existence; her father and Maria take care of her. Romeo will not be able to give her the life to which she is accustomed. Despite their all-consuming passion, they must consider these problems. Rather than using Shakespeare's or Villarreal's resolution, the actors may find their own way out of this crisis. The actors should also be encouraged to do improvisations on Shakespeare's *Romeo and Juliet*.

See index for other improvisations from this source.

Source: *A Little Princess,* a musical play adapted by Susan Kosoff and Jane Staab, from the novel by Frances Hodgson Burnett

Characters
One male, one female: Mr. Barrow, an attorney; Miss Minchin, proprietor of Miss Minchin's Select Seminary

Place
Miss Minchin's sitting room at the seminary, London; the late nineteenth century

Background
Although Miss Minchin has never truly liked her star student, Sara Crewe, she has indulged and pampered her because Sara's father, Captain Crewe, is rich.

Situation
In the middle of Sara's extravagant birthday party, Mr. Barrow arrives unexpectedly to inform Miss Minchin that Captain Crewe has died and left Sara penniless. Miss Minchin is absolutely taken aback by Mr. Barrow's news. She feels betrayed. Her dreams of financial security for herself and the school are dashed. And she has lost money that she spent on Sara with the expectation of being reimbursed. Mr. Barrow absolves his law firm of any obligations and responsibilities to Sara. He warns Miss Minchin that turning Sara out into the street would be a bad reflection on the school. Mr. Barrow is eager to leave as quickly as possible, with Miss Minchin holding the bag, and Miss Minchin, still slightly in shock, begins to blame Sara for what has happened.

Comments
Miss Minchin and Mr. Barrow are a lot alike in that they are governed by their own self-interests and needs. They care nothing about Captain Crewe's death except for how it affects them personally. And, while they want to keep up the appearance of propriety, they really care nothing about Sara's fate.

This is a scene in which the conflict is right up front and yet very polite and controlled. The two people dislike in one another what is true of themselves. Mr. Barrow remains in control of the situation because he has taken Miss Minchin by surprise and because he is able to leave. Miss Minchin is genuinely shocked by the news, but she feels sorry for herself and angry at Captain Crewe and Sara.

Source: *Little Women,* a novel by Louisa May Alcott

Characters
Two females: Jo March, in her early teens; Mrs. March, her mother

Place
The sitting room of the March home in Concord, Massachusetts; the mid-nineteenth century

Background
Despite the austerity of their financial situation and other external pressures, the four March sisters (Meg, Jo, Beth, and Amy) and their parents live a happy life full of the security that comes from their deep love for each other. No matter the odds, it seems that their sense of family enables them to endure.

  Jo has just learned that her sister Meg is involved in a serious relationship with a man named John. As an avowed spinster, Jo is furious that her sister would ever consider—let alone accept—a proposal of marriage. Most of all, she cannot accept the idea that anything might change in the nature of their family life.

Situation
This scene begins with Jo throwing a book on the floor in a fit of fury. Mrs. March comes in and immediately guesses why her daughter is upset. In trying to help Jo resolve her feelings, Mrs. March reveals that John has already declared his intention to marry Meg.

Comments
Jo is struggling with two major discoveries in this scene; she is still reeling from the news about Meg's involvement with a man, when her mother tells her that Meg will be marrying this man. To Jo, these revelations signal the destruction of the close-knit March family. Mrs. March understands Jo's anguish and wants to help her come to terms with the changes that are an inevitable result of growing up.

  See index for other improvisations from this source.

Source: *The Mambo Kings,* a film by Arne Glimcher based on the novel *The Mambo Kings Play Songs of Love* by Oscar Hijuelos, screenplay by Cynthia Cidre

Characters
Two males: Nestor Castillo; Caesar Castillo, his brother

Place
A hotel room in New York City; the late 1950s

Background
Caesar and Nestor came to New York City from Havana, Cuba, in 1952. They had been very successful musicians in Cuba but were forced to flee to the United States because a nightclub owner had threatened Nestor's life. Nestor's girlfriend, Maria, married the nightclub owner to keep him from killing Nestor, but insisted that Caesar take Nestor to the United States, out of harm's way. Maria also begged Caesar never to tell Nestor the full story. Nestor thus believed that Maria had betrayed him. Broken-hearted, Nestor married Dolores, an American girl, and they have had two children. Caesar and Dolores, however, have been in love since the moment they met, but have concealed their love from Nestor.

Situation
Caesar has found Nestor in bed with another woman. As soon as she leaves, Caesar attacks Nestor for being unfaithful to Dolores, reminding him that he has two children. Nestor says that Caesar forced him to come to the United States against his will. He wanted to stay in Cuba and marry Maria. He believes that Caesar has ruined his life. Out of patience with Nestor's ingratitude, Caesar finally tells him the truth behind their departure from Cuba. This is the first time that Nestor realizes Maria didn't jilt him, that she loved him more than he ever imagined.

Comments
This is a major discovery for the actor playing Nestor, but what is done is done: he is now a married man with two children. Caesar is driven to tell all to Nestor to make him understand that they only came to the United States to save Nestor's life. An added element of subtext in the scene is Caesar's love for Dolores, which he does not reveal. If *he* were married to her, he would not cheat on her. The brothers' strong bond is also an essential element of this situation.

See also the following improvisation.

Source: *The Mambo Kings,* a film by Arne Glimcher based on the novel *The Mambo Kings Play Songs of Love* by Oscar Hijuelos, screenplay by Cynthia Cidre

Characters
One male, one female: Nestor Castillo; Lydia, Caesar Castillo's girlfriend

Place
A nightclub in New York City, where Nestor and Caesar perform as musicians after hours; the late 1950s

Background
Until quite recently, Nestor believed that his girlfriend Maria dumped him to marry a Cuban nightclub owner and that Caesar had selfish motives for relocating the brothers' nightclub act to the United States. He did not know that Maria and Caesar were, in fact, sacrificing their own happiness to protect him from the murderous intentions of the nightclub owner. Caesar, however, nettled by Nestor's ungrateful attitude and infidelity to his wife, Dolores, has recently revealed the truth to him.

Instead of feeling grateful to Caesar and Maria for saving his life, Nestor is irate that no one told him that Maria still loved him. If he had known, he would have stayed in Cuba—and been killed. Nestor is now married to Dolores and is the father of two children. He does not know that his brother and Dolores fell in love the minute they met each other, but have done nothing about it because Dolores is married to Nestor.

Situation
Lydia, Caesar's girlfriend, and Nestor are talking in the nightclub after it has closed for the night. Nestor is furious with Caesar because he feels his brother has ruined his life. He tells Lydia that he has made a deal behind Caesar's back to break the partnership and go out on his own. Lydia reveals that Caesar has always loved Dolores (Nestor's wife), but sacrificed his love for Nestor. Caesar loves Nestor more than anything in the world, and Lydia knows that Nestor's leaving would break Caesar's heart. To prevent this, she makes this revelation to Nestor.

Comments
The actor playing Nestor is faced with a major discovery: Caesar and Dolores love each other but, for Nestor's sake, have never acted on it. Lydia must protect the man she loves, while at the same time feel the hurt of knowing that Caesar has not loved her for years; up until now she has had no one with whom to share her sorrow.

See also the preceding improvisation.

Source: "Manila House," a short story by Bienvenido N. Santos in *Scent of Apples: A Collection of Stories*

Characters
One male, ensemble: Val, the host of a special dinner; five Filipino men, his guests

Place
A dining room in Manila House, San Francisco; the 1940s

Background
Val has invited his friends to dine with him, and they come dressed in their finest. This is a festive occasion; the purpose is to reminisce about life in the Philippines.

Situation
Val speaks with the chef in the kitchen, overseeing the special dishes. People are laughing, eating, drinking, and talking—having a good time. The waitress is very attentive to all their needs.

    During dinner, the men fall into a discussion of the economics of the Philippines, how their country was devastated during World War II. Leo tells them that the peasants of the Philippines are up in arms and will not return to their farms under the old conditions of serfdom. This discussion and argument goes on for a while. Eventually, Val tells the group a story about his father, a landowner, who treated his tenants with affection and respect, which they reciprocated. As a child, Val was friends with all of them. There was no unrest on his father's land. But then, some strange men arrived and began stirring up trouble. While his father was listening to their complaints one day, the men rushed upon him—among them his old tenants—and killed him.

Comments
This improvisation has no conflict in it; the focus is on discovery. The important element for the actors is the change in atmosphere. The first mood is one of excitement and festivity. Nobody expects Val to tell this story; when he does the atmosphere changes abruptly and silence falls over the room. Even the waitress stops and listens. Val wants this to be a joyous occasion, but the discussion in favor of the tenants and the condemnation of all landowners disturb him. He obviously feels the need to defend his father. This incident should be a vivid "memory" in the actor's mind. See the history of the Philippines in "Immigration Blues."

    See also improvisations from the following sources: "Immigration Blues" and "Footnote to a Laundry List."

Source: *The Matsuyama Mirror,* a play adapted by Velina Hasu Houston from an ancient Japanese fairy tale

Characters
Ensemble; Two or three females: Aiko, a Japanese girl, twelve years old; Okaasan, her mother; Tooriko, Aiko's sixteen-year-old sister (optional)

Place
Aiko and Tooriko's bedroom in Matsuyama; Japan; the late seventeenth century

Background
This story is about a little girl's coming of age. Aiko has been having a difficult time growing up; all she wants to do is play with her dolls.

Situation
Okaasan tells Aiko what happens when a little girl becomes a lady; her father takes away her dolls and brings a handsome suitor who will take her for his bride. Okaasan says that growing up starts in the body, in the abdomen, and she tells Aiko about bleeding. Aiko is appalled.

Comments
This is a sensitive issue for students and needs to be handled accordingly. The right atmosphere must be present in the group. The actor playing the mother must consider the best way to explain this phenomenon to her daughter. If the actor playing Aiko is not menstruating yet, she really may need some answers; if she has already begun to have periods, she must try to remember how she felt when they began.

Young actors may laugh in embarrassment when doing this scene, and it may be difficult for the actor playing Okaasan to explain menstruation to Aiko. Many adults find this to be an unapproachable subject; some mothers never tell their daughters about menstruation. Ask the actors to explain this bodily function as best they can without going into graphic detail; this is not a physical hygiene class.

Aiko's sister, Tooriko, may be included in this improvisation. Tooriko feels quite superior to Aiko because she knows about becoming a woman. She thinks Aiko is strange because she doesn't want to grow up. Tooriko does not relate to Aiko in the nurturing way that the mother does.

See also the following improvisation.

Source: *The Matsuyama Mirror,* a play adapted by Velina Hasu Houston from an ancient Japanese fairy tale

Characters
Ensemble; Two females, one male: Aiko, a Japanese girl, twelve years old; Tooriko, her sister, sixteen years old; Otoosan, their father

Place
Their home in Matsuyama, Japan; a cold winter night in the late seventeenth century

Background
Aiko has found growing up difficult, and she has been playing with her dolls all the time. Her mother, Okaasan, has been attempting to ease this transition. Older sister Tooriko sees Aiko as a child who will never become a woman. Otoosan, her father, has gone off with a traveling party and has run into a heavy snowfall. Because it is past the time that he is due home, Okaasan takes a horse and rides into town to check on him.

Situation
It has been many hours since Okaasan left, and Aiko, against Tooriko's will, is about to go off in search of her mother. Otoosan arrives, but he is alone. He tells the girls that Okaasan had an accident with the horse in the snow; her head struck a rock and she died. He then insists that the children open the gifts he has brought them. Aiko cannot believe that she will never see her mother again. Tooriko and Otoosan tell her that it is not their custom to weep; Otoosan says that she should be as happy as she always is when he returns from a journey. Aiko does not want her gift, but Otoosan gives it to her anyway. It is a mirror, something Aiko has never seen before. When she looks in the mirror, she sees her mother as a young girl. As hard as Otoosan and Tooriko try to convince her that it is not her mother in the mirror, Aiko is certain that it is.

Comments
The actors must understand and respect the reserved nature of these people, for whom it was not customary to indulge in emotion. Although they may feel deeply, the outward display of emotion must be stifled. Otoosan is also very sad, but he is doing his best to help his daughters accept their loss. Aiko is more demonstrative, and this embarrasses Tooriko. Aiko cannot understand why they should not be allowed to express their grief.

See also the preceding improvisation.

Source: *The Moon by Night,* a novel by Madeleine L'Engle

Characters
Ensemble; Three females, three males: Vicky, fifteen years old; Suzy, her younger sister; Victoria, her mother; Rob, her younger brother; John, her older brother; Wallace, her father

Place
Inside a tent on a camp site in the Grand Canyon

Background
The Austins are on a camping trip.

Situation
Suzy comes running to announce that something has happened to Victoria. Rob runs ahead into their mother's tent and returns with the news that Victoria has had a baby. (She has not been pregnant!) Vicky, John, and Wallace enter the tent to find a baby sleeping beside Victoria. She wakes up and is as bewildered as the rest of the family by the infant's presence. Suzy wants to keep the baby. The parents explain why this is not possible.

Comments
In a very short amount of time, the children become attached to the new baby. They want to adopt it, as children want to take in an abandoned kitten or puppy. Each member of the family will have his or her own reaction to the baby.

See also the following improvisation.

Source: *The Moon by Night,* a novel by Madeleine L'Engle

Characters
Ensemble; Four females, four males: Vicky, fifteen years old;   Suzy, her younger sister; Victoria, her mother; Rob, her younger brother; John, her older brother; Wallace, her father; a young mother; a park ranger

Place
A camp site in the Grand Canyon

Background
The Austins are on a camping trip. They have just discovered a baby sleeping beside Victoria in her tent and are wondering where it came from and what to do with it. Suzy wants to keep the baby, but Wallace and Victoria have explained why they cannot. They have had the child in their possession long enough to have become attached to it.

Situation
The baby's mother arrives at the Austin's camp site with a park ranger. With no job and no husband, she had decided that her baby would be better off

without her. Needing someone to care for the child, she chose the Austins. Now, however, she has changed her mind and wants her baby back.

Comments
The actor playing the birth mother needs to probe her character's background. What brought her to such a desperate act? Why did she choose this family? She can create her own motivations. And the actors can find their own resolution for the situation. Maybe the mother decides to take back her baby, maybe she doesn't. The Austin family must contend with their feelings of attachment to and protectiveness toward the baby.

See also the preceding improvisation.

Source: *Newcomer,* a play by Janet Thomas

Characters
Ensemble; One male, one female, one male or female, ensemble: Mai Li, Vietnamese, sixteen years old; Benny, Chinese American, sixteen years old; a high school teacher; high school students

Place
A public high school

Background
Mai Li was sent to the United States by her mother, who remained behind in Vietnam. Her mother told Mai Li that the people in the United States would like her and take care of her. She gave her daughter a bundle of clothes, a gold necklace (to be used as payment to the boatman who took Mai Li out of Vietnam), and a family photograph, which Mai Li carries with her at all times. Upon her arrival in the United States, Mai Li spent several weeks in a refugee camp. Today is her first day of school.

Situation
Mai Li speaks no English, and it seems that nobody can communicate with her. The teacher asks Benny to speak to Mai Li—he is the only student who can speak Chinese—but Benny refuses. He does not want to look foolish in front of his peers. Suddenly, the fire drill bell rings. Mai Li drops to the ground and covers her head with her hands. When told to line up and prepare to leave the building, she remains cowering on the ground. Benny goes to touch her, and she screams. He begins to talk to her in Chinese and reports to the teacher that Mai Li believes that bombs are dropping.

Comments

The important exercise in this improvisation is the actor's experience of being unable to communicate with the people around her. The other actors can talk in a nonsense language as if they were communicating. Mai Li is the only one who doesn't understand. When Benny and Mai Li speak, the actors can create their own language (if they don't speak Chinese), which only they comprehend. This improvisation can also be used for other newcomers with different native languages.

Source: *Nightjohn*, a novella by Gary Paulsen

Characters

Ensemble; One male, two females: Nightjohn, an African American man in his late thirties; Sarny, a twelve-year-old African American girl; Sarny's mother

Place

The slaves' quarters on a Southern plantation; just before the Civil War

Background

Nightjohn is an extraordinary person—a freed slave who returns to slavery to teach others how to read and write during a time when slaves were severely punished for learning to read. For example, Sarny's grandfather had two fingers chopped off because he knew the alphabet.

Situation

Late one night, when everyone is asleep, Sarny's mother discovers Nightjohn teaching Sarny the alphabet by writing the letters in the dirt on the ground with their fingers. Sarny is very eager to learn, but her mother is terrified that Sarny will be punished if the white slave owners ever find out that she has learned the alphabet. She wants Nightjohn to stop teaching Sarny.

Comments

The other slaves do not know that Nightjohn is an emancipated slave. He had run away to the North, where he was liberated. He has sacrificed his freedom to teach his people the written word. He would most likely reveal this information to Sarny's mother. Sarny is very excited to be learning and won't easily relinquish her chance to be educated by Nightjohn.

See index for other improvisations from this source.

Source: *The Odyssey,* an epic poem by Homer

Characters
Two males: Odysseus, the king of Ithaca; Telemachus, his twenty-two-year-old son

Place
Outside the city of Ithaca in Greece; 800–700 B.C.

Background
After leading his troops to victory in the Trojan War, Odysseus angered the god Poseidon and ended up on a dangerous, twenty-year journey home to his loyal wife, Penelope, and his son, Telemachus. During Odysseus' absence, Ithaca has been under siege and many suitors have been vying for Penelope's hand in marriage. These men hang around the palace, eating her food. They plan to murder Odysseus when he comes home. Inspired by the gods, Telemachus goes on a journey in search of his father.

Situation
Telemachus has just returned to Ithaca, his quest for Odysseus having been unsuccessful. Odysseus, however, has found his way home at last. On the outskirts of the city, he encounters Telemachus. Realizing that this is his son, Odysseus reveals his identity, but Telemachus is very suspicious. He has never seen his father, and he doesn't believe that this man is telling the truth. He assumes that Odysseus is an enemy. Odysseus must convince Telemachus that he truly is his long-absent father.

Comments
Telemachus is naturally reluctant to believe that Odysseus is his father; throughout his life, enemies have surrounded him. The majority of the men with whom he is acquainted are thieves who are greedily waiting to seize his mother and the palace. Once Odysseus convinces Telemachus of his true identity, it is a profound moment for both of them.

See also the following improvisation.

Source: *The Odyssey,* an epic poem by Homer

Characters
One male, one female: Odysseus, the king of Ithaca; Penelope, his wife

Place
The city of Ithaca in Greece; 800–700 B.C.

Background

After leading his troops to victory in the Trojan War, Odysseus angered the god Poseidon and ended up on a dangerous, twenty-year journey home to his loyal wife, Penelope, and his son, Telemachus. During Odysseus's absence, Ithaca has been under siege and many suitors have been vying for Penelope's hand in marriage. These man hang around the palace, eating her food. They bring her many gifts, hoping to win her over. And they plan to murder Odysseus upon his return.

Penelope tells the men that she will weave a tapestry. When it is finished, she will choose a suitor. She promised Odysseus that she would wait twenty years for his return. If he had not come back to her by then, she would remarry.

Odysseus has made his way home at last. However, it is not safe for him to appear among Penelope's suitors; they all want to kill him. The goddess Athena disguises him as a beggar, so that he can approach his home in anonymity.

Penelope's time is up. She agrees to marry the man who can draw Odysseus's bow and shoot an arrow through the rings of twelve axes. After all the suitors have failed at this task, the "beggar" asks to take part in the competition, although he declares he will not claim his prize. He draws the bow and, to everyone's amazement, he succeeds. He is transformed from his disguise as the beggar to his real appearance as Odysseus. He and Telemachus then kill all the suitor-thieves who attempted to usurp Odysseus' rule in Ithaca.

Situation

Odysseus tells Penelope that he is her husband, but she does not believe him. Even after his disguise has disappeared and he is revealed as himself, Penelope is doubtful. It is only when Odysseus tells her several details of their life together—details that only he could know—does Penelope believe he is the man for whom she has waited faithfully for twenty years.

Comments

The details which Homer had Odysseus describe to Penelope were the coverings of their marriage bed. However, the actors can invent their own cherished memories. These two people, separated for two decades, loved each other enough to remain faithful and to wait for this monumental reunion. They have both matured and gone through many changes, to which they must adjust.

The Odyssey is a great metaphorical poem. It is a contemporary story in the sense that it is about a man who has had an extraordinary adventure, and about a husband and wife who have paid the terrible price of war.

See also the preceding improvisation.

Source: *Parenthood,* a film by Ron Howard

Characters
Two females: Mother, in her early forties; Julie, her teen-aged daughter

Place
The living room of their home

Background
The mother does not like Julie's new boyfriend. Although Julie told her mother the relationship is over, she has continued to see him.

The mother went to Fotomat to pick up a roll of film that she had dropped off to be developed. By mistake, Fotomat gave her photographs that are really Julie's: nude pictures of Julie and her boyfriend having sex. Not only is Julie still dating this objectionable young man, but she is—quite evidently—having sex with him as well.

Situation
With photographs in hand, Mother confronts Julie.

Comments
This is a devastating moment for both Julie and her mother. A lot depends on the kind of relationship they have had until now, but it cannot be an all-understanding relationship or there is no conflict. Remember, the mother dislikes this boy; she must have a reason, which the actor needs to investigate. The actor playing Julie also needs to be clear about her relationship with the young man. Both actors should clearly imagine the content of the photographs.

Source: *The Posthumous Papers of the Pickwick Club,* a novel by Charles Dickens

Characters
One male, one female: Samuel Pickwick, a middle-aged bachelor; Mrs. Martha Bardell, a middle-aged widow

Place
Samuel Pickwick's apartment in London; the nineteenth century, early afternoon

Background
Having just entertained a gentleman from the Pickwick Club at afternoon tea, Pickwick has decided that life would be altogether easier if he

hired a manservant. But he wants to ask the approval of his landlady, Mrs. Bardell.

Situation

Mrs. Bardell is dusting the furniture. Pickwick asks if she doesn't agree that two can live as cheaply as one. Immediately misinterpreting this as a proposal of marriage, Mrs. Bardell replies that it depends on the person. Pickwick agrees and proceeds to enumerate the attributes of an ideal manservant, which Mrs. Bardell takes to be a description of herself. Among Pickwick's selling points is that Mrs. Bardell will always have company. Pickwick declares that he has made up his mind. What does *she* think?

Comments

A note to the actor playing Pickwick: Never refer to the manservant as such. Both Pickwick and Mrs. Bardell assume that they are talking about the same thing. He is delighted that she will accept the arrangement, and, of course, she is delighted that Mr. Pickwick has proposed to her.

　　This is a classic comedy of errors and mistaken identity: two people think they're talking about the same thing but are actually talking at cross purposes. The actors must concentrate on what they believe the other person is reacting to and carry on as though they understand each other perfectly.

Source: *Pink Cookies,* a play in the works by Jorma Taccone (improvisation written by UCLA student Jorma Taccone)

Characters

One male, one female: Andrew, a seventeen-year-old senior in high school; Jessica, eighteen years old, Andrew's best friend

Place

The front porch of Jessica's house

Background

Andrew and Jessica have been friends for six years. They have been in and out of love with each other—and had a brief romantic relationship that "just sort of happened." Although they are no longer dating, they are still attracted to each other and have remained close friends.

　　Andrew recently started experimenting with heroin. Intelligent, emotional, and depressed, Andrew is terribly confused about the purpose and direction of his life. Jessica is intelligent and stubborn; she has not tried heroin and is worried about Andrew's use of the drug. Two weeks ago, Andrew was tested for HIV.

Situation
Andrew arrives at Jessica's house with the results of the AIDS test: he is HIV-positive. Although he has had unprotected sex in the past (after Jessica) and shared needles, he has no idea from whom he could have contracted the disease. Jessica is the first person he tells, for two reasons: (1) She is his best friend and the only person to whom he can really talk, and (2) six months previously, the two were a couple and had had unprotected sex. Andrew must tell Jessica that she *may* have the virus too. It is even possible that he contracted it from her.

Comments
The two may go for a walk or move about in some way; the scene does not have to be played sitting down. Remember that Andrew and Jessica are both angry and scared, but they are old friends and still love each other deeply.

Source: *The Prime of Miss Jean Brodie,* a play adapted by Jay Presson Allen from the novel by Muriel Spark

Characters
Two females: Jean Brodie, an English teacher; Sandy, one of her students

Place
Jean Brodie's classroom in a girls' school in Scotland

Background
Jean Brodie is a flamboyant, stimulating teacher with enormous influence over "The Brodie Girls." For years, she has been living vicariously through them and predicting their futures. Jenny, she decided, should have a love affair with Teddy Lloyd, the art teacher, while dependable Sandy wou'd not be as attractive to men but would make a good spy. Insulted and angry, Sandy set about proving Jean Brodie wrong by becoming Teddy Lloyd's lover herself. However, every portrait Teddy painted looked like Jean Brodie, including Sandy's. Sandy realized at last that Teddy was in love with Jean Brodie.

Miss McKay, the headmistress, had been attempting to dismiss Jean Brodie for some time; she believed that Miss Brodie did not set a good example for the students. Sandy supplied Miss McKay with the evidence she needed to fire Jean Brodie: Miss Jean Brodie sent Mary McGregor, one of "her girls" disguised as a man, off to fight in the Spanish Civil War. Dimwitted Mary would have done anything Miss Brodie told her to do, and she was killed fighting on the wrong side. Sandy believed that Miss Brodie was responsible for Mary's death. When Miss McKay heard the story, she fired Jean Brodie.

Situation
Jean Brodie has just been dismissed by Miss McKay. She is devastated. She has devoted her life to this school, to her "girls." She returns to her class-room and finds Sandy waiting for her there. Miss Brodie believes that Sandy is her confidant and great admirer, so she tells her what has hap-pened. As the conversation progresses, it becomes apparent that Sandy is the one who betrayed Miss Brodie.

Comments
The actor playing Sandy must be clear about her motivation for betraying Jean Brodie. Miss Brodie took something important away from Sandy— her sense of being attractive to members of the opposite sex. Jean Brodie has always been the one in control of other people, particularly her girls. She has trusted Sandy above and beyond anyone else and respects her in-telligence. She views this incident as total betrayal. She is probably not capable of seeing her own culpability.

Source: *Rebecca,* a novel by Daphne Du Maurier

Characters
One male, one female: Maxim de Winter; Mrs. de Winter, his wife

Place
A cabin on the Manderley estate in Cornwall, England; the late 1930s

Background
Mrs. de Winter is Maxim's new wife. His first wife, Rebecca, drowned at sea a year ago. Rebecca was worshipped by the household staff at Manderley, and they have made the new Mrs. de Winter feel unwanted. She is convinced that she will never be able to replace Rebecca and that Maxim will never really love her.

Situation
The boat in which Rebecca drowned has been retrieved. Max confesses to his wife that he hated Rebecca and that he killed her himself. He identified another woman's body for burial. He tells Mrs. de Winter that one week after their marriage, Rebecca had informed Max that she did not love him and she had married him only in order to be mistress of Manderley. He describes Rebecca's unfaithfulness to him, which resulted in her becoming pregnant by another man. She had told him that the child would grow up at Manderley bearing his name. While she was laughing at him, he shot her and carried her body to the boat. He drove a spike into the planks so that

the water would come in, slowly sinking the boat. His great fear now is that they will identify the body and that he will be found a murderer.

Comments

The actor playing Mrs. de Winter can discover her own reaction to the news. She does love Max; however, she must have mixed feelings—on the one hand, relief that he did not love the idolized Rebecca; on the other hand, the realization that her husband is a murderer.

The actor playing Max should find this confession of murder very difficult but, at the same time, be glad to get it off his chest. Max has been repressing these horrible events for some time. He loves the new Mrs. de Winter more than anything in the world and fears that his confession will kill her feelings for him.

See index for other improvisations from this source.

Source: *The Rest of My Life*, a UCLA student film by Mark Lawrence

Characters
One female, one male: April, in her early teens; Nigel, in his late teens

Place
Two locations on the telephone: a public phone booth on a country road near the beach and a phone in a music store

Background
April's parents, who live in Los Angeles, are moving back to Iowa. She is very angry with them for uprooting her. They haven't even given her a good reason for the move. At the same time, April is crazy about Nigel. They made love for the first time last night. She is convinced that he is the knight in shining armor who will rescue her from her mundane existence.

April's father loves to fish, so the family will be making one last stop at the shore before going on to Iowa. April is expecting Nigel to pick her up at the beach and deliver her to eternal ecstasy.

Situation
The family is at the beach. April, in her high-heeled shoes and carrying a suitcase, leaves her parents behind and struggles up to the main road, where she waits for Nigel to come by on his motorcycle. A number of motorcycles pass, but none of them is his. He is almost an hour late, so April finds a telephone booth and calls him. Nigel tells her that he has just

been made manager of his uncle's music store. He can't leave. It soon becomes apparent that he doesn't like April as much as she likes him. April is shattered.

Comments
This is a story about the pain of growing up. April is at that awkward age. She wears too much makeup, her dress is very short, and she can hardly walk in her very high heels. She is ashamed of her parents and has put all her faith in a boy who doesn't reciprocate her feelings. This is April's first heartbreak, and it hits her hard. Nigel isn't cruel; this relationship just does not have the same intensity for him that it does for April.

See index for other improvisations from this source.

Source: *The Story* (an original improvisation, based on an actual event, written by UCLA student Stephanie Armstrong)

Characters
Two females: Dinah; Beth—both are high school students

Place
A parked car

Background
Dinah stole a credit card from the purse of a teacher she does not like. She convinced Beth to come with her to the mall to run up some charges on the card. Dinah was buying one last pair of shoes before they left—and she got caught using the stolen credit card. Both girls were arrested.

Situation
Dinah and Beth are out on bail and must collaborate on an alibi. They are seniors in high school and at risk of being expelled and losing scholarships if they don't figure out a story to save themselves.

Comments
This may not be a highly moral situation, but it is a true one. The two actors must call on their imaginations to concoct a story. Their survival is based on its believability. They may also find an entirely different solution to this problem.

Source: *Waterland*, a film by Stephen Gyllenhaal based on the novel by Graham Swift, screenplay by Peter Prince

Characters
One male, one female: Tom Crick; Mary Crick, his wife

Place
Their home in Pittsburgh, Pennsylvania

Background
Tom teaches history at a private school in Pittsburgh. He and his wife, Mary, came to the United States just after World War II. When they were teen-agers, Mary became pregnant. An abortion was performed under unsanitary conditions: it left Mary sterile. It was a traumatic experience from which she never recovered. Later, the couple married. They moved to the United States when Tom secured his teaching position. In social situations, Mary is given to casually announcing that she is pregnant. This, of course, is distressing to Tom; he knows it's impossible.

Situation
Tom comes home one day and is startled to hear a baby crying in the bedroom. He rushes upstairs to find Mary holding an infant. She insists that it is their child. When he continues to question Mary, the truth comes out: she stole the baby from an unattended carriage in the supermarket. The baby's mother left the carriage near the check-out counter, apparently to pick up a few items that she had forgotten. Mary says that she just wheeled the carriage out and the baby smiled at her; it didn't cry. The couple must deal with the implications of what Mary has done.

Comments
The background information regarding the abortion is important in this improvisation. The actors should discuss or, perhaps, even improvise the emotions surrounding that traumatic experience. This baby is very important to Mary. Tom knows, of course, that the police must be notified, since the baby's mother must be frantic. Mary is convinced that this is her child and doesn't understand why she should give it up. Tom has to take the baby away from her, but gently. A doll or some similar object should be used as a substitute.

2

Confrontation/ Conflict

If drama, by definition, is about conflict, then acting is about confrontation. Although there may be subtle differences between the two, they usually go together hand in glove. Both conflict and confrontation make exciting theater. Actors must learn to paint their characters into a corner, to stack the deck so that characters are thrust into inevitable confrontation with one another. In other words, conflict consists of wanting something from someone that he or she won't or can't give. In these situations, actors must work hard to make their needs strongly felt and to attain their objectives.

Actors often assume that to create conflict they must instigate a heated argument. However, as Lee Strasberg said, "The actors can do the whole scene without a single word. You could sit for half an hour just making little sounds and noises and could still build up the whole sense of the conflict between you and him" (the actors) (Strasberg 1965, 277). The situations in this chapter have been selected to help actors learn to face conflicts from which they cannot escape. They need to rely on their intuition and improvising spirit—as opposed to their logic and dialogue.

CONFRONTATION/CONFLICT SITUATIONS

One male, one female
Anne of Green Gables
Christmas Eve With the Trumans
"Dénouement"
The Godfather III

Peer Pressure
The Wedding

Two females
The Assignment
The Cat Ate My Gymsuit
Eating with Jude
"Footnote to a Laundry List"
The Joy Luck Club
Miss Saigon
"The Reunion"
Steel Magnolias
Vilma Martinez
Wedding Band

Two males
The Deadly Crush
Dreaming of Rope Ladders
Henry IV
Langston Hughes: Poet of the People
"The Old Chief Mshlanga"

Ensemble
Dead Poets Society
Death and the Maiden
Nine Armenians
Scorpions
The Slave
To Kill a Mockingbird

Source: *Anne of Green Gables,* a novel by L. M. Montgomery

Characters
One female, one male: Marilla Cuthbert, a spinster; Matthew Cuthbert, a bachelor, Marilla's brother

Place
Green Gables, a house in Avonlea, on Prince Edward Island, Canada's smallest province; the early twentieth century

Background

Matthew and Marilla made arrangements with an orphanage in Halifax, Nova Scotia, to take one of the orphaned boys to work on their farm in exchange for room and board. Matthew went to pick up the orphan at the train station, only to discover that the orphanage had sent a girl, Anne. Matthew took Anne back to Green Gables. En route, he was completely charmed by her. Marilla, however, is certain that a girl will be of no use to them.

Situation

Anne is in bed when Matthew and Marilla sit down to dinner. Marilla is determined to send Anne back to the orphanage; she doesn't believe that a girl will be able to do the work that needs to be done on the farm. Matthew expresses his desire for Anne to stay, but Marilla's mind is made up. What she has seen of Anne's flair for the dramatic has made Marilla uncomfortable. Reluctant to fight with her, Matthew leaves the table without eating his dinner.

Comments

Marilla is clearly the dominant figure in this relationship, but she is troubled by Matthew's passionate determination to keep Anne. Matthew has never disagreed with her like this. The strength of his feelings may surprise Matthew himself. The actor playing Matthew should be clear in his mind what it is about Anna specifically, that has so impressed him. The actors should feel free to depart from the established story line if they find another way to resolve the situation.

See index for other improvisations from this source.

Source: *The Assignment* (an original improvisation, based on an actual event, written by UCLA student Evangeline Monroy)

Characters

Two females: Marissa; Lyn—both are junior high or high school students

Place

A hallway at school

Background

Marissa and Lyn have known each other for three years. They hang out with the same circle of friends. One day at school, Lyn asked Marissa about an assignment, a paper (neither the subject nor the topic is important, but both should be agreed upon in advance by the actors) with which Lyn had been having problems. Both very serious students, Lyn and Marissa often discussed assignments. Marissa had already completed her paper, so Lyn asked to borrow it to get a sense of the assignment. Lyn returned Marissa's paper the next day.

A couple of weeks later, the papers were passed back to Lyn and Marissa, with notes from the teacher to see him after class. The teacher spoke with each of them separately and informed them that they would have to see the dean; he did not tell them why. Marissa didn't know that Lyn had gotten the same note until she saw Lyn leaving the dean's office just before Marissa's own appointment with him. The dean told her that she was suspected of plagiarism. Of course, it was Marissa who had loaned her paper to Lyn, but apparently Lyn told the dean that *she* had loaned her paper to *Marissa*. Marissa was shown both papers—they were identical. Unless one of the girls confesses, both girls will be expelled.

Situation
Marissa confronts Lyn about the plagiarism.

Comments
Lyn's main reason for lying was that she couldn't come up with an idea for the paper; desperate and afraid of getting anything less than an A (her father is very strict and will not tolerate low grades), she copied Marissa's work. The outcome of the improvisation is in the actors' hands, but the focus of the conflict is Marissa's innocence of plagiarism.

Source: *The Cat Ate My Gymsuit,* a novel by Paula Danziger (improvisation written by UCLA student Ryan Cadiz)

Characters
Two or three females: Carrie; Carrie's mother; a saleswoman (optional)

Place
A department store

Background
Carrie is a self-described sixteen-year-old blimp with mousy brown hair and wire-rim glasses—scared of everything. Both Carrie and her mother are frightened of Carrie's father because he is verbally abusive. He often gives them shopping money to assuage his guilt about his harsh behavior. Carrie has always refused to change into her gymsuit in the girls' locker room because she believes that there are better ways to die than of humiliation.

Tonight, Carrie will be attending her first real high school party, and she and her mother must shop for a new outfit for her to wear. They are shopping with "guilt money" from Carrie's father: after walking into the kitchen and observing Carrie scoop out a second helping of ice cream, he had called her lazy and fat. Actually, Carrie was having another bowl of ice cream because she was happy—a smart boy named Joel had asked her if she were going to Nancy Sheridan's party, and she had realized that he was asking her for a date.

Situation
Carrie and her mother are shopping for the new outfit. Carrie is in a hurry to get home, so that Nancy, her best friend, can teach her how to dance before the party begins. A saleswoman has just steered them out of both the petite and the junior miss sections into what Carrie calls, "the young whale section." Her mother tries to sell her on a colorful tentlike contraption; the saleswoman wants her to buy the one-piece dress with a large collar that angles up and away. Carrie is leaning more toward a purple, long-sleeved blouse and matching slacks that will only make her look like an overgrown grape with glasses. Carrie's mother keeps promising her that, once they buy the outfit, they can head over to the jewelry department to find something to draw attention to Carrie's face.

Comments
The actor playing Carrie must remember that she wears her body uncomfortably, like a burlap sack. Even if the actor is not heavy, she must feel heavy. The awkwardness of puberty is coupled with her weight problem. She actively participates in hiding her body and is not yet ready to be proud of who she is. The actor playing Carrie's mother must remember that she believes it is her job to soothe everyone into denial. If she can pretend that everything is fine, then she can create a world of easy solutions.

Source: "Christmas Eve With the Trumans," (as heard in a sermon told by Brother Satyananda, based on an incident from the life of Harry S. Truman, in *First Ladies* by Margaret Truman

Characters
One male, one female: President Harry Truman; Bess Truman, his wife

Place
Their home in Missouri; Christmas Eve, 1945

Background
This situation took place during World War II, when the United States was fighting the war in the Pacific. President Truman had been faced with making horrific decisions; whether or not to drop the atomic bomb on Japan may have been the toughest, having the widest implications.

Truman's wife, Bess, never enjoyed being in the public eye. She was upset with her husband; due to the demands of the presidency, he was neglecting both Bess and their daughter, Margaret.

Situation
Truman has been working hard on Christmas Eve day. Despite a blizzard, the president is able to fly home for Christmas Eve so that he can spend Christmas day with his family. When he arrives, Bess is very cold to him. Truman explains that he has done one hundred things that day that he did not want to do. He tries to express to her how important his family is to him and that he could not make these decisions without their support.

Comments
The actor playing President Truman is contending with a number of physical and emotional states. For one, he must be exhausted from his presidential responsibilities. He is excited about getting home, but he is also hungry, angry with the cold response from Bess, guilty about neglecting Bess and Margaret, preoccupied with politics, and desperately in need of his family's love and support. Somehow, he must make Bess see the situation from his point of view. Also, the actor should have some idea of the work Truman was doing all day.

Bess Truman is a human being first, a simple woman who never asked for this high position; it was thrust on her. All she wanted was a quiet life in Missouri with her husband and child. Christmas is a sacred time for her, and it means a great deal to her to have her husband at home on Christmas Eve.

Source: *Dead Poets Society,* a film by Peter Weir, screenplay by Tom Schulman

Characters
Four males, one female: Todd, a teen-ager; the father of Todd's roommate, Neil; Todd's mother; Todd's father; the headmaster

Place
The headmaster's office at a prestigious prep school

Background

Through the inspiration and encouragement of Mr. Keating, an innovative teacher, Todd's roommate, Neil, discovered a passion for acting. Neil's father had other plans for his son and was furious when he discovered him acting in a play. He told Neil that he was to be withdrawn from prep school and sent to a military academy. Neil committed suicide, using his father's gun.

Neil's father holds Keating responsible for his son's death. He has begun a movement to oust Keating from the school.

Situation

In this scene, Todd has been called to the headmaster's office, where he finds his parents and Neil's father. They all want Todd to sign a document condemning Keating: they apply a great deal of pressure on him to do so. Todd believes that Keating is the best teacher the school has ever had, but he also knows that he will be expelled if he refuses to sign the document.

Comments

Todd knows that Keating is not to blame for Neil's death. If anyone is responsible, it is Neil's father. While Todd sympathizes with Neil's father, he finds it hard to contribute to the ruin of Keating, an innocent person whom he respects. The actor playing Todd must have a strong sense of what makes Keating such an extraordinary teacher. And he must also feel some responsibility toward Neil, his friend. Todd is intimidated by the adults who surround him; they have the power to do him harm. The actor will need to examine Todd's relationship with Neil, with his parents, and with the headmaster. It is understandable that Neil's father needs to blame someone for his son's death. This is his way of dealing with his grief.

See index for other improvisations from this source.

Source: *The Deadly Crush* (an original improvisation based on a widely reported news story, written by UCLA student Evangeline Monroy)

Characters
Two males: Adrian; Eric

Place
Adrian's home in Minneapolis, Minnesota

Background
Adrian and his close friend Delia appeared on a nationally syndicated talk
show. The topic of the show was "Same-Sex Crushes." Delia convinced
Adrian to talk about his crush on their mutual friend, Eric. Eric also
agreed to be on the program, but he hadn't a clue why he had been
brought there. Eric wasn't even aware that Adrian was gay, much less that
Adrian was infatuated with him. Adrian was very candid on the show, describing specific sexual fantasies that he has had about Eric.

Situation
Several days after the program, feeling humiliated, Eric goes to Adrian's
house to confront him about the confession.

Comments
In reality, Eric killed Adrian. The murder was obviously premeditated,
since Eric went to Adrian's house carrying a loaded gun. However, it is
for the actor to determine whether he is set on this decision—or if something Adrian says or does during one improvisation detonates a sudden,
homicidal rage in Eric. The actor playing Eric will need to find reasons
why homosexuality repels him so profoundly.

Source: *Death and the Maiden,* a film by Roman Polanski based on the novel by Ariel Dorfman

Characters
One female, two males: Paulina; Gerardo, her husband; Dr. Roberto
Miranda, their guest

Place
Gerardo and Paulina's beach house; just before dawn; 1990

Background
Although this situation took place in Chile in 1990, it could take place in
any country establishing a democratic government after a long dictatorship. A commission was appointed to investigate the crimes of the former
Chilean dictatorship under General Pinochet, and Gerardo, a lawyer, was
asked to serve on it. His is a delicate position; many of the officials who
committed the crimes are still in power.
     Paulina was opposed to Pinochet's regime, and she was tortured for
her beliefs. Although several years have passed, her mental wounds have
not yet healed.

As he was driving home one night, Gerardo's car blew a tire. Dr. Roberto Miranda stopped and offered him a ride home, which Gerardo gladly accepted. He invited Miranda to be their guest for the night. When Paulina met Miranda, she recognized his voice. It was the voice of the doctor who, repeatedly during her imprisonment, raped her and then sent an electric current through her body to see how much she could tolerate. Whenever the current was increased, the doctor played a tape recording of Schubert's *Death and the Maiden*. To this day, whenever she hears this piece of music, Paulina becomes ill.

During the night, while the two men slept, Paulina tied Miranda to a chair, stuffed something is his mouth, and held a loaded gun on him until he awoke.

Situation

Miranda realizes that he is in restraints and tries to free himself. He then sees Paulina sitting in front of him with a gun. She tells him that she recognized his voice and that she knows who he is. She is playing a cassette tape-recording of Schubert's *Death and the Maiden*, which she found in the doctor's car. Gerardo enters and, much to his dismay, finds Paulina holding their guest hostage. She explains that Miranda is the doctor who tortured her. Gerardo is embarrassed that his wife would treat a guest in this manner, especially someone who rescued him on the road. He believes Paulina is still mentally disturbed from her experience and too eager to uncover the identify of her tormentor.

Comments

The dilemma for Gerardo is whether to believe his wife, whom he loves. If she is mistaken, this is a serious offense—especially so for someone newly appointed to public office. He needs to decide for himself whether Miranda is innocent or guilty. He should have no preconceived notion. All he knows are the few things that Paulina has told him about her past experience.

The actor playing Paulina needs to have specifics in mind that convince her of this man's identity. She cannot be absolutely positive, however, time has passed and she never saw Miranda's face. His manner of speaking, his scent, his expressions, and his touch should all be clear in her mind.

The actor playing Miranda needs to decide whether he is innocent or guilty. If he is not guilty of this crime, he may have committed actual or imaginary crimes against other women, about which he feels guilty. If he *did* torture Paulina, the actor should have a clear understanding of the circumstances and of his motivation.

Source: "Dénouement," a short story by Jeff Rosenberg (improvisation written by UCLA student Jeff Rosenberg)

Characters
One male, one female: Evan Richard Kennedy, the youngest of four brothers, in his early twenties; Mary Ann Kennedy, his mother

Place
The snowy front yard of the Kennedys' two-story colonial house in Buckfield, Maine; April 1987

Background
Five years ago, during a Christmas Eve dinner party, Evan told his family that he was gay. His lover, Barry, a dancer, was present. A huge argument ensued, and Evan left home that same night. Soon after, Evan and Barry moved to Los Angeles, where they both pursued careers as actors and dancers. Evan gradually lost touch with his family. Evan and Barry lived together for three years. Then, during a brief separation, Barry contracted HIV. Evan took him back and cared for him during the difficult last months of his life. Near the end, when Evan tried to contact Barry's family to inform them of his condition, they refused to speak with him.

Situation
It has now been two months since Barry's death. Evan has returned to attempt a reconciliation with his family. His father, George, has made a real effort to welcome Evan back into the family, but Evan's mother, Mary Ann, is having a more difficult time. Convinced that Evan has AIDS, she serves him his meals with disposable utensils and on Styrofoam plates, and she refuses to stay in the same room with him for any length of time, exclaiming that he has come home to die. On the morning of his second day at home, Evan overhears his mother say that she wishes she had never given birth to him. Extremely hurt, Evan makes his presence known, runs upstairs, grabs his suitcase, and heads out the front door. Mary Ann follows him, and, in the cold of the April morning, the two have an explosive confrontation on the front lawn.

Comments
Remember that both Evan and Mary Ann love each other, though during this scene they might often say hurtful things. They are both afraid: Evan, of possibly dying without the love of his family, and Mary Ann, of Evan dying. Both actors should try to think of specific events in their own lives to bring to the scene and, in light of these past events, see if reconciliation is actually possible.

Source: *Dreaming of Rope Ladders,* a play by UCLA student Jason Sinclair Long

Characters
Two males: Raymond; Peter, in his early twenties, the tutor of Raymond's dyslexic ten-year-old daughter, Gwen

Place
Raymond's middle-class home

Background
Raymond's wife died giving birth to his youngest daughter, Gwen. Gwen is severely dyslexic; Raymond hired Peter to teach her to read and write. Gwen adores Peter.

Sarah, Gwen's older sister, blames Gwen for their mother's death and thoroughly resents her presence. Jealous of all the time the tutor was spending with Gwen, Sarah seduced him and then told her father that Peter was sexually abusing Gwen.

Situation
After much prodding from Sarah to interrogate Peter, Raymond confronts Peter with this accusation. Peter, of course, truthfully denies it. However, he eventually reveals that he has had sexual relations with Sarah.

Comments
When Raymond finds out that Peter has been sexually involved with Sarah, he dismisses him. This is difficult for Gwen and Peter; she is very attached to him, and his leaving will be devastating to her.

See index for other improvisations from this source.

Source: *Eating with Jude,* a UCLA student film by Anne Kelly

Characters
Two females: Jude; her neighbor

Place
Jude's kitchen

Background
Jude is the best cook on the block. Her neighbor's husband loves her cooking. Every chance he gets, he sneaks over to Jude's house to eat.

Situation
The neighbor's wife asks Jude to stop feeding her husband. He refuses to eat anything at home, she says, because it doesn't taste as good as Jude's food.

Comments
This situation is a switch on the theme of sexual infidelity. In this case, all the husband is coming for is food. Jude is very proud of her cooking and enjoys feeding him, especially since she has no husband of her own. It would be hard for her to give up this pleasure. The neighbor's wife is desperate because she can't keep her husband home; every time she turns around he is sneaking off to Jude's house. She takes this most personally and sees it as a poor reflection on herself.

Source: "Footnote to a Laundry List," a short story by Bienvenido N. Santos in *Scent of Apples: A Collection of Stories*

Characters
Two females: Miss Magdalena Barin, a teen-ager; the dean of the Columbia College of Education

Place
Columbia College of Education, New York City; 9 A.M. on a summer day, the 1940s

Background
A meeting of the committee on discipline has been called to interrogate a female student, Miss Barin, who stands accused of having illicit relations with a faculty member, Mr. Sulpicio Vivo, by his wife. Mr. Vivo had introduced his wife to Miss Barin at a campus dance on Saint Valentine's Day. Mrs. Vivo invited Miss Barin to a birthday party at her home; this was last Sunday, the last time they met. Mrs. Vivo had a policeman follow Miss Barin. He tried to persuade her to sign a statement admitting that she was having an affair with Mr. Vivo, but Miss Barin refused, saying it was not true.

Although Miss Barin is a sophomore at the college of education, she is still in her teens. She lives in a boarding house and shares a room with other girls. This is where Mr. Vivo came to visit her. Some of his shirts were found in her room. Mr. Vivo bought her things, but she claims that she always returned them. She has no parents but receives support from an aunt who is a teacher. Miss Barin wants to be a teacher. The last time she saw Mr. Vivo was a few minutes ago at the gate of the university; he told her he was leaving for Manila.

Situation

Miss Barin is being interrogated by the dean of the college in front of other faculty members on the discipline committee. The dean questions her about the alleged events. Miss Barin insists that she and Mr. Vivo were only friends and never had the kind of relationship of which she is accused.

Comments

The punishment, if she is found guilty of "immorality," is expulsion from the university. This would prohibit her from gaining admission to any other public or private school. Although Miss Barin is emphatic that she and Mr. Vivo are just friends, she must answer the questions and justify her actions. The actor playing Miss Barin needs to familiarize herself with the given facts and fill in the blanks for herself before doing this improvisation. Women in the 1940s had less freedom and fewer rights than women do today. Mr. Vivo, a male with a high-ranking position, is not held accountable. The class may be used as the other faculty members on the discipline committee. See history of the Phillippines in "Immigration Blues."

See also improvisations from the following sources: "Immigration Blues" and "Manila House."

Source: *The Godfather III*, a film by Francis Coppola, based on the novel by Mario Puzo, screenplay by Francis Coppola and Mario Puzo

Characters
One male, one female: Michael Corleone, the Godfather; Mary, his daughter

Place
The Corleone home

Background
Mary and her first cousin, Vinnie, have fallen in love. Michael Corleone will eventually turn his command over to Vinnie, and he knows that his enemies will kill someone precious to Vinnie—Corleone's daughter—to keep Vinnie down.

Situation
Corleone begs Mary to give up her relationship with Vinnie. As the Godfather, he warns her of the dangers she would face as Vinnie's wife.

Comments
Michael Corleone is a very powerful man, and he is not used to being disobeyed. But Mary loves Vinnie and wants to marry him. Corleone knows that this marriage would be a death sentence for Mary, but he is also aware that he is asking her to sacrifice her love for Vinnie.

Eventually Vinnie does become the Godfather, after he promises Corleone that he will never see Mary again. The scene in which Vinnie and Mary part would also be a good improvisation. The actors are warned not to attempt to play stereotypical Mafia hoods: Corleone and Vinnie are people with deep feelings about their family.

Source: *Henry IV,* a play by William Shakespeare (improvisation written by UCLA student Jason Bushman)

Characters
Two males: Henry IV, King of England; Prince Henry (casually called Hal), his eighteen-year-old son

Place
A chamber in the king's palace; the sixteenth century

Background
Prince Hal has had quite a freewheeling adolescence. While most eighteen-year-olds in his position would be preoccupied with their eventual role as king, Hal prefers carousing with the dregs of society in pubs and committing petty crimes. His motivation for these activities is his need for a "normal" childhood away from the public eye. He does, however, have some sense of duty toward the throne.

Hal's father, King Henry, is obsessed with being the perfect monarch. He has recently heard of a rebellion by the Percy family brewing in the north and knows he must squelch the uprising himself. Because he gained the throne in an unethical manner, King Henry believes that he can trust no one in his court (other than his children) to lead the military operation against the Percys.

Situation
Hal comes home from a night of revelry, unaware that he will even be seeing his father. King Henry, however, has been awake all night long, contemplating his method of attack in the north. The king, who has not seen his son for several days, confronts him about his recent disorderly conduct. Apparently, Hal's reputation is spreading and is actually affecting the public's opinion of the king. King Henry compares his slacker son with

the brave and noble Henry Percy in the north. Even though Henry Percy, who is eighteen years old, is the leader of the rebellion, the king admires his determination to uphold a sense of family honor, which is not evident in Hal. Hal does not wish to give up his double life, but it seems that he must make a choice.

Comments

The key to King Henry is his anxiety and vulnerability. Even though he must play the role of the strong father, Henry, in fact, could quite easily be destroyed by Hal's irresponsibility. Even though Hal has had *quite* a bit to drink during this night, his inebriation should not be extreme. Slurred speech, staggering, and so forth will only detract from the essential situation. In Shakespeare's play, Hal vows to change his life and to lead soldiers in the army to fight the Percy family, though this is certainly not the only way to resolve the situation. The key issue for Hal is responsibility and what he loses by accepting it.

Source: *The Joy Luck Club*, a film by Wayne Wang based on the novel by Amy Tan, screenplay by Ronald Bass and Amy Tan (improvisation written by UCLA student Trung Bach)

Characters

Two females: Waverly, in her mid-twenties; Auntie Lindo, Waverly's mother

Place

A barber shop

Background

Auntie Lindo was abandoned as an infant by her mother. Her marriage was arranged by matchmakers, but she managed to avoid it by fooling everyone into believing an inventive story. Auntie Lindo has struggled to ensure that her daughter retains traditional Chinese views. She is afraid that Waverly's assimilation into the culture of the United States will drive a wedge between them.

Waverly, a chess champion as a child, received tremendous honor for her achievements. Raised in the United States, Waverly has become accustomed to liberal western ways and beliefs. Her struggle to cope with Auntie Lindo's conservatism is the source of frequent mother-daughter conflicts. In particular, the two have had many disagreements since Waverly's divorce from a Chinese husband.

Situation
Waverly tells her mother that she is going to marry a man who is not Chinese.

Comments
Auntie Lindo still longs for her mother, who sent her away as a child. Her escape from an arranged marriage suggests that she is a woman of her own convictions, but her conservative background influences the ways in which she relates to her daughter. She wants Waverly to be obedient—to follow and obey all rules.

Waverly is independent and broad-minded. She is rebellious, yet respectful of her mother. Waverly once said to her mother, "You don't know the power you have over me," and this remark underlies their whole relationship.

Source: *Langston Hughes: Poet of the People,* a play by Mary Satchell

Characters
Two males: Langston Hughes, the African American writer, as a teenager; James Hughes, his father

Place
The study in James Hughes' home near Mexico City; the summer of 1920

Background
Mr. Hughes wants his son to study engineering in college so that one day he can run the family's ranch. Langston, however, wants to be a writer.

Situation
Mr. Hughes enters the study to see if his son is doing his accounting problems for school, but finds Langston doing nothing. Langston tells Mr. Hughes that, though he has tried, he is not interested in accounting; he wants to write. His father believes that Langston will be wasting his life if he becomes a writer, and he does his utmost to persuade his son to study engineering, something he feels is really worthwhile. However, Langston is determined to do what *he* believes to be worthwhile.

Comments
Langston's decision to become a writer, especially a poet—the hardest of all in terms of earning a living—is devastating to Mr. Hughes. He visual-

izes his son's life going down the drain. Langston is confident about his ability to write, but it is difficult to disappoint his father.

Langston Hughes went on to become one of the United States' great poets. Two of his most famous poems are "The Negro Speaks of Rivers" and "Harlem Night Song." He published many books of poetry, plays, novels, and essays. In the end, his father was proud of him.

Source: *Miss Saigon,* a musical by Alain Boublil and Claude-Michel Schönberg (improvisation written by UCLA student Marie Gulmatico)

Characters
Two females: Kim, a Vietnamese woman; Ellen, an American woman

Place
Ellen's hotel room in Bangkok, Thailand; the 1970s

Background
Three years ago, Kim, a girl from the provinces, was forced into prostitution at a brothel in Saigon. Chris, a soldier working at the American Embassy, spotted Kim her first night out. They fell in love immediately. He promised to take her to the United States, but during the chaos of evacuation was unable to find her and was forced to leave without her.

Believing that she is married to Chris, Kim left Saigon for Bangkok, where she worked as a prostitute and gave birth to a child fathered by Chris. She sustained herself with thoughts of an eventual peaceful future with her husband and their child in the United States.

Chris did everything he could to find Kim. After years of fruitless effort, he finally gave up the search, married, and tried to start a new life. His wife, Ellen, helped him to put the traumas of the Vietnam War behind him, and she loves him dearly. She does not know how serious Kim and Chris' relationship was, but she knows that they had a child.

Through a Vietnam War veterans organization, Chris and Ellen discovered that Kim and the child were living in Bangkok. The couple have journeyed to Thailand. Chris is out combing the city for Kim, while Ellen waits in the hotel room.

Situation
Kim knows that Chris is in Bangkok and discovers where he is staying. She goes to his hotel room expecting to be reunited with her husband at last. Instead, Ellen greets her at the door. Ellen thinks that Kim is the maid. Through the ensuing conversation, Kim discovers who Ellen is.

Comments

Do not stereotype Kim as the prostitute. Prostitution is a means of survival for her and her child. Kim has gone through hell and back to be with Chris. Her ultimate dream, beyond being with Chris, is to provide a safe home for her child in the United States. Ellen loves Chris but also empathizes with Kim's situation. Each actor should avoid portraying her character as a victim.

Source: *Nine Armenians,* a play by Leslie Ayvazian

Characters

Ensemble; Five females, two males: Ani, in her late teens; her mother; Non, her grandmother; Ginya, her younger sister; Aunt Louise; Uncle Garo; Raffi, her younger brother—all are Armenian (The number of characters is flexible.)

Place

An airport in the United States

Background

Ani's grandfather had tried to teach her about her Armenian heritage, but she has had a hard time identifying with it. When her grandfather died, she decided to go to Armenia. Her grandmother, parents, aunt, and uncle know that the country is in turmoil and do not want her to go.

Situation

The whole family goes with Ani to the airport. They still plead with her to change her mind; they fear she may not survive the hardships of Armenia.

Comments

The actors may find it helpful to know something of the history of Armenia—it is a long and tragic one, starting centuries before the common era. Armenia is a small country, located where Turkey, Iran, and the former Soviet Union meet. Three seas surround it: the Black Sea, the Caspian Sea, and the Mediterranean Sea. A great mountain, Ararat, is the source of its rivers. Armenia is rich in oil fields, which have been plundered by its neighbors for generations. And it has endured three waves of genocide. In 1915, Turkey committed wholesale slaughter of the Armenian people. Over one million Armenians were murdered, and many more died of starvation. Six million Armenians have fled their homeland and are now scattered around the world. Ani's grandmother lived through the decimation of her people in 1915 and is worried about her granddaughter's safety. In Armenia today, food and fuel are scarce; the winters are bitterly cold.

Ani's departure stirs up painful memories, particularly for her grand-mother. Ani, having been brought up in the comfort of suburbia, really has no conception of life in Armenia. She is sorry that she ignored her grandfather's attempts to make her aware of her background, and she is determined to undertake this mission. She feels that she must do this for him. There is also a part of Ani that is scared and would rather stay home with her family.

Source: "The Old Chief Mshlanga," a short story by Doris Lessing in *Somehow Tenderness Survives: Stories of Southern Africa*, selected by Hazel Rochman

Characters
Two males: Nkosis Jordan, a white African; Chief Mshlanga, an elderly black African

Place
The home of Nkosis Jordan, South Africa; the 1980s

Background
Nkosis Jordan's fields were trampled by the goats from Chief Mshlanga's kraal. Nkosis confiscated all the goats, sending a message to the chief that if he wanted them back he would have to pay for the damage. Up until this time, the two men have had an amicable relationship.

Situation
The chief arrives at the home of Nkosis to plead for the return of his goats. He claims that his people cannot afford to lose all twenty goats at once—it would mean starvation during the dry season. Nkosis feels that the damage to his crop entitles him to keep the goats.

Comments
Neither man is rich, although the chief believes that Nkosis is a man of wealth. Nkosis does have the upper hand; due to the current social situation, the chief cannot go to the police. All the land inhabited by white settlers once belonged to Chief Mshlanga and his tribe. The chief is a man of dignity and highly regarded by his people. When he steps into the white man's world, however, he is treated as a servant.

Nkosis is not an evil man; he is still a beneficiary of apartheid. He is following the rules established by the society in which he lives. Both men want justice, but Nkosis has an advantage because of his position.

Of course, the South African system of apartheid plays a role in this situation; the actors should be aware of the racial hierarchy that existed at this time. (In the story, the chief uses an interpreter because he does not speak English. The actors might want to incorporate that element into the improvisation.)

Source: *Peer Pressure* (an original improvisation written by UCLA student Spencer Thiel)

Characters
One male, one female: Kevin; Erica, his girlfriend—both are in their teens

Place
The living room in Kevin's parents' house

Background
Kevin and Erica have been dating for several months and have begun to fall in love. Before meeting Erica, Kevin was involved in sexual relationships, but only a few. He has not yet slept with Erica, because she is saving herself for marriage. She is afraid that she will end up like her mother, who was only seventeen when she had Erica. Kevin's friends are constantly making fun of him because he is not having sex with Erica. Kevin desperately wants to maintain his friendship with Erica, but he has told her several times that if she doesn't sleep with him soon he will break up with her. Erica is worried that if she doesn't capitulate, she will lose Kevin.

Kevin's parents have gone away for the weekend, and he sees this as an opportunity to begin the sexual part of his relationship with Erica.

Situation
Kevin and Erica are sitting on the couch watching television. They start kissing, but Erica begins to feel uncomfortable and pulls away. Infuriated, Kevin again threatens to leave her if she doesn't have sex with him.

Comments
It is important that the actor playing Kevin explore his inner conflict. He is being pulled in all directions by his friends, by his sexual urges, and by his love for Erica. Likewise, the actor playing Erica needs to explore the range of emotions she is experiencing. She loves Kevin and suspects that she will not regret sleeping with him. At the same time, Erica does not want to end up like her mother, and she does not feel that she is emotionally ready for a sexual relationship.

Source: "The Reunion," a short story by Maya Angelou in *Hot and Cool: Jazz Short Stories,* edited by Marcela Breton

Characters
Two females: Philomena, a young black woman; Beth Ann, a young white woman

Place
A jazz nightclub in Chicago, Illinois; 1958

Background
Philomena has bitter childhood memories of the wealthy white couple for whom she and her parents worked. Beth Ann, the couple's daughter, did many cruel things to Philomena. Once, when Philomena attempted to play the piano, Beth Ann slammed the key cover down on Philomena's hands.

Situation
Philomena is now a talented jazz pianist employed by an upscale nightclub with a predominantly black clientele. Beth Ann enters the nightclub with her husband, a black man. Philomena, still haunted by the unhappy childhood memories, recognizes her. On her break between performances, Philomena gets up the courage to confront Beth Ann.

Comments
The actor playing Philomena should create very specific memories of the hurtful incidents she suffered at the hands of Beth Ann and her parents. The wounds are deep. Beth Ann might attempt to justify what she did to Philomena as a child; she may or may not acknowledge that she did anything wrong. Why did Beth Ann marry a black man? In Maya Angelou's short story, the two women are not reconciled. Although the actors may find a different resolution, they are cautioned not to let the scene become sentimental. The actors are also advised to take into account the racial climate of the United States in 1958.

Source: *Scorpions,* a novel by Walter Dean Myers

Characters
Ensemble; Three males, one female: Jamal Hicks, twelve years old; Dwayne Parsons, twelve years old; Mr. Davidson, the school principal; Mrs. Parsons, Dwayne's mother—all are African American

Place
Mr. Davidson's office in a high school in Harlem, a section of New York City

Background
Jamal's older brother, Randy, was the leader of a gang known as the Scorpions. Randy is now in jail, and, until his release, he wants Jamal to take his place as the leader of the Scorpions. Some of the gang members have objected to Jamal's leadership and are threatening him. One of the Scorpions who likes Jamal has given him a gun for protection.

Jamal has also been having a hard time at school. Dwayne Parsons, one of his classmates, is always trying to pick fights with him. One day, Dwayne and Jamal got into a fight in the school storeroom. Jamal was losing, so he pulled the gun on Dwayne. Dwayne told his mother, Mrs. Parsons, who has now come to see the principal.

Situation
Jamal is called to the principal's office to confront Dwayne and Mrs. Parsons. Mr. Davidson has to hear the story from both sides before he can call the police. He tells Mrs. Parsons that he can be sued for accusing someone of something they haven't done; he must also consider the school's reputation. Jamal denies having had a gun and claims that Dwayne is mad at him because he tore Dwayne's shirt.

Comments
Each person has something to protect: Jamal wants to stay out of trouble with the police; Dwayne is afraid for his life; Dwayne's mother is afraid for her son's life; and Mr. Davidson is concerned with the reputation of the school and, ultimately, the security of his job.

See index for other improvisations from this source.

Source: *The Slave*, a play by LeRoi Jones

Characters
One female, two males: Grace, a white woman in her forties; Walker Vessels, a black man in his forties, Grace's former husband; Bradford Easley, a white man in his forties, a university professor, Grace's present husband

Place
The living room in Grace and Bradford's home; the early 1960s

Background
Unable to stomach Walker's increasing militancy and insane hatred of whites, Grace divorced him several years ago. She then married Bradford, and they live with Grace's two daughters from her previous marriage. Somehow, Walker had been able to separate Grace from other white people in his mind and to believe that he loved her. He never forgave her for leaving him.

A race riot, instigated by Walker, is raging outside in the streets.

Situation
In the midst of the riot, Walker bursts into Grace and Bradford's home. He holds them at gun point and tells them that he has come to take his two daughters away. Grace and Bradford desperately attempt to dissuade him.

Comments
The actors playing Grace and Bradford must not forget that they are in great danger. Also remember that this play is set in the early 1960s, during a period of great tension between blacks and whites. That Grace's second marriage is to a white man is relevant. Walker and Grace did have two children together, which created a bond, but Walker's hatred of whites and of Bradford is out of bounds. He has become twisted by his hatred, jealousy, and feelings of rejection. The plays ends with everyone dead; in this improvisation another resolution may evolve.

Source: *Steel Magnolias,* a play by Robert Harling

Characters
Two females: Shelby, in her twenties; Shelby's mother

Place
The kitchen of Shelby's parents' home

Background
Shelby has a serious case of diabetes. When her insulin is low, she has convulsions. Her mother has lived with the fear of losing Shelby all her life. A doctor told Shelby that having a child would probably prove fatal to her. Now Shelby is married, and she has just gotten pregnant.

Situation
Shelby's mother, in the midst of baking, is breaking eggs into a bowl. Shelby announces that she is pregnant. Her mother, knowing this could

mean her daughter's death, is very upset by the news. Shelby has the task of convincing her mother how important it is to her to have the baby.

Comments

Both actors need to accept the reality of the doctor's prognosis. The actor playing Shelby needs to find for herself the significance of having her own child rather than adopting. And the actor playing her mother needs to do everything she can to persuade Shelby not to have this child. To her, Shelby's decision to continue the pregnancy is equivalent to suicide.

Source: *To Kill a Mockingbird,* a novel by Harper Lee

Characters

Four males, one female, ensemble: Tom Robinson, a twenty-five-year-old black man; Atticus Finch, a white lawyer; Mr. Gilmer, a white lawyer; Judge Taylor, a white man; Mayella Ewell, a nineteen-year-old white girl; other court officers and spectators, black and white

Place

A courtroom in Maycomb County, Atlanta, Georgia; 1930

Background

Mayella Ewell accused Tom Robinson of attempting to rape her. Tom is uneducated and living in the South at a time when blacks had few rights; Mayella would be labeled as "poor white trash." Her demeanor suggests that she has had a hard life. Her family is large, and her father is abusive. Tom has been brought to trial; he is being defended by Atticus Finch. Mr. Gilmer is the prosecuting attorney for Mayella.

Situation

Mayella takes the witness stand and is questioned, first by Mr. Gilmer and then by Atticus. She recounts that she was on her front porch when Tom passed by. She claims that when she turned around to go inside her house, Tom jumped on her from behind. Not only did he rape her, she insists, but he also hit her several times. Atticus, in his cross-examination, reveals that Mayella's father drinks and is often physically abusive to her, although she will not admit it. He tries to get her to declare whether it was Tom or her father who hit her in the face. Because she is lying, her answers become quite confused.

Tom Robinson takes the witness stand and is questioned by Atticus. Tom is married, with three children. He works picking pecans, chopping wood, and doing other odd jobs. Tom recounts that Mayella often asks him to do little chores for her when he passes by. He always does them because Mayella never seems to have much help or money. Tom testifies that he never went on the Ewell property without an invitation. On the day in question, Mayella asked him to come into the house to fix something. He noticed that it was unnaturally quiet around the Ewell place, which was usually filled with children.

Mayella told him that she had sent the children out for ice cream. She asked him to step on a chair to get a box down from the top of a chifforobe. As he was reaching for it, she grabbed him around the legs. He fell off the chair and she jumped on him, kissing him. When he heard Mayella's father coming, he broke from her as gently as he could and ran. Prosecutor Gilmer cross-examines Tom and accuses him of lying, insisting that Tom raped Mayella. Gilmer is quite disrespectful in his questioning.

Comments

The actors are warned not to get caught up in courtroom procedure. A certain amount of background material has been given, but the characters on the witness stand may not use all this information; it depends on the questioning. (On the witness stand, under stress, people often forget pertinent facts anyway.)

Mayella is lying about everything, while Tom is telling the truth. The actors may add their own "facts" as long as the basic story is not altered. Atticus must prove Tom's innocence—virtually an impossible task at this time in the South's history. Although it is pretty evident that Mayella is covering up for her actions and that the sexual violence was really perpetrated by her father, the jury brings in a verdict of guilty. It is difficult for both Tom and Mayella to take the stand; neither of them is very articulate, and the actors need to take this fact into account. This trial is a travesty of justice, but Atticus is brave in his efforts to defend Tom. Although Tom knows deep down that he has little chance in this kangaroo court, he must do what he can to save his own life. Mayella is attempting to save herself from humiliation in front of the whole town. The court is filled with spectators, black and white.

Source: "Vilma Martinez," an incident from the life of Vilma Martinez, as told in *Notable Hispanic Women* edited by D. Felgen and J. Kamp

Characters

Two females: Vilma Martinez, a junior high school student; a guidance counselor

Place
The guidance counselor's office; the 1970s

Background
At one time, Mexican American children were expected to go to a different high school, one that prepared them for menial work rather than for college.

Situation
The guidance counselor suggests that Vilma attend a vocational school; she believes that Vilma will be more comfortable with other Mexican American immigrants. However, Vilma wants to go to Jefferson High School, so that she will be prepared for college. She will have to fight for her right to attend Jefferson, because it is not the norm.

Comments
The actor playing the guidance counselor needs to accept the prejudice that prevailed at that time. She is unable to see Vilma any differently than the way that society has taught her to see Mexican Americans. She is convinced that Vilma will be happier at a school in which most Mexican American children enroll. (Students love playing authority figures, such as counselors.)

The actor playing Vilma needs to believe in herself enough to persuade the counselor to break the pattern. Her whole future is at stake. Remember, neither of them knows of Vilma's impending success.

In fact, Vilma did go to Jefferson High School and then to college. In 1982, she became a lawyer in a large law firm handling business cases. She worked for an organization called MALDEF and became an important figure in public education, serving on the governing board of the University of California system. She testified before Congress in an attempt to gain voting rights for Mexican Americans and to get election materials printed in Spanish as well as in English. President Carter asked Vilma Martinez to choose ambassadors to represent the United States in other countries. She served on committees to appoint judges for California courts. Many powerful people in the United States government recognized her abilities and called on her for help.

Source: *The Wedding,* a novel by Dorothy West

Characters
One male, one female: Clark Coles, an African American man; Shelby, his daughter, a mulatto woman in her late teens or early twenties

Place
Their home in the South; the early twentieth century

Background
Clark, Shelby's father, married a white woman, Corrine, and they had two daughters, Shelby and Liz. Clark and Corrine's marriage has not been fulfilling, but the two have remained together for the sake of the children. For many years, Clark has had a mistress, a black woman named Rachel. He recently decided to leave Corrine and marry his true love, Rachel.

Tomorrow Shelby is to be married to Meade, a white man. Their wedding has been in the planning stages for months.

Situation
Clark announces that he wants Shelby to cancel her impending marriage to Meade. He interprets her choosing to marry a white man as a rejection of himself, a black man. He accuses her of being afraid to marry within her own race.

Comments
Shelby has had no prior indication of her father's attitude before this moment. Through all these months of planning the wedding, he has said nothing. Although Shelby loves Meade, Clark succeeds in placing doubts in her mind. What she doesn't realize is that all of this has come up because of the emotional turmoil in Clark's life.

See index for other improvisations from this source.

Source: *Wedding Band,* a play by Alice Childress

Characters
Two females: Julia, a young black woman; Herman's mother, a white woman

Place
The front yard of Julia's house in the black section of Charleston, South Carolina; 1918

Background
While the war is raging in Europe, a deadly influenza epidemic is sweeping over the world, killing millions in its path. It has now reached Charleston. At the same time, race relations are at the boiling point, as the old South is being dragged into the new century. African Americans are still treated as virtual indentured servants.

Herman, a white man, and Julia, a black woman, have been in love for ten years. Because it is illegal for them to marry—or even to have a relationship—they can never be seen together in public. So, they have been meeting secretly in Julia's home. Herman's mother knows of this relationship and is outraged by it. Herman has been stricken with influenza and needs medical attention.

Situation

Herman's mother has come to take him to a hospital. As Herman is being taken out of Julia's house, his mother confronts Julia about her relationship with Herman. She wants Julia to forget her son. Julia has given ten years of her life to this man. They love each other.

Comments

The actors need to understand the historical context in which this play takes place. In the South, it was impossible for blacks and whites to mix. In the eyes of Herman's mother, this relationship is a disgrace; she thinks of Julia as inferior. But Julia is strong; she can stand up to this woman in spite of her "inferior" position in life.

This improvisation can be continued with another scene between Julia and Herman's mother. Herman is dying, and he has come to Julia. His mother asks Julia to let him die in his own home. Julia has to make this decision.

3

Fantasy

People spend a great part of their lives fantasizing—imagining themselves living in another time or place or becoming other people. For the actor in particular it is beneficial to move away from the naturalistic world and into the realm of make-believe. The actor's task is to experience and identify with make-believe situations as though they are real. Michael Chekhov wrote, "The imagination of an actor is not that of an ordinary person. I want to know how to do things which I am not able to do" (1985, 41).

Stanislavski once suggested to a student that he imagine himself to be a tree. Just saying that you are a tree doesn't make you believe it. You have to ask yourself certain questions, such as: If I were a tree, what would I do? Where am I? What are my surroundings? How do they affect me? What do I hear? What do I see? What is my purpose? What are the surrounding circumstances that would move me emotionally or incite me to action? Once the actor has definite visual images, he is living the fantasy. In Stanislavski's words: "Every movement you make on the stage, every word you speak, is the result of the right life of your imagination" (1936, 67).

The situations in this chapter allow actors to create a world that does not exist, that is pure fantasy. In *Lessons for the Professional Actor*, Michael Chekhov suggests that there are three stages in exercising the imagination: the first is to imagine things we already know; the second is to imagine things we've never seen but have heard about; and the third is to imagine things that do not exist. Even though the actor is inventing elements that never have been or, perhaps, never can be, sometimes the most fantastical things prove to be true, such as the existence of life on other planets. Human beings possess the ability to see things that do not exist, to create mental pictures. The actor's ability to create a mental picture is essential, and these improvisations should be a stimulus. The characters are real, feeling human beings in fantastical situations. After attempting these improvisations, actors will return to more realistic circumstances with a fresh, perhaps more inventive, perspective.

Stanislavski said "imagination plays by far the greatest part." In his book, *An Actor Prepares*, Stanislavski makes reference to a drawing of a design, planned for the last act of a Chekhov play about an expedition to the arctic. It was painted by a man who had never left the suburbs of Moscow; he painted from his imagination. Stanislavski then points out sketches for a play about life on other planets. In this case, the artist is relying on fantasy.

FANTASY SITUATIONS

One male, one female
The Infernal, Interdimensional Experiments of Doctor McFee
Liliom
Shakuntala
*The Tragedy of Tragedies, or The Life and Death of Tom Thumb the
    Great*

Two females
Fatal Beatings

Two males
Fatal Beatings
The Giver

Ensemble
A Midsummer Night's Dream

Source: *Fatal Beatings*, a film by Richard Curtis, Rowan Atkinson, and Ben Elton (improvisation written by UCLA student Adam De La Pena)

Characters
Two males or females: A headmaster, any age; Mr. or Mrs. Perkins, any age, the parent of a prep school student

Place
The headmaster's study in an English prep school

Background
Like many parents, Mr. and Mrs. Perkins want their son to have the very best education, so they enrolled him in an expensive and well-known English preparatory school. Their son has always done well in school and has never been unruly.

Situation
Mr. or Mrs. Perkins is called in to speak with the headmaster about some disciplinary problems with their son. The headmaster tells the parent that their son has not been going to any classes or turning in his homework because he is dead. (This is not regarded by the school as an excuse.) It is later revealed that death came by way of a beating administered to punish the son for neglecting to check out a library book with a library card. The headmaster threatens to expel the child if his behavior does not improve.

Comments
It is very important that the actor playing the headmaster treat this situation with the utmost sincerity and conviction that this dead child's behavior is a problem of grave concern. The parent must understand that the headmaster is a highly respected man. Their son's future depends on his opinion. They have no reason to doubt anything the headmaster tells them. This is a comment on the sometimes petty incidents in the educational system that get blown out of proportion.

Source: *The Giver,* a novel by Lois Lowry

Characters
Two males: Jonas, twelve years old; the Elder Giver, an old man

Place
A spacious room, filled with luxuriously upholstered furniture and thousands of books

Background
In this rigidly structured, rule-oriented, science fiction society, everything is geared to "sameness." Couples can have only two children: one male and

one female. Babies are assigned to parents. Anyone who does not live by the rules is expelled from the community. People are required to take pills when they have "stirrings" (feelings of any depth). At age twelve, children are given a profession, for which they are trained. Jonas is not assigned to a profession but has the honor bestowed upon him of becoming the "receiver of memory." All he has been told about this position is that he should report to the House of the Old after school each day. He is not to discuss his training with anyone, he may not take medication, and he may lie about what he is doing.

Situation

This is Jonas's first meeting with the elder, who is the present receiver for the community. The elder has been doing this job since the age of twelve; now it is time for him to prepare Jonas to take his place. His task is to transmit to Jonas all the memories of the past—the memories of the whole world from past generations.

The elder begins to transfer his memories into Jonas' mind. He starts with pleasant remembrances, such as the memory of snow. No one in this community has a memory of such things as snow, mountains, and the sun; they live in a climate-controlled world. Also, in their world there are no colors—everyone has the same skin and hair color; clothes are colorless; there are no colors in nature; everything is gray. No one chooses a mate, or children, or a job. People know nothing of war, birthday parties, holidays, museums, animals, love, anger, sadness, happiness, or music. The elder must give all of these memories to Jonas. And as he transmits a memory, the elder loses that memory forever.

Comments

Of course, the elder cannot give all these memories to Jonas in just one day. For the sake of this exercise, however, the actor should choose the memories he wants to impart. They should be both painful and pleasant. The actor playing Jonas must receive the memories as if he were an empty vessel or a blank slate, experiencing these sensations for the first time. The elder must be very clear in his descriptions and create images as he transmits the memories. He can use personal experiences, events in history, and so forth.

Jonas asks the elder for his favorite memory. The actor should choose his own. It will be a challenge to guide the other character into feelings of sadness, anger, and love—for the first time. How do you explain these emotions? The actor "receiving" needs to be able to absorb these revelations. In this community all pain—mental and physical—is immediately repressed, so he also needs to convey the first experience of physical pain. This is a difficult acting exercise, but a valuable one.

Source: *The Infernal Interdimensional Experiments of Doctor McFee,* a comic book by Johnny Tornado (improvisation written by UCLA student Damon Poeter)

Characters
One female, one male: Beth Buxemberg, a former beauty pageant queen, in her mid-thirties; Dr. Cyrus McFee, an elderly (and rich) scientist

Place
A hospital room

Background
Dr. McFee has been experimenting in extradimensional travel his whole life. Last week, he finally succeeded in transporting himself to another dimension, where he saw bizarre and unspeakable things. As a scientist, he has been able to maintain his sanity, but he has been affected by one significant thing in his return to our dimension: he now can physically see words as they are formed by other humans and can capture them with his hands and eat them as if they were food. He has become addicted to these words that only he can see, and he will do anything to continue catching them and eating them—even risk his life. Words live for only ten seconds after leaving the mouth, and, as they are living, they try to get away from pursuers, so Dr. McFee must chase them and snare them quickly.

Beth Buxemberg is Dr. McFee's wife. She married him ten years ago for his vast wealth, hoping that he would die and leave her a substantial amount of money. In the last few years, however, she has grown to love the eccentric old coot and will be sorry when he passes on. Dr. McFee's kids despise Beth and think of her as only a gold digger. Dr. McFee has written no will, and it is assumed that his estate will simply be split among the children, leaving Beth out in the cold.

Situation
Since his latest dimensional trip, after which Beth found him unconscious in the laboratory, Dr. McFee has been hospitalized. The doctor has told her that any sudden movements would cause Dr. McFee to hemorrhage and die. Beth has called in an attorney to draw up a will and is trying to convince Dr. McFee to leave his money to her. The attorney has not yet arrived, and Beth struggles to keep her husband alive until he does. She is also aware that the children could show up at any second. Meanwhile, Dr. McFee has awakened and feels the urge to eat words.

Comments
The actor playing Dr. McFee really does see words as delicious and intoxicating food; his dimensional travel is completely real, not the hallucina-

tions of a mad scientist. In fact, Dr. McFee is in all ways a coldly rational scientist, a bit absent-minded in day-to-day life, perhaps, but in his studies completely meticulous and logical. It is important that this strange addiction be one hundred percent real to the actor. The actor playing Beth should feel both a love bond with her husband and a strong desire to make sure he gives his money to her—she needs to be able to convey both her ambition and her very real feelings for the doctor in a way that does not compromise either of these driving forces.

Source: *Liliom*, a play by Ferenc Molnar

Characters
One male, one female: Billy Bigelow, in his twenties; Louise, his teen-aged daughter

Place
The porch of Billy's home

Background
Billy Bigelow was a barker at the carousel, where he met Julie Jordan. Jealous of his attentions to Julie, Mrs. Mullin, his boss, forbade Billy to allow Julie on the carousel again. Billy refused to comply and was fired. He and Julie fell in love and married. However, Billy could not get work and became abusive. One day Julie announced that she was pregnant. Desperate to earn money to support the child, Billy agreed to take part in a robbery, during which he was shot and died.

Situation
Fifteen years have gone by, and Billy is still in purgatory. An angel tells him that he has one day on earth to do something good in order to get into heaven. Billy goes back to meet his daughter, Louise. He sees that she has become promiscuous and that her heart has been broken many times. This is the day before her graduation from high school. He talks to her; she can see and hear him.

Comments
Louise, naturally, is frightened and bewildered. Billy might be a crazy person. He must persuade her that he is really her father. She has heard terrible things about him from all the kids and adults—he was a thief, he struck her mother, he was a no-good bum—and she has believed these things for many years. Because they are true, the actor must not deny them. Billy, however, has a short time to convince Louise that there is

more to his character than she has heard; he loved her mother very much, for example. Billy must give Louise hope about her future. (The Rodgers and Hammerstein musical, *Carousel*, is based on this play.)

Source: *A Midsummer Night's Dream*, a play by William Shakespeare

Characters
Ensemble; Two females, two males: Helena; Hermia; Lysander; Demetrius

Place
A wood some distance from Athens, Greece, a favorite haunt of the fairies

Background
Helena is in love with Demetrius. He used to tell her he loved her, but now he despises her and loves Hermia instead. Hermia's father, Egeus, wants her to marry Demetrius because he is of a noble Athenian family, but Hermia loves Lysander. Hermia pleaded with her father—*Helena* loves Demetrius and should marry him—but her plea fell on deaf ears. If Hermia refuses to marry Demetrius, she will be put to death in four days: this is the legal punishment for disobedience.

Hermia told Lysander of her predicament. Lysander arranged for her to flee beyond the boundaries of the city, where he planned to meet her. Hermia, delighted with the plan, told Helena, who told Demetrius, whom she knew would follow Hermia to the wood.

Oberon, the king of the fairies, observed Demetrius and Helena fighting. He asked Puck, his shrewd and mischievous sprite, to put the juice of a flower called Love in Idleness on the eyelids of Demetrius when he was asleep; the juice would cause him to fall in love with the first thing he saw upon awakening. Oberon told Puck to make sure that Helena was nearby, so that when Demetrius woke up he would see Helena first and love her.

However, Puck mistook Lysander for Demetrius, and put the love juice in his eyes. When Lysander woke up, he saw Helena and forgot his love for Hermia. Puck, realizing his mistake, also put the juice in Demetrius' eyes.

Situation
Demetrius and Lysander awake and, seeing Helena, they both fall madly in love with her. Helena is furious with them because she believes they are teasing her. It seems to her a cruel joke when Demetrius knows how she feels about him. Hermia arrives and sees her beloved Lysander chasing after Helena. Helena thinks that Demetrius, Lysander, and her once dear

friend Hermia are all in a plot to make fun of her. Hermia is as amazed as Helena; she doesn't know why Lysander and Demetrius, who both used to love her, are now the lovers of Helena.

Comments

Hermia and Helena were close friends before this strange occurrence. The two men cannot remember their previous feelings about the two women; they have eyes only for Helena. Needless to say, this causes much confusion and anger. At the end of the play, the fairies straighten it all out and Demetrius ends up with Helena and Hermia with Lysander.

Source: *Shakuntala,* an ancient Indian play by Kalidasa (improvisation written by UCLA student Stacy Rothman)

Characters
One male, one female: King Dushyanta; Shakuntala, his wife

Place
The king's palace

Background
King Dushyanta was traveling through Shakuntala's town and, by chance, they met and fell in love at first sight. Soon after, the two were married. One day Shakuntala was very rude to a stranger who was passing through the town. The stranger placed an evil curse on Shakuntala: if she failed to wear the ring given to her by King Dushyanta, she would become unrecognizable to him.

A great war divided the country, and King Dushyanta sent Shakuntala away to a place of safety. During their separation, Shakuntala accidentally lost the ring.

Situation
At last the war is over, and Shakuntala has returned to the palace. She finds her way to her beloved husband—and he does not recognize her.

Comments
The actors should remember the romantic and love-filled past that these two characters shared. In Kalidasa's play, the ring is found by a fisherman, and the lovers are reunited to live happily ever after. However, at the time that this situation takes place, Shakuntala must deal with the idea of losing her husband—while he is sitting right in front of her. Although he does not recognize Shakuntala as anyone of particular importance, King

Dushyanta must agonize over wanting to remember the happiness the two had once shared.

King Dushyanta and Shakuntala should still feel an emotional bond during the scene, which supports the theme that true love will always triumph. He may not know who she is, but his feelings for her are still somewhere inside.

Source: *The Tragedy of Tragedies, or The Life and Death of Tom Thumb the Great,* a novel by Henry Fielding

Characters
One female, one male: the Princess Huncamunca; Lord Grizzle

Place
The court of King Arthur in England; 1731

Background
Princess Huncamunca was King Arthur's daughter and equally in love with both Lord Grizzle and Tom Thumb, who was the size of a thumb. Both men were very much in love with her.

Situation
Princess Huncamunca announces to Lord Grizzle that she has just married Tom Thumb. He is astonished; he had expected to marry her himself. She proposes that she marry both of them. However, Lord Grizzle does not want to share her with another man.

Comments
The actor playing Lord Grizzle can decide what to do about Huncamunca's proposal. This is a farcical piece, but the actors should still portray these characters as real people.

The Tragedy of Tragedies is a political satire, poking fun at historical personages: the womanizing King George II, his wife, and their hero, Prime Minister Walpole, who, in Fielding's novel, is reduced to the size of a thumb.

4

Relationship

This chapter focuses on situations in which the primary element is the relationship between two characters. If it is a long-standing relationship, the actors should research the history of these people to discover what they like or dislike about each other. The relationship between two people in a scene is about much more than the factual connection or the formal arrangements between them. It is about the multiplicity of feelings in the relationship—the full emotional attitude of each character toward the other character. Also, it is useful to endow other characters with a secret—something you know about them that they do not know you know. It is these kinds of background details that will determine the ways in which characters relate to one another truthfully.

Milton Katselas once told an acting class that all relationships must be Clytemnestra and Agamemnon. It is not all simple reality; it is also a Greek chorus. The relationships in this chapter must all be approached with that sense of importance. These characters' lives are interwoven with and crucial to each other. The actors must concentrate on each other. They cannot simply stand alone and talk.

Love is an element in all relationships, even if it is only the *desire* to love and to be loved. In *Audition*, Michael Shurtleff writes that love is a "given" in every scene; characters always want love from each other. The actor should learn which kind of love is present in the relationship—passionate, familial, obsessive, spiritual, affectionate—and how it affects the interactions of the characters. "The desire for love, to give it or receive it and preferably both and simultaneously, is the chief propellant in human beings. An actor had best learn that love comes in all forms, and in many more forms than only those he himself admires" (Shurtleff 1978, 29).

RELATIONSHIP SITUATIONS

One male, one female
Ah, Wilderness!
Anna Karenina
The Big, Bad World
La Bionda (The Blonde)
Camilla
"A Couple of Kooks"
Cronaca di un Amore
Emma
The Hunger Waltz
Lady Jane
The Language of Flowers
Little Women
Machinal, Episode Three: Honeymoon
The Man in the Ceiling
"Masculine Protest"
Les Misérables
Our Town
Proposals
Return Engagements
The Seagull
Sleepless in Seattle
Starting Over
The Taming of the Shrew
Valley Song

Two females
The Award
Baby
Emma
Proposals
The Rest of My Life
The Wedding
A Yellow Raft in Blue Water

Two males
Convicts
Dead Poets Society
The Man in the Ceiling
"Masculine Protest"
Men, Myths, and Dogs
The Pinballs
Swingers

Ensemble
Childhood
Climbing Fences
Dreaming of Rope Ladders
Scorpions
A Yellow Raft in Blue Water

Source: *Ah, Wilderness!*, a play by Eugene O'Neill

Characters
One male, one female: Richard Miller, sixteen years old; Muriel McComber, fifteen years old

Place
A strip of beach on the harbor

Background
Muriel and Richard are in love. Muriel's father does not approve of Richard, and he has told Muriel that she must never see Richard again. The young people have not met for some time. During their separation, Richard spent a drunken night on the town with an older woman, which he now regrets.

Muriel has made arrangements for a clandestine meeting, and Richard has been waiting anxiously for her to appear.

Situation
Muriel arrives. She is eager to see Richard, but he greets her nonchalantly. Disappointed by his reception, Muriel turns to leave, whereupon Richard admits how broken-hearted he has been without her. They reminisce about their miserable existences during their separation. Richard tells Muriel about his drunken escapade with the older woman, and Muriel is overcome by jealousy.

Comments
In the play, this scene ends with Muriel and Richard's first kiss—and a new declaration of love for each other. No matter how the improvisation ends,

the actors should remember that Muriel and Richard are absolute roman-
tics in the throes of their first love. The actor playing Muriel should be
specific about the trials that she endured during their separation. (For example, she has not been allowed to leave the house for a month, and she
must be in bed every night by 8 P.M. sharp.)

See index for other improvisations from this source.

Source: *Anna Karenina,* a novel by Leo Tolstoy (improvisation written by UCLA student John Elerick)

Characters
One male, one female: Alexey Karenin; Anna, his wife

Place
Karenin's study in his mansion in Saint Petersburg, Russia; the late eighteenth century

Background
In a previous scene, Anna told Karenin that she has been having an affair
with a dashing member of the Czar's guards, Count Vronsky. Although
his male pride was stung, Karenin, a top official in the Saint Petersburg
government, was more concerned about his reputation should the news
of Anna's infidelity get out. He insisted that she stay under his roof and
see Vronsky elsewhere, only under the most discreet circumstances. However, this condition soon becomes untenable for Anna, who considers
Karenin an unfeeling, self-centered tyrant.

Situation
Anna has come to Karenin's study to ask for a divorce. She is certain that
she will never be happy with her husband and that she wants to marry
Vronsky. Karenin tells her that a "higher power" binds them as husband
and wife and that he cannot break that bond by divorcing her. Anna does
not back down. Karenin then plays his trump card. He tells her that a divorce would mean relinquishing all rights to their six-year-old son, Sergey;
Anna would never be permitted to see him again. She must either give up
Sergey or stop seeing Vronsky.

Comments
Anna faces the great conflict of sacrificing either her son or the man she
loves. She has not had an affair before and considers Vronsky the one true
love of her life. She respects Karenin but cannot abide his religious hypoc-
risy, having observed that religion, for him, is more appearance than sub-

stance. She also cannot stand his cold, self-centered ambition. But he holds her fate in his hands.

Karenin should not be played one-dimensionally. Though inflexible in his beliefs, he can be moved by a woman's tears and has a deep love for their son. He is proud of the career he has built, one of the most respected in Russia. (Note, however, that he has one maddening habit: he cracks his knuckles when he is under stress!)

Source: *The Award* (an original improvisation written by UCLA student Laura Wales)

Characters
Two females: Amy, fourteen years old; her mother

Place
Amy's bedroom

Background
Eight months ago, while Amy's mother was out of town, Amy saw her father leave the house in the middle of the night with a strange woman. Amy started spying on her father and discovered that he was having an affair. She listened in on his phone conversations and learned that he was planning to fly to Texas with this woman for a weekend "business trip." Amy has kept all of this a secret; she is afraid of the consequences should her mother find out.

Situation
Amy's father is out of town and will not return for several days. Amy and her mother have just returned from a junior high school awards ceremony, during which Amy was given a prize for her leadership. She is proud of her award and wants her mother to join her in celebrating the occasion. However, her mother starts yelling at her about a phone message that Amy forgot to relay to her. When Amy gets upset, her mother says that perhaps Amy needs to start seeing a counselor. Finally, Amy blurts out the news that her father is having an affair.

Comments
Amy did not intend to confess her secret to her mother. She has held everything inside; she does not want to face the possibility of her parents' getting a divorce. Although she is aware of problems in the marriage, Amy's mother never supposed that her husband was cheating on her. She has been trying to relive her own youth vicariously through her daughter, and this has led her to be hard on Amy.

A note to the actors: several questions should be answered before attempting this improvisation. What was the awards ceremony like? What was the misplaced telephone message? Why was it important to Amy's mother? How do Amy and her mother relate to Amy's father? What is it that finally triggers Amy to divulge her secret?

Source: *Baby,* a novel by Patricia MacLachlan

Characters
Two females: Larkin Byrd, twelve years old; Lily Byrd, her mother

Place
Lily's art studio on an island off the east coast of the United States

Background
Six months ago Lily had a baby boy, who lived for only one day. The baby was buried, and nobody talked about it any more. Shortly after this sad event, a baby named Sophie was left at the Byrds' doorstep in the hopes that they would care for her until her mother returned. Sophie has lived with the Byrds for several months now, and Lily gives all her attention to the baby. Larkin has just been to the cemetery, where she saw her baby brother's headstone. There was no name on it, only the word *Baby.*

Situation
Larkin confronts Lily about her baby brother. She expresses her resentment that she never saw the baby and that he was never even given a name. Larkin goes on to say that she has watched Lily being a good mother to Sophie, while neglecting Larkin. Then she sees that her mother is painting a picture of a baby. Lily tells her that the painting is of Larkin's baby brother. Larkin asks if they can name him.

Comments
Larkin's visit to the cemetery should be improvised before this scene is attempted. Larkin's anger at her mother for not talking about her baby brother's death has been building up for some time, so it has been difficult to watch Lily's display of affection toward Sophie. Undoubtedly, Lily never meant to neglect Larkin, and she has never really explored her own grief over the loss of the baby. This scene is a revelation for both of them. They could name the baby together.

See index for other improvisations from this source.

Source: *The Big, Bad World* (based on an original improvisation written by UCLA student Natalie Avital)

Characters
One male, one female: Ted, a high school teacher; Daphne, his former student

Place
The waiting room of an abortion clinic

Background
Ted was Daphne's teacher at the local high school. The two have always been attracted to each other; after Daphne graduated, they began a clandestine affair. Several months into the relationship, Daphne discovered that she was pregnant. Headed for college and ready to start a new, exciting phase of her life, she knew that it would be impossible to bear and raise the child.

Situation
In this scene, Daphne is at an abortion clinic with Ted, waiting to have the procedure performed. Ted and Daphne are very much at odds with each other, even though both of them realize that there is no place for a child in their lives. They are trying to talk through and justify their separate reasons for terminating the pregnancy.

Comments
It is important to remember that both of these people are very intelligent: this is not a TV talk show scenario. Their feelings are genuine. They have long struggled with their own insecurities about their intense connection, and this pregnancy has given them something to pull through together.

Source: *La Bionda* (*The Blonde*), a film by Sergio Rubini, screenplay by W. Gian Filippo Ascianone, Umberto Marino, and Sergio Rubini

Characters
One male, one female: Tommaso Montefusco, in his twenties or thirties; Christina, a beautiful young girl

Place
Tommaso's apartment in Milan, Italy

Background

Tommaso is studying to be a watchmaker in Milan. He is engaged to be married, but the match was arranged by his family and he is not enthusiastic about it. As Tommaso was on his way home from school one day, a young woman, Christina, ran in front of his car. He was unable to avoid hitting her, and she fell to the ground, unconscious. Fortunately, she was only slightly hurt and was released from the hospital the same day. She went to see Tommaso in his apartment.

Situation

Christina tells Tommaso that she has amnesia; she has no idea who she is or where to go. He attempts to convince her to return to the hospital, but she refuses. She wants *him* to help her retrieve her identity, although she fears that she is not a good person and has not led a good life.

Comments

The actor playing Christina can invent a past life for her, but at this point Christina can remember nothing about it. That Christina suspects that her life is not good should be suggestive to the actor. The important task here is to explore a relationship in which two unlikely people are brought together by circumstances. Although their worlds are very different, neither of them is happy. Christina is wearing an expensive, sophisticated dress, torn in the accident. Tommaso is a simple person, with little money or excitement in his life.

Source: *Camilla*, a novel by Madeleine L'Engle

Characters

One male, one female: Jacques Nissen, in his thirties; Camilla Dickinson, fifteen years old

Place

Jacques Nissen's apartment, near the Museum of Modern Art in New York City

Background

Jacques Nissen has been having an affair with Camilla's mother, Rose. Anguished and confused, Rose recently attempted suicide. Camilla knows that Rose has promised her husband that she will never see Jacques again. Meanwhile, Jacques has asked Camilla to come to his apartment to talk. Reluctantly, she keeps the appointment. She is still very shaken by her mother's attempted suicide. She is planning to tell Jacques that her parents have reunited and that her mother will no longer be seeing him.

Situation
When Camilla arrives at Jacques's apartment, she overhears him having an intimate conversation on the telephone and is surprised that he has become involved with another woman so soon after ending his affair with Rose. Jacques offers Camilla sherry. He then attempts to justify his relationship with her mother. Rose, Jacques explains, is the type of woman who needs tenderness and emotional protection, and Camilla's father is not an affectionate man. Camilla finally tells Jacques that her mother never wants to see him again. He responds by revealing that he was speaking to *Rose* on the telephone when Camilla arrived.

Comments
Jacques knows that Camilla hates him, and his objective is to win her over. Camilla is protective of her father and wants to keep her parents together. It is a shock to her that Rose and Jacques are still in contact after her mother promised not to communicate with him again. Camilla will hate her mother for a long time after this incident.

See index for other improvisations from this source.

Source: *Childhood,* a play by Thornton Wilder in *All the World's a Stage: Modern Plays for Young People,* edited by Lowell Swortzell

Characters
Three females, two males: Caroline, twelve years old; Dodie, ten years old; Billee, eight years old; Mother; Father

Place
The living room of their home

Background
Caroline, Dodie, and Billee play games that their mother labels as awful, dangerous, and morbid. In these games, the children imagine that their parents have been killed in a terrible accident; orphans, the children are free to do whatever they want. Or they imagine that their mother has been away visiting their grandmother for years and years. Caroline instigates these games. When their parents are at home, the children avoid them as

much as possible. Dressed all in black for mourning, the children are im-
mersed in their awful, dangerous, and morbid games.

Situation
Mother and Father confront Caroline, Dodie, and Billee about these
games. They want to know why the children insist on imagining these terrible things.

Comments
In Wilder's play, the parents never confront the children; they just discuss
the games in private. The children and parents remain estranged and never
get to know each other any better. Since the parents and children actually
discuss the games in this improvisation, perhaps something might be resolved. On the other hand, the discussion could backfire and alienate parents and children even more. Clearly, something is wrong in the children's
lives that they create such bleak fantasies. They may feel frightened by
their games and grateful to the parents for rescuing them; they may also
resent their parents' invasion of their private fantasy world.

The actors portraying the children should play the actual games before interacting with the parents; the actors playing the parents should
discuss the problem between themselves before approaching the children.

Source: *Climbing Fences,* a UCLA student film by Mark Lawrence

Characters
Ensemble; One female, two males: Laura; Steve; John—all are junior high
school students

Place
A bench on the school grounds

Background
Laura and Steve have been good friends since childhood. They have a pet
bird, which they rescued and raised together. This bird has been a real
bond between them. Lately, Laura has been neglecting Steve and the bird.
She is growing up and her interests are elsewhere; Steve hasn't quite kept
up with her.

Situation
Laura is sitting on a school bench waiting for John, a boy with whom she has
become romantically involved. Steve approaches Laura to tell her that the bird

is sick; he wants her help. Until recently, this would have been important news to Laura, but now her only concern is her appearance to John. Steve's presence is an embarrassment to her; he obviously does not fit into John's circle. As she is attempting to get rid of Steve, John arrives. While Laura and John are in their own flirtatious world, Steve tries to be a part of it.

Comments

This is not a scene of great conflict (except for the conflict within Laura, who is torn between leaving her childhood behind and becoming an adult with a boyfriend). Rather, this is a scene about the pains of growing up. Steve is left out and has to cope with losing his best friend. He does not know about male–female relationships yet. Laura is experiencing her first romance, which is awkward for her, but it is the most important thing in her life right now. John is also new to this, but he is very confident and wouldn't be caught dead with a kid like Steve.

Source: *Convicts,* a screenplay by Horton Foote

Characters
Two males: Horace Robedaux, white, thirteen years old; Leroy, black, in his twenties

Place
A pasture in Texas; Christmas Eve day, 1902

Background
When young Horace's father died, Horace's mother, who lived in a small house in Houston with his baby sister, found that she could no longer support her son. He was sent to live with his aunt and uncle sixty miles away on a plantation worked by convicts from a neighboring prison. Horace works for meager wages, which he is saving to purchase a tombstone for his father's grave.

Leroy is working on the plantation to pay off a fine for getting in a fight. His wages are seven dollars a week; his fine is over five hundred dollars. While he was in prison, Leroy killed a man. Horace has been given a gun with which to guard Leroy.

Situation
This is the first time the two have met. Leroy believes his days are numbered; it's only a matter of time until somebody kills him. He says that he might as well kill himself first and asks to borrow Horace's knife to do the job. Horace refuses. He desperately wants to talk about his father. He has

not recovered from the loss, and he has a hard time concentrating on anything else.

Comments
Actors, remember how lonely these two people are. Although Leroy killed a man, there must have been some justification for what he did. In this scene, both characters reveal a lot about themselves. However, these revelations should not become exposition; they should come from a deep need for human contact.

Source: "A Couple of Kooks," a short story by Cynthia Rylant in *A Couple of Kooks, and Other Stories About Love*

Characters
One female, one male: Suzy, sixteen years old; Dennis, sixteen years old

Place
Dennis' parked car on a country road; October

Background
Suzy and Dennis are two very careful people who love each other. Suzy has accidentally become pregnant. She and Dennis are both still in high school and cannot support a baby. An attorney and a social worker are in the process of finding a home for the child after Suzy gives birth. Dennis read somewhere that a fetus can hear sounds from outside the womb, so they have begun talking to the baby.

Situation
This location—a country road—is where Dennis and Suzy have come many times to sit for hours in solitude, just looking at the trees. Suzy is now in her ninth month of pregnancy, and the baby is large in her stomach. This is their last chance to talk to the baby they've grown to love. They must explain why someone else will be rearing it. Each one takes their turn talking to the baby.

Comments
Suzy and Dennis would have made excellent parents. They have devoted nine months to doing everything they could for this child—talking to it, playing music. Being sixteen and pregnant can be very alienating; Suzy doesn't feel that she belongs anywhere. The actors need to think about what they might want the baby to know about them, their life, their fu-

ture. After doing this improvisation, the actors may derive some nice monologues from the rest of the short story.

Source: *Cronaca di un Amore* (*The Story of a Love Affair*), a film by Michelangelo Antonioni, screenplay by Michelangelo Antonioni, Daniele D'Anza, Sylvio Giovannetti, Francesco Maselli, and Piero Tellini

Characters
One female, one male: A married woman; her lover

Place
A street near the woman's home

Background
This situation is based on events that actually occurred in Malibu, California, in the 1940s. The woman is married to a wealthy, older man whom she does not love. He became suspicious of her and initiated an investigation into her background. He discovered that his wife had been involved in a mysterious accident. The man with whom she was then involved had a girlfriend who fell down an empty elevator shaft. The woman and her lover both realized that she was about to fall, but did not warn her; it was easier to have her out of the picture. Their complicity in her death has haunted them for years.

When the lover sought out the woman to inform her that a detective had been asking questions, they realized that they were still passionately in love. He asked her to leave her husband, although they both knew that the lover was too poor to support her in the luxurious lifestyle she craved. The woman persuaded him to kill her husband; they could then be together and still live comfortably. He was reluctant, but she finally convinced him.

The lover planned to shoot the husband as he was driving over a bridge late at night on his way home from work, thus causing the car to crash. The plan was set, but just before the lover fired his gun, the husband's car had a blow-out, swerved, crashed—and the husband was killed.

When the woman saw the police arriving at her house, she assumed that her lover had murdered her husband and that their plan had been discovered. She rushed out of the house to avoid the police and to find her lover.

Situation
The woman finds her lover and tells him that the police are already after her. She is in a panic. Her lover tells her that he did not kill her husband.

However, although there is no longer anything to keep them apart, he realizes that their lives have been destroyed by their evil actions and that they cannot be together. She cannot follow his reasoning and begs him to stay with her.

Comments
The passion between these two people drives them to irrational acts. You could say that the lover's tragic flaw is his conscience, while the woman's tragic flaw is her need for wealth. The two have devoted most of their lives to finding a way to be together. Now that they have finally succeeded, they have lost.

A note to the actors: do not concentrate on the background story, although it is important to know that this is the second time that the woman and her lover have been involved in the death of another person. The relationship is tainted. Through this improvisation, the characters discover the moral decay that casts a shadow on their love for each other.

Source: *Dead Poets Society,* a film by Peter Weir, screenplay by Tom Schulman

Characters
Two males: Neil, a teen-ager; Neil's father

Place
Neil's room at a prestigious prep school

Background
Neil's father worked hard to send Neil to prep school; he wanted his son to have advantages he'd never had. His goal for Neil is to become a doctor, and he has ordered Neil to steer clear of any extracurricular activities at school and to devote all of his energy to his studies.

However, Neil auditioned for the school's production of *A Midsummer Night's Dream* and was cast in the role of Puck. This was the most important thing that had ever happened to Neil; he realized that he wants to become an actor. His father found out about this situation just before opening night.

Situation
Neil's father confronts him after the opening night performance and orders him to drop out of the play.

Comments

Each actor must understand what is at stake for his character. The father has devoted his life to his son, who, it seems to him, is throwing it all away. Also, he wants Neil to make up for what he, himself, hasn't achieved.

Neil is good in this play. He's having the most wonderful time of his life; suddenly he is very popular with the other students. If he drops out of the play, he'll never be able to face them again. However, Neil also knows that if he disobeys his father, he will be withdrawn from the school. (In Weir's film, the father withdraws Neil, supposedly to place him in military school, and Neil commits suicide. This information is given only to alert the actors to the seriousness of this matter. The actors should make no decision ahead of time as to the resolution of the conflict.)

See index for other improvisations from this source.

Source: *Dreaming of Rope Ladders,* a play by UCLA student Jason Sinclair Long

Characters
Ensemble; Three females, one male: Gwen, ten years old; Sarah, her sister, fifteen years old; Dora, Raymond's new girlfriend; Raymond, father of Gwen and Sarah

Place
Their home

Background
The sisters' mother died while giving birth to Gwen, and Sarah has always held Gwen responsible. Gwen is severely dyslexic; she needs special tutoring. Their father, Raymond, is employed by the military to investigate the use of illegal drugs within its ranks. He was recently brought up on charges of drug usage himself: the decision as to his innocence or guilt is pending. Sarah knows that he's guilty, but Gwen, who worships him, does not. Sarah is a vindictive and destructive child. Gwen is innocent and affectionate; she takes a good deal of abuse from Sarah.

Situation
Raymond has not been home much lately; he has been spending a lot of time at a particular café. Today, he brings home a waitress named Dora and announces that she has come to live with them.

Comments

Gwen immediately sees Dora as a mother and is happy to welcome her. Sarah detests Dora's "invasion"—no one can replace her real mother. So, Sarah intends to make Dora's life as difficult as possible. She will also resent any relationship that might develop between Dora and Gwen.

It might have helped if Raymond had given the children some warning about Dora. The actors can explore what happens when Dora becomes a member of the family.

See index for other improvisations from this source.

Source: *Emma,* a novel by Jane Austen

Characters

One female, one male: Emma, a young woman; Knightley, a young man

Place

The garden of a country house in England; the early nineteenth century

Background

Emma is a matchmaker, obsessed with finding a husband for her rather plain friend, Harriet. However, all the matches she has plotted for her friend have ended in failure. Meanwhile, Harriet has fallen in love with Emma's dear friend, Knightley. He and Emma have had a close, but strictly platonic relationship until now. But Emma has recently become aware that she is in love with Knightley. She has told neither Harriet nor Knightley about it, and now she fears that Knightley loves Harriet.

Situation

Emma and Knightley meet in the garden. Knightley has said that he has something important to relate to her, and she assumes that he is going to tell her that he is in love with Harriet. Instead, he is there to tell Emma that he loves *her*, although he is unaware of Emma's feelings for him. If Emma knew what was really on his mind, she would be eager to have him speak. As it is, she does not want him to say a word for fear that he will announce his marriage to Harriet.

Comments

The excitement of this love story is that both of these people have just discovered that they love each other, though neither of them has any idea that their love is reciprocated. Any admission of their newfound feelings could be risky for both of them. They have been friends since childhood, and the whole fulcrum of their relationship has now been altered.

See also the following improvisation.

Source: *Emma*, a novel by Jane Austen

Characters
Two females: Emma; Harriet

Place
Harriet's home in the English countryside; the early nineteenth century

Background
Emma has made a great effort to find the right husband for her dear friend, Harriet, but all of her attempts have failed. Emma had earlier convinced Harriet not to marry a young farmer (who really was the right person for her), because she had higher hopes for her friend. Meanwhile, Harriet has revealed to Emma that she is in love with Emma's dear childhood friend, Knightley. Emma and Knightley have just realized that they are in love with each other.

Situation
Emma must inform Harriet that she, Emma, is going to be married to Knightley.

Comments
This is a particularly difficult situation because Harriet is ecstatically in love with Knightley, and Emma is her dearest friend.

See also the preceding improvisation.

Source: *The Hunger Waltz*, a play by UCLA student Sheila Callaghan

Characters
One male, one female: Walter; Gwen, his wife

Place
The couple's home, somewhere in the United States; the eighteenth century

Background

Today, Gwen met Beth, who was working in her vegetable garden. Gwen stopped to give her some advice on how to plant tomatoes. They quickly became friends. There was an immediate attraction, which led to a kiss on the mouth. Greg, a young employee of Walter and Gwen who has a crush on Beth, was eavesdropping on the two women. He reported what he had seen to Gwen's husband, Walter, who had just returned from hunting.

Situation

Gwen comes home, and Walter confronts her about Greg's report. Walter tells Gwen that he wants a child. She informs him that she does not want to have one.

Comments

A note to the actors: keep in mind the time period in which this play is set. These women are taking an independent stance, which was uncommon in those days. Both Gwen and Walter have made major discoveries about their relationship. Until today, Gwen probably had no idea that she might become romantically involved with another woman.

Source: *Lady Jane,* a film by Trevor Nunn, screenplay by David Edgar, story by Chris Bryant

Characters

One female, one male: Lady Jane, in her late teens; Edward, her husband, in his early twenties

Place

Lady Jane's bedchamber in a castle in England; 1553

Background

Against their wishes, Lady Jane and Edward submitted to an arranged marriage one year ago. They live in the same castle but maintain separate apartments. They have never touched each other. Both were extremely bitter about the arranged marriage. For the past month, however, they have begun to actually talk to and see each other as people.

Situation

Edward has come to Lady Jane's bedchamber to return a book she lent him. It is late, and Jane is reading in bed. This is the moment when Jane and Edward realize that they are in love.

Comments

The actors must find what it is that changes their relationship at this particular moment. What is the book Edward is returning, and how did he come by it? The instant in which the characters realize that they're in love has to just happen; it can't be forced. In all love scenes, actors need to be aware of the moment the characters fall in love. Karl Menninger of the Menninger Clinic, said on a television interview in the 1970s that romantic love happens in an instant.

Source: *The Language of Flowers,* a free adaptation by Edit Villarreal of William Shakespeare's *Romeo and Juliet*

Characters

One female, one male: Julieta Bosquet, fourteen years old; Romeo Martinez, fifteen years old

Place

The front yard of Julieta's house in East Los Angeles, California; late evening on Dia de los Muertos (the day of the dead), a Mexican holiday that falls on the same night as Halloween

Background

Julieta, the daughter of a banker, is second-generation Mexican American. She does not speak Spanish; her father wants her to assimilate into the culture of the United States. Julieta's father is divorced and involved in an affair with Maria, Julieta's maid. He is delighted that Julieta will be marrying the non-Latino man to whom she is presently engaged.

Romeo, a bilingual house painter, has been living in the United States illegally for eight years with his mother. He is on the rebound from a failed romance; to cheer him up, his friend, Stanley, persuaded him to crash a Halloween party at Julieta's house. Romeo and Julieta had never met. They danced together, kissed, and immediately fell in love.

Situation

It is late in the evening after the party, and Julieta is waiting to meet Romeo in front of her house. Romeo is in the shadows nearby, and he overhears her professing her feelings for him. He eventually reveals both himself and his love for Julieta. They realize that the profound class difference between their families will make their relationship very difficult. Julieta's father will never allow her to be involved with someone like Romeo.

Comments

Romeo and Julieta don't know much about each other, but they are aware of the difficulties and dangers that will accompany their romance. For one thing, Julieta is engaged, and there are big wedding plans. It will not be easy to tell her father that she is in love with someone else. Another element at play involves gang turf: Romeo is in forbidden territory.

According to Villarreal, Julieta's falling in love with Romeo symbolizes her falling in love with Mexico and her heritage. In Shakespeare's *Romeo and Juliet,* Juliet was only twelve years old, which would make her marriage to Romeo illegal today. Therefore, the characters—and the actors playing them—can be older. It is suggested that the actors also improvise Shakespeare's *Romeo and Juliet.*

See index for other improvisations from this source.

Source: *Little Women,* a novel by Louisa May Alcott

Characters

One female, one male: Jo March; Laurence ("Laurie")—both are in their early twenties

Place

In the woods near the March residence in Concord, Massachusetts; the mid-nineteenth century

Background

There are five girls in the March family. Their father, Colonel March, has been away at war for some time, leaving Mrs. March and the girls to fend for themselves. Jo is a highly intelligent young woman, whose major interest is writing. Laurie has lived next door to the Marches for many years. Unlike the March family, his family has money. When they were all children, Jo used to dress her sisters and Laurie in costume and put on theatricals in their home. Laurie and Jo are very good friends and share many intellectual curiosities. He has been studying at Harvard College and has recently returned to Concord.

Situation

Upon his return from Harvard, Laurie confesses his love for Jo. He proposes to her, offering her not only his love, but also a life full of the luxuries that her family has been denied. He wishes to take her to England to live; she protests that she is not fashionable enough. Jo points out that they will only quarrel, since they are both so stubborn. She tells Laurie that he is her dearest friend, but she cannot be his wife.

Comments

Jo has a conversation with her mother after refusing Laurie's proposal. Her mother tells her, "You have so many extraordinary gifts, how can you expect to lead an ordinary life . . . go and embrace your liberty and see what wonderful things come of it." The actors must understand that this novel is set in the nineteenth century, when it wasn't easy for an unmarried woman to make her way in the world. It was difficult for Jo when Laurie went off to Harvard; she wished that she could go, too, but women were not allowed to attend college. It took courage for Jo to turn Laurie down. He was surprised and hurt by the rejection.

Jo went to New York City and, in time, became an established writer. In fact, she is Louisa May Alcott, who wrote *Little Women*.

See index for other improvisations from this source.

Source: *Machinal, Episode Three: Honeymoon,* a play by Sophie Treadwell

Characters

One male, one female: The husband, a middle-aged man; the young woman, his bride

Place

A small, dingy hotel room overlooking a casino; the 1940s

Background

The husband is the wealthy vice president of the company for which the young woman works as his secretary. She married him out of desperation: he promised that, if she married him, he would provide for her impoverished mother. The young woman is a virgin and has never lived with anyone but her mother. She is terrified of her husband and finds him unattractive. He tells her the same crass stories over and over.

Situation

The newlyweds have just arrived at their honeymoon destination after a long train trip. The hotel room is not at all what the young woman had expected. Her husband had promised her that there would be a view of the ocean, and there isn't. Instead, there is a view of a casino. The sounds of a jazz band float through the window.

The husband demands that she undress, but the young woman is afraid. She does everything she can to avoid contact with him, while he does everything he can to have her sexually.

Comments

Let the actors discover the outcome for themselves. Naturally, the husband has certain expectations for his wedding night, and he cannot relate to this young woman's feelings of fear. He is crass, while she is very sensitive. The festive sounds from the casino across the street contribute to the mood of the scene. It is interesting that the characters in the play are not given names: they are referred to as "husband" and "young woman."

Source: *The Man in the Ceiling,* a novel by Jules Feiffer

Characters

Two males: Jimmy, twelve years old; his father

Place

The cellar of Jimmy's house

Background

Jimmy has no aptitude for sports or school work. His teachers acknowledge that he is bright and imaginative, but they contend that he just doesn't "apply himself." He can't do multiplication or write reports; his reading skills are below grade level. Jimmy's dream is to be a great cartoonist, and he spends all his time drawing. He thinks that multiplication isn't important for a cartoonist to know. Jimmy's mother works in the attic of their home, drawing fashion sketches. Jimmy's father does not have the artistic disposition; Jimmy says that he hardly ever wastes his breath on any subject other than baseball.

Situation

Jimmy does all his drawing in the cellar. He is sitting, with his drawing board on his lap, when his father comes downstairs to talk to him—an unusual event. Jimmy's father explains his attitude about artists: he doesn't think of them as real men. Drawing is for women. Jimmy's father cites Uncle Lester (who writes musicals) as an example of a man who should go out and get a real job. Basically, his message is that he believes Jimmy is wasting his time. As Jimmy's father keeps talking about Jimmy's preoccupation with drawing, Jimmy keeps hoping that his father will ask to see some of his cartoons.

Comments

Jimmy admires his father and wants to win his respect. The fact that his father has even come downstairs to talk to him is a major event. Jimmy is proud of his cartoons and wants to show them to his father. At first, he may have thought that his father came to see his drawings.

It's hard to realize that no one approves of, or even understands, your particular dream or passion; it's even harder to be told by your father that you are wasting your time. This improvisation is similar to one about the great poet, Langston Hughes, which appears in Chapter 1 of this book. Both stories have happy endings. In this instance, Jimmy is actually Jules Feiffer, the author of *The Man in the Ceiling,* who went on to win many prizes for his cartoons, plays, and screenplays.

See also the following improvisation.

Source: *The Man in the Ceiling,* a novel by Jules Feiffer

Characters
One male, one female: Jimmy, twelve years old; Lisi, his sister, thirteen years old

Place
Lisi's bedroom

Background
Jimmy is a good cartoonist. He spends all of his time in the cellar of his house, drawing. He and his friend, Charley Beemer, are working on a comic book they're calling "Bullethead." Jimmy looks up to his friend and lives for Charley's positive appraisal of his work. Recently, Jimmy showed Charley some brilliant new pages for "Bullethead" and was shocked and disappointed to hear Charley say that he'd have to do better than that. Since then, Jimmy has been in a slump. For two weeks, he hasn't drawn a thing—and he won't even go near the cellar, where he ordinarily spends all of his time.

Jimmy's sister Lisi usually screams and shouts to get her way. She treats her father with respect; otherwise, she is uncooperative and unpleasant. Not long ago, Lisi and Jimmy had a huge argument. Jimmy had been busy, working on "Bullethead," and he foisted Lisi off on his mother, who wanted someone to do an errand for her. Lisi was furious, there was a scene, and the two haven't made up yet. Things have been pretty tense between them lately. Jimmy never shows his cartoons to Lisi; once she made fun of him and embarrassed him in front of their father.

Situation
Lisi tells Jimmy that she wants to talk to him—now! She demands that he come to her room. Having nothing better to do, he goes. However, he doesn't respond immediately; he torments her by keeping her waiting for a minute before he enters. He can't imagine what she wants.

Lisi confronts him with the fact that he has not been drawing for two weeks. The whole family knows that he has not been going to the cellar. Lisi says that she knows he has stopped drawing because he is intimidated by Charley Beemer. She tells him that he is more talented than Charley is and shouldn't listen to anything Charley says. Jimmy is flabbergasted: Charley is his idol; he draws whatever Charley tells him to draw.

Comments

This situation deals with a major change in the relationship between a brother and a sister. Jimmy is startled; he was pretty sure Lisi had called him into her room to attack him. She has never been on his side before. Lisi's statement that he is talented and doesn't need his friend's affirmation of his good work is also a major discovery for Jimmy. It may take a while to convince him that what Lisi says is true. And it may also take some time to *get* to the subject; there is still a great deal of tension from their previous conflict.

See also the preceding improvisation.

Source: "Masculine Protest," a short story by Frank O'Connor in *Collected Stories*

Characters

One male, one female: Denis, a twelve-year-old boy; his mother

Place

Their home in a small town in Ireland; the early twentieth century

Background

Denis lives with his parents and his younger sister, Martha. Their father works long hours for the county council in Dublin, so they don't see much of him. Denis feels that his mother is always finding excuses to get rid of him; she gives him money to go to the movies (to get him out of the house), and she is always away from home visiting friends.

Situation

Today is Denis's birthday. He is very excited about it. He has planned to bring some friends home to demonstrate he has a mother who cares for him; but his mother tells him that she won't be at home. Her announcement makes Denis cry—and she accuses him of being unmanly. Denis is devastated; it would have meant so much to him to have his mother share his birthday celebration.

Comments

The actor playing Denis may react any way he wants: for instance, he may cry, yell at his mother, beg her to stay. He is struggling to win her love and respect; instead, she hurts his pride. His mother's not staying is confirmation to him that she does not care about him. In O'Connor's story, Denis runs away to Dublin following this incident. The actor playing Denis' mother needs to find her own reasons for going out with friends all the time. After all, her husband is rarely home, so she has to create her own life.

See also the following improvisation.

Source: "Masculine Protest," a short story by Frank O'Connor in *Collected Stories*

Characters

Two males: Denis, a twelve-year-old boy; his father

Place

Denis home in a small Irish town twenty miles from Dublin; the early twentieth century

Background

Denis ran away from home because his mother told him that she would not be home for his birthday. When he reacted to her announcement with tears, she accused him of being unmanly. He ran away, riding his bike to Dublin. A bartender befriended him and helped him make a phone call to his father. Arrangements were made for Denis to take a bus home.

Situation

When Denis arrives home, his mother is, as usual, not there. Denis is not sure how his father will react to his running away.

Comments

He is relieved that his mother is not in and hopes that his father will not tell her what he has done. Denis sees his act of running away as his "masculine protest," an act of rebellion against his mother. This incident alters the relationship between Denis and his father.

See also the preceding improvisation.

Source: *Men, Myths, and Dogs,* a UCLA student film by Anthony Pringle

Characters
Two males: Father; Roy, his teen-aged son

Place
The kitchen of their home

Background
Roy lives with his father and mother, who are happily married. Recently, Roy and his friend picked up Ginny and her friend; all four went to Ginny's house to make love. Roy was in bed with Ginny, when her mother suddenly came home. She had a man with her—Roy's father! Terrified lest they be caught, the boys took off, leaving some of their clothes behind. Subsequently, Roy's attitude toward his father reflects his suspicions of his father's infidelity.

Situation
When Ginny returns Roy's clothes, Roy's father begins to get the picture. He confronts Roy about his strange behavior. Eventually, Roy reveals that he believes his father is having an affair with Ginny's mother. But the truth is that the father, who installs tile for a living, was there to retile the kitchen.

Comments
The actor playing the father should let the situation unfold. He wants his son to confess what is bothering him. The father must deal with his own feelings about his son's suspicions. Also, Roy wasn't at Ginny's house under the most virtuous of circumstances and has been feeling guilty about this. Both father and son are disillusioned with each other. Their relationship needs to go through a transformation in this improvisation.

Source: *Les Misérables,* a novel by Victor Hugo

Characters
One male, one female: Jean Valjean, a middle-aged man; Cosette, a young woman

Place
Their apartment in Paris; the early nineteenth century

Background
Under the cruel laws of France at the time, Jean Valjean spent ten years in the galleys (jail) for stealing a loaf of bread for his hungry family. After his

release from jail, Jean was required to report to the police for parole, which he failed to do. He became such an upright citizen—in fact, by hard work and good luck, he became the mayor of a small town—that no one would ever suspect that he had a prison record.

A police inspector has been hunting Valjean for years. When Valjean heard that another man had been apprehended as Jean Valjean, he attended the court trial. Unable to sit by and watch an innocent man be accused, he revealed his true identity. He then went into hiding with his adopted daughter, Cosette. They lived in a convent, where Valjean worked as a gardener and Cosette was raised by the nuns. Eventually, they moved back to the city. Cosette, now a beautiful young woman, met Marius, a twenty-two-year-old student, at a political rally where he was fighting for prison reform. They fell in love.

Situation
Jean realizes that the police will never stop hunting for him, and he decides that he and Cosette must move to England immediately. Because the French populace is rioting in the streets of Paris at the time, it will be easy to slip away unobserved. Cosette tells Jean that she does not want to go; she is in love with Marius and cannot leave him. This is the first Jean has heard of Marius, and he is wounded that Cosette has kept her lover a secret from him. Jean is also devastated, because he is in love with Cosette himself; he has never told her this before now. Cosette has always thought of Jean as her father, and she is shocked to realize that he has romantic feelings for her.

Comments
This is a painful moment for both of them. Their love for each other is profound, but two kinds of love have been confused: parental love and romantic love. Jean has devoted his whole life to making Cosette happy, and she is indebted to him. She would not hurt him for the world. Both Jean and Cosette feel disillusioned and betrayed.

Source: *Our Town*, a play by Thornton Wilder

Characters
One female, one male: Emily Webb; George Gibbs—both are juniors in high school

Place
Grovers Corners, New Hampshire

Background
Emily and George have been next-door neighbors and good friends since

early childhood. They know almost everything there is to know about each other's lives and their respective families. Their long-standing relationship has allowed them to take each other for granted.

Situation
Emily is walking home from school, when George catches up with her and offers to carry her books. They have both just been elected class officers. George asks Emily why she is angry with him. It seems that Emily has found George totally preoccupied with baseball to the exclusion of family and friends; she says that he has become conceited and stuck up. Rather than reacting defensively, George appreciates Emily's criticism. He invites her to have an ice cream soda with him. As they sip their sodas, they talk about their friendship and future plans.

Comments
This is the very conversation between George and Emily that convinced them that they were meant for each other. What they say about their relationship is significant, but far more momentous is the realization each has about the other and the implications of their respective realizations. Because the characters have known each other since childhood, the actors will have to spend time establishing their history and past relationship.

Source: *The Pinballs*, a play by Aurand Harris, adapted from the novel by Betsy Byars

Characters
Two males: Harvey, a young boy; his father

Place
Harvey's bedroom in a foster home

Background
Upset over a business deal, Harvey's father had been drinking. He confused the forward and reverse gears in his new car and ran over Harvey, crushing both of his legs. Harvey is in leg braces and a wheelchair now and living in a foster home with two other children, because his father was declared unfit to care for him. Harvey's mother joined a commune three years ago to "find" herself. Harvey has written to her many times, but she has never replied.

Situation
Harvey's father has come to give Harvey a birthday present. It's a few days early, because he has a business meeting on his son's actual birthday. His gift to Harvey is a pair of boxing gloves, which Harvey is obviously in no

position to use. This is the first confrontation between the two since Harvey was removed from his father's custody. Harvey demands to see the letters that his mother wrote back to him, but his father insists that there are no letters. Harvey can't believe his mother didn't answer his letters—especially the ones about his appendectomy, his measles, and his two broken legs. He suspects his father has torn up her letters.

Comments
The actors should decide what the father and son want from each other during this visit. The father has no idea how much Harvey is hurt emotionally, but the fact remains that he did come to see his son. There really is no resolution to this situation. The concept to be explored in the scene is the relationship between two people who need each other, hurt each other, fail to connect, and wind up even more isolated from each other than they were before.

Source: *Proposals,* a play by Neil Simon

Characters
One female, one male: Josie Hines; Ken Norman—both are in their early twenties

Place
The back yard of the Hines' summer house in the Poconos in Pennsylvania; the 1950s

Background
Ken, a good-looking young lawyer, met Josie at a Democratic convention. They have been engaged for a few months and are busily planning their wedding. Ken's parents are prominent members of the community. While Josie's parents have separated, and Josie has been estranged from her mother, she has since formed a close relationship with Ken's mother.

Situation
Josie has just realized that she cannot go through with this marriage: she is not so much in love with Ken as she is with his family, his law degree, and the Democratic convention. She is very fond of Ken and doesn't want to hurt him, but she simply must break off the engagement. Ken is deeply in love with Josie, and he takes this news very hard.

Comments
Josie remembers that when her mother divorced her father he was devastated, and she doesn't want to do the same thing to Ken. Although he is

a successful lawyer, Ken crumbles when he learns that Josie wants to break the engagement. He will do anything he can to keep her.

See also the following improvisations.

Source: *Proposals,* a play by Neil Simon

Characters
One female, one male: Josie Hines; Ray Dolenz—both are in their early twenties

Place
The back yard of the Hines' summer house in the Poconos in Pennsylvania; the 1950s

Background
Josie has just broken off her engagement to Ken Norman, Ray's best friend. Ken's father delivered the eulogy at the funeral of Ray's father; when Ray was in an automobile accident, Ken donated blood. Last summer, Josie and Ray were romantically involved. When Ray broke up with her, Josie begged him to change his mind, but he would not.

Situation
Ray shows Josie a suicide note from Ken. (Ken has not committed suicide.) Ray is furious with her for causing his friend so much pain. He insists that she change her mind and marry Ken. Josie reminds Ray that he would not change his mind for her. Ray, however, is determined that the discussion be restricted to Josie's relationship with Ken.

Comments
Josie is in love with Ray. She doesn't want him begging her to marry Ken; she wants him begging her to marry *him*. Ray is in love with Josie but is trying not to be. He believes that he is doing this to save Ken. The underlying reason (which emerges later in Simon's play) is that Ray doesn't feel worthy of Josie.

See also the preceding and following improvisations.

Source: *Proposals,* a play by Neil Simon

Characters
Two females: Josie Hines, in her early twenties; Annie Robbins, Josie's mother

Place
The back yard of the Hines' summer house in the Poconos in Pennsylvania; the late 1950s

Background
Annie divorced Josie's father, Burt, and married another man, with whom she now lives in Paris. Josie and her father have lived together since the divorce, and she has seen how lonely he is without his wife. Burt also has a weak heart, and he doesn't have much longer to live. Annie has come from Paris to see him and to attempt to patch up her relationship with Josie.

Situation
Annie is about to leave, but first wants to clear the air with Josie. She explains that the reason she left Burt was because he worked so hard that he never had time for her. She still cares for him. And she knows that Josie has never forgiven her for deserting him.

Comments
This conflict may or may not be resolved. Josie loves her mother, but her resentment is deep and has gone unexpressed for many years. Annie wants to bring the anger out into the open. Josie is her only child, and they need each other's love. Subtext: Josie is having problems facing her father's impending death and resents her mother's reference to it.

See also the two preceding improvisations.

Source: *The Rest of My Life,* a UCLA student film by Mark Lawrence

Characters
Two females: April, in her early teens; Donna, her mother

Place
A beach in Malibu, California; the late 1980s

Background
April is at that awkward age. Everything her parents do embarrasses her, and now they have decided to move back to Iowa from Los Angeles. April is furious with them. They haven't even told her why.

Until a few minutes ago, April had hoped to be rescued from this fate by Nigel, the young man she has been dating. When he failed to show up, she called him at work and found not only that was he not planning to pick her up, but that he didn't care for her as much as she cared for him.

Situation
Having been rejected by Nigel, April leaves the phone booth, devastated. She returns to the beach in defeat. Her father is fishing. Her mother offers her a sandwich, and they begin to talk. April asks why they're going to Iowa. Her mother finally reveals that April's father, an engineer, has been laid off. They're bankrupt. They've lost their house. They're moving back to Iowa to start again.

In the second part of this improvisation, April goes to join her father on the rock where he is fishing. When April was a little girl, she loved to fish with him. But, once she became a teen-ager, she lost interest—to her father's great sorrow.

Comments
Until now, April has been horrid to her parents. There is a major change in her attitude toward them after Nigel's rejection. This is the first time that, as a teen-ager, she talks to her parents as people. The three of them share heartbreak.

See index for other improvisations from this source.

Source: *Return Engagements,* a play by Bernard Slade

Characters
One female, one male: Daisy Lawrence, an actor, in her twenties; Raymond MacKay, a bellboy, in his twenties

Place
A hotel room near Stratford in Ontario, Canada; early morning

Background
Daisy is getting married today, but she has just spent the night with the bellboy in the hotel. She is an American actor (definitely not a star) appearing in a play in Canada; her whole family and, of course, the groom and his family, are arriving today from the United States for the wedding.

Situation
Daisy wakes up in the hotel room and finds, sleeping next to her—the bellboy. She cannot understand why she did this. What was she thinking? She must now get up, get dressed, and get . . . married. Raymond wakes up thinking he has finally found the love of his life. He has planned out the whole summer with Daisy. It comes as a great shock to him that this is her wedding day.

Comments
Why Daisy slept with Raymond last night is, for her, the biggest "why" in the world, but she must find the answer. In Slade's play, she discovers that she doesn't really love her fiancé; she loves Raymond because he makes her laugh. Two keys to Raymond's character are Daisy's description of him: "You look like a cocker spaniel who wants in," and his description of himself: "Outside I'm Raymond MacKay, but inside I'm Cary Grant." His goal in life is to be comfortable in his own skin.

Source: *Scorpions,* a novel by Walter Dean Myers

Characters
One male, two females: Jamal Hicks, twelve years old; Sally, his younger sister; Mrs. Hicks, their mother—all are African American

Place
The living room of their apartment in Harlem, a section of New York City

Background
Jamal's elder brother, Randy, was the leader of a gang called the Scorpions. Randy is now in jail, and, until his release, he wants Jamal to take his place as the leader of the Scorpions. Some of the gang members are opposed to Jamal's leadership and have been threatening him. One of the Scorpions, who likes Jamal, has given him a gun for protection. Jamal pulled the gun on a classmate, who was always picking fights with him. When he was called to the principal's office, Jamal denied having a gun.

Because of his ties to the Scorpions, Jamal was recently fired from his first job. He needed the money to pay for an appeal to get Randy out of jail and to help his mother pay the household expenses.

Situation
Jamal comes home to find his sister, Sally, cooking supper. She tells him that their mother left the house immediately after getting a phone call from the jail where Randy is being held. Sally says that she heard Jamal had a gun at school; she questions him about it and about his involvement with the Scorpions. Jamal denies both. Sally is worried that Jamal will end up like Randy. Finally, Jamal admits that he has a gun and begs Sally not to tell their mother about it. He explains that he took it to school because Dwayne is always picking on him, and Dwayne's a lot bigger. Sally says if Jamal doesn't let her see the gun, she'll tell their mother.

Mrs. Hicks returns and tells them that Randy has been stabbed. He's in the hospital now, wrapped in bandages, with a tube down his throat. She says she's got to get Randy out of jail before he gets killed.

Comments
Subtext for Jamal and Sally: they know that Jamal has a gun and is involved with the Scorpions. If their mother knew, it would destroy her.

See index for other improvisations from this source.

Source: *The Seagull*, a play by Anton Chekhov

Characters
One female, one male: Pauline Andreyevna, a young woman; Eugene Sergeyevitch Dorn, a middle-aged doctor

Place
A country house in Russia; the late nineteenth century

Background
Pauline, who is in an abusive marriage with Shamreyeff, is having an affair with Dorn, a successful doctor. Because Dorn has a reputation to uphold, they must always meet in secret.

When Dorn appeared to be overly attentive to Arcadina, the famous actress who is visiting Pauline and Shamreyeff, Pauline became jealous. In front of visitors, Shamreyeff hit Pauline, yelled at Arcadina, and stormed out of the room. The guests followed, leaving Pauline alone with Dorn.

Situation
Pauline begs Dorn to marry her, to take her away from her miserable life with Shamreyeff. Dorn refuses: the scandal would ruin his status and reputation as a doctor.

Comments
Dorn is in love with Arcadina; she is not in love with him. This may (or may not) be revealed in this improvisation. *The Seagull* is a play about unrequited love. Chekhov's characters often love the wrong persons, which is certainly the case in this play. Pauline has made her entire happiness dependent on her dream of leaving Shamreyeff and marrying this eligible doctor. It is in desperation that she finally blurts out her desire.

Source: *Sleepless in Seattle,* a film by Nora Ephron, screenplay by Nora Ephron, David S. Ward, and Jeff Arch (improvisation written by UCLA student Brian C. Bethel)

Characters
One male, one female: Walter; Annie

Place
A posh restaurant in New York City

Background
Annie and Walter are engaged and have gone to New York City to celebrate Saint Valentine's Day. Annie is having second thoughts about getting married, due to her sudden infatuation with a man she heard on a radio talk show.

Situation
Annie and Walter are having dinner at a restaurant overlooking New York City. Annie has also made arrangements to meet Sam (her radio talk show man) at the top of the Empire State Building. Annie must decide whether to stay with her safe and stable fiance or to call off the wedding and go after her dream, who could be waiting on top of the Empire State Building.

Comments
Annie is not sure that Sam will be waiting for her. The actor playing Annie needs to decide how to tell Walter that she wants to risk everything for the possibility of meeting Sam. Walter has no inkling that there is a problem with the relationship.

Source: *Starting Over* (an original improvisation written by UCLA student Amy Lucas)

Characters
One female, one male: Barbara; Charles—both are in their late twenties, they are not of the same race

Place
The arrivals lounge in an airport

Background
Barbara has returned from a year of travel around the world. She left home to escape a difficult situation: both her family and her boyfriend

Charles' family were intolerant of interracial relationships. She has kept in touch with Charles over the past year, but their exchange of letters has become more and more infrequent. Barbara's travels have been lonely, and she has missed her home desperately. After much soul searching and growing, she is ready to come back and renew the relationship. Her fear is that Charles has been influenced by his family's beliefs.

Situation
Charles promised to pick Barbara up at the airport the day she returned. He arrives and, for the first time in a year, they confront each other.

Comments
Barbara and Charles still love each other very much. However, they have both gone through changes in the past year. Each needs to decide what these changes are and how they will affect the relationship.

 In the actual situation, Charles was African-American and Barbara was Caucasian. In this improvisation however, any combination of races can be used.

Source: *Swingers,* a film by Doug Liman, screenplay by Jon Farreau

Characters
Two males: Mike; Richard—both are in their early twenties

Place
A diner

Background
Mike's girlfriend, Michelle, broke up with him after a two-year relationship. It has been six months since their separation, and she has not called him. Michelle has started seeing another man. Mike is still very upset and has not dated anyone since the breakup with Michelle.

Situation
Mike is at a diner with his best friend, Richard. Mike wants advice from Richard on how to get Michelle back. Richard's advice is to forget about her and find somebody new. However, his advice falls on deaf ears; all Mike can think or talk about is Michelle. He doesn't believe that there will ever be anyone else for him.

Comments

This scene may be played humorously or seriously. Mike is unable to envision other alternatives. He is obsessed with Michelle; although he has sought solace from his friend, he really cannot accept it. Six months is a fairly long time, but Mike still has not recovered. Richard tells him that, by the time he manages to forget Michelle, she will decide she's ready to come back to him—and this is exactly what happens. But Richard's words are cold comfort to Mike now. Most any actor playing Mike will have experienced rejection (directly or indirectly) and should be able to empathize. Richard genuinely wants to help Mike; he sees that his friend is hurting.

Source: *The Taming of the Shrew,* a play by William Shakespeare

Characters

One male, one female: Petruchio; Kate

Place

A room in Kate's father's home in Padua, Italy; the sixteenth century

Background

Kate is the eldest daughter of Baptista, a well-off Paduan. She is noted for her fiery temper and uncontrollable spirit—thus her name: Katharina the Shrew. It has been difficult for Baptista to find a suitor for Kate; the eligible men would prefer to marry Bianca, Kate's younger, gentler sister. Petruchio, having heard reports of Kate's temper, is intent upon marrying her and turning her into an obedient wife.

Situation

This is the initial meeting between Kate and Petruchio. He begins by praising her, announcing that her father has consented to their betrothal and that the dowry has been agreed on. Kate is extremely rude to Petruchio, physically and verbally, to discourage his pursuit. Petruchio, however, is persistent, determined to woo her, and more than equal to her abuse.

Comments

Kate is a woman ahead of her time, who probably disdains arranged marriages. She also may have feelings of jealousy toward Bianca. The actor can search out her own motivations for Kate's rebelliousness. The competition between Petruchio and Kate is part of the fun. In the last act of the play, Petruchio ends up taming Kate, and she ends up loving him. Therefore, the potential—and the fire—in their relationship need to be there from the start. The actor playing Petruchio must decide why he wants to win Kate over. Why not find an easier conquest?

Source: *Valley Song,* a play by Athol Fugard

Characters
One male, one female: Abraam "Buks" Jonkers, an old, "colored," tenant farmer; Veronica Jonkers, Abraam's teen-aged granddaughter

Place
A remote village in the Karoo, a vast, semi-desert region in the heart of South Africa; the 1990s, shortly after the dismantling of apartheid (the systematic policy of racial segregation)

Background
Veronica lives with her grandfather on land that is owned by whites. Veronica's mother had run away to Johannesburg to find a better life, leaving Veronica in her grandfather's care. Buks expects that Veronica will stay with him. His life consists of the hard work of planting pumpkin seeds every season and the thrill of watching them grow into pumpkins.

Situation
One day, Veronica receives a letter from a girlfriend, who now lives in Johannesburg. Buks is amazed that Veronica received a letter of her own, so he opens it. Veronica scolds him for this, although she knows that he cannot read. He demands that she read it to him. At first, she makes up the letter as she goes along, but Buks knows what she is doing and insists that she read exactly what the letter says. It is an invitation from her friend to come to Johannesburg, where many good jobs are available.

Veronica tells Buks that she has been singing in the village; the people give her money, which she has been saving. She wants to go to Johannesburg to study singing and become a professional singer. Buks is furious and forbids her to leave. He tells her that she can have a very good job cleaning the white man's house—and she should be grateful for that.

Comments
This scene contains several varieties of challenge. One is the challenge that Buks must face in letting Veronica go; he can't keep her so safe that he smothers her with his love. Veronica faces the challenge of stepping into an uncertain future with only her faith in herself to protect her. And also

implicit is the challenge of letting the old South Africa go, of recognizing that it is going to be a different world.

In Fugard's play, Buks initially takes Veronica's money and throws it away—and that breaks her spirit for a time. Although Buks eventually lets her go, he never really understands why she wants to leave. Veronica represents the new freedom in South Africa, and she is ready to soar. The struggle is between two generations and a new world.

Veronica and Buks both love and need each other. Each is selfish in their own way—and frightened of the separation. However, Veronica is certain that going to Johannesburg is her only salvation; she would suffocate in this little village.

"Colored" was one of four official racial categories in South Africa under the old system of apartheid. The other categories were white, black, and Asian. *Colored* is defined as anyone of mixed racial descent. Veronica and Buks speak Afrikaans.

Source: *The Wedding,* a novel by Dorothy West

Characters
Two females: Liz, a young mulatto woman; Gram, her white grandmother

Place
Liz's home in the Deep South; the early twentieth century

Background
Liz is the daughter of Josephine, a white woman, and Hannibal, a black man. Her baby, Laurie, is darker skinned than Liz. Gram has never really accepted Josephine's interracial marriage, the union that produced Liz.

Situation
Liz tries to persuade her grandmother to hold Laurie, but Gram refuses; Laurie is black.

Comments
The actors should not judge Gram too harshly; she is a product of her time and of a bigoted upbringing. She simply cannot bring herself to touch Laurie; for Gram, it is as if the child has leprosy. However, there is probably an internal conflict, for a grandmother's tendency is to love all generations of her offspring. This scene is painful for Liz, who is devoted to her daughter and fond of her grandmother. At the very end of West's novel, Gram finally does hold the child; she might do so in this improvisation.

The actors should use props to suggest the baby's crib and the baby herself, because the infant is at the center of the improvisation.

See index for other improvisations from this source.

Source: *A Yellow Raft in Blue Water*, a novel by Michael Dorris

Characters
Two females: Rayona, fifteen years old, Native American and African American; Christine, Rayona's mother, forty years old, a Native American

Place
A parked car at the side of the road in the middle of nowhere; late evening

Background
Rayona's mother and father have had a rocky marriage for sixteen years. One fight followed another, and Rayona's father was always threatening to leave. Today they had another bad fight, which has left Christine extremely upset. They are having trouble paying the rent, and Christine is finding it difficult to earn any money.

Today, the possibility of a divorce is more than just a threat; Christine tells Rayona that her father is in love with a twenty-two-year-old woman. Distraught, Christine drives off with Rayona. She plans to smash the car and kill herself, leaving the insurance money to support Rayona.

Situation
It is late at night; they are in the middle of nowhere. Christine pulls over to the side of the road and tells Rayona to get out of the car.

Comments
Essentially, Christine is asking for Rayona's complicity in attempting suicide. The actor portraying Rayona can decide whether she gets out of the car. Rayona's choices: she can defy her mother; she can attempt to change her mother's mind; she can get out of the car. The actor playing Christine needs to remember that, although Christine is slightly deranged at the moment, she believes that she is doing the best thing for Rayona. She will undoubtedly have to reveal her reasons to Rayona for wanting her to get out of the car.

See also the following improvisation.

Source: *A Yellow Raft in Blue Water,* a novel by Michael Dorris

Characters
Three females: Christine, forty years old, Native American; Rayona, fifteen years old, Christine's daughter, half Native American and half African American; Aunt Ida, Christine's mother, Native American

Place
An Indian reservation in Montana

Background
Rayona's father is divorcing Rayona's mother, leaving Christine unable to care for Rayona either financially or emotionally. After attempting suicide, Christine told Rayona that Rayona would now be living with her Aunt Ida. Aunt Ida is actually Christine's mother and Rayona's grandmother. Since Ida had had Christine out of wedlock, she claimed to be her aunt to avoid gossip.

Situation
Christine and Rayona arrive at the reservation. Aunt Ida does not expect them, and she is not particularly happy to see Christine. Christine announces that Rayona will be living there, turns around, and leaves. Rayona tries to stop her mother, but Christine jumps in her car and drives off. Rayona and Aunt Ida are left alone, face to face.

Comments
Rayona does not expect to be left alone with this woman. Even though Ida is Rayona's grandmother, the two have never met. Rayona must be feeling many things, for example, fear, shock, sorrow, and anger. The fact that Aunt Ida is actually Rayona's grandmother may or may not be revealed at this time.

See also the preceding improvisation.

5

Solo Moment

The nature and content of the situations in this chapter range from commonplace to the exotic. What unites and defines solo moments is their private nature. Not to be confused with Strasberg's "private moments"—scenes of intimacy (such as bathing oneself), instances of being "private in public" (Strasberg, 1965, 115)—solo moments occur when an actor is onstage alone. Whether or not they involve climactic developments in a scene or in a characters life, solo moments must always allow for a full and rich sense of the actor, as well as the situation at a specific point in time. In enacting solo moments, actors may or may not speak; indeed, they may not even discover, until in the moment, whether the nature of the scene evokes a verbal or nonverbal response.

Some people talk to themselves, others do not. Talking to oneself is usually involuntary; often people are not even aware that they are doing it. The same principle applies to the actor in the solo moment. Uta Hagen, in *A Challenge for the Actor* (1991), discusses the many reasons people have for talking to themselves. One is derived from the explanation of a psychologist, Dr. Palaci, who wrote that "the underlying reason for verbalizing when alone is a need to gain control over one's circumstances." People also talk to themselves to keep from forgetting something, to organize their thoughts, to prevent boredom, to express anger (by using expletives), and to solve a problem in the midst of a crisis.

Emotional preparation is of the utmost importance. The actor must fantasize, inventing everything that has happened up to this particular point in time. The actor must also resist the temptation to supply the audience with exposition. It is important to remember that when people talk to themselves, they know the scenario. Their verbalized comments are simply the random bubbles that arise from whatever is percolating underneath.

SOLO MOMENT SITUATIONS

One female
Anne of Green Gables
Baby
Camilla
The Color Purple
A Dark-Adapted Eye
The Diary of Anne Frank
First Dance
"Geraldo No Last Name"
In the Cemetery
Kindred
Life
Little Women
The Miracle Worker
The Moon by Night
Mrs. 'Arris Goes to Paris
The New Car
"The New Dress"
Nightjohn
Rebecca
"Sire"
"The Story of an Hour"
Tous les Matins du Monde (All the Mornings of the World)
The Wedding
A Yellow Raft in Blue Water

One male
Ah, Wilderness!
"American History"
"The Bear"
City Hall
Dead Poets Society
"Desiree's Baby"

Dinner Theatre
Escape From Slavery
The Fisher King
Going After Cacciato
The Journey of the Fifth Horse
"Masculine Protest"
Péllèas and Mélisande
Scorpions
Shunkan Heike Nyogo-ga-shima
The Stationmaster's Wife
"A Sunrise on the Veld"
The Tragedy of the 1996 Mount Everest Expedition

Source: *Ah, Wilderness!*, a play by Eugene O'Neill

Characters
One male: Richard Miller, sixteen years old

Place
A strip of beach on the harbor

Background
Richard Miller is in love with Muriel McComber. Muriel's father found letters filled with romantic poetry that Richard had sent to Muriel, and he believes that Richard is a corrupting influence on his daughter. As a result, he has not allowed Muriel to leave the house for a month. He also forced her to write a letter to Richard ending their relationship. Richard, hurt and angry, went out with an older woman and got drunk.

Situation
Muriel has sent a note to Richard, arranging for a clandestine meeting on the beach at 9 P.M. Note in hand, Richard waits anxiously in the light of a new moon for Muriel's arrival. Faint strains of music can be heard from a nearby hotel.

Comments
A hopeless romantic, Richard is absolutely smitten with Muriel. He also deeply regrets his drunken escapade. He comforts himself with snatches of poetry and thoughts of Muriel.

See index for other improvisations from this source.

Source: "American History," a short story by Judith Ortiz-Cofer in *Who Do You Think You Are? Stories of Friends and Enemies,* a collection selected by Hazel Rochman and Darlene Z. McCampbell

Characters
One male, ensemble (optional): Mr. DePalma, a white high school teacher; high school students, predominantly of Puerto Rican descent

Place
A classroom in P.S. 13, a high school in Paterson, New Jersey; November 22, 1963

Background
Mr. DePalma is a science teacher, physical education coach, and disciplinarian. He breaks up playground fights, escorts violent teen-agers to the principal's office, and presides over homeroom for troublemakers.

Situation
President John F. Kennedy was assassinated today. Mr. DePalma stands in front of his class, crying audibly. There is giggling in the room. He tells the students that the president is dead.

Comments
Mr. DePalma is very moved by the president's death, but he is in a room full of students who cannot relate. In Ortiz-Cofer's story, he screams at the class, calling them idiots. The actor can do what he needs to do, but he is not reaching the students. Experiencing a tragedy with no one to share your grief is frustrating and lonely. This improvisation may be done with either an actual or an imaginary class.

Source: *Anne of Green Gables,* a novel by L.M. Montgomery (improvisation written by UCLA student Kelli Tager)

Characters
One female: Anne Shirley, a twelve-year-old orphan

Place
The kitchen in Anne's home

Background
Anne has just been adopted by an elderly sister and brother, Marilla and Matthew Cuthbert. She is determined to make a good impression, but her temper and imagination consistently get her into trouble.

Situation

Anne discovers, to her horror, that a little mouse has drowned in her plum pudding sauce because she forgot to cover the bowl. This situation is even more horrible for her since she made the pudding for a special dinner with her teacher that night.

Comments

The scene can be extended to include Marilla in the kitchen. If Marilla is present, the actor playing Anne can try to work up the courage to tell her about the mouse, but keep in mind the consequences if Anne's mistake is found out. Once the mouse is discovered, it is for the actor to decide what to do with the "corpse."

See index for other improvisations from this source.

Source: *Baby,* a novel by Patricia MacLachlan

Characters

One female: Larkin Byrd, twelve years old

Place

A small cemetery on an island off the East Coast of the United States

Background

Six months ago, Larkin's mother had a baby boy, who lived for only one day. He was quietly buried in a small cemetery on the top of a hill near the ocean. Nothing more was said. Recently, the Byrds found a baby in a basket left on their driveway. A note in the basket asked the Byrds to take care of the infant Sophie until her mother was able to return. Everyone in the family adored Sophie, especially Larkin's mother.

Situation

Larkin's father has just advised the mother not to get too attached to Sophie. Larkin runs out of the house to the cemetery where her baby brother is buried. She locates a tiny headstone with no name on it; it simply reads "Baby," with a date showing that it lived only one day. Larkin stands there, looking down at the stone.

Comments

Sophie's arrival stirs memories of Larkin's baby brother. Looking down at the stone with no name on it is a lonely and sad moment for Larkin. All the surrounding stones have names carved on them. Even Sophie, the abandoned baby, has a name. Larkin has wanted to talk about her dead baby brother, but her parents have always refused to discuss him.

See index for other improvisations from this source.

Source: "The Bear," a short story by William Faulkner in *Uncollected Stories of William Faulkner*

Characters
One male: A fifteen-year-old boy

Place
Rural Mississippi; the 1880s

Background
All his life, the boy has heard stories about a huge bear, Old Ben, that haunts the wilderness in his region. At the age of eleven, he became fascinated by the tales of Old Ben and learned to be a skillful hunter so that he could track down the bear. For four years he trailed Old Ben. During that time, he shot one buck.

Situation
Finally, the boy tracks down Old Ben. He is close enough to shoot him easily. He stands with a gun in his hands, facing Old Ben—but is unable to shoot the bear.

Comments
The boy knows that the bear is near; after four years he is familiar with its ways and its movements. His familiarity with the wilderness has made him a good hunter. He has also learned that a good hunter must not show any panic, because wild animals sense genuine fear and react dangerously to it. Although terrified, he needs to be alert and cautious. In his pursuit of Old Ben, the boy has acquired respect for the woods and for the bear, and he has learned that hunting is not just about tracking and killing.
   The actor has to visualize the wilderness and the tremendous bear. There is the moment of knowing that it is close—hearing and smelling it. Then comes the actual encounter. The actor needs to find out for himself why he chooses not to shoot.

Source: *Camilla,* a novel by Madeleine L'Engle

Characters
One female: Camilla Dickinson, fifteen years old

Place
Camilla's bedroom in an upper-middle-class apartment in New York City

Background
Camilla is in love with Frank. Frank's parents are separating, and he has
been sent away suddenly to live with his father in Cincinnati. Camilla
knows that he said good-bye to his friends, but not to her. She is being
sent off to school herself, so they will probably never meet again. Frank
was her first love. He was supposed to meet her after school today, but he
never appeared. Luisa, Frank's sister, has brought Camilla a farewell letter
from Frank.

Situation
Camilla reads the good-bye letter from Frank.

Comments
The actor playing Camilla should decide what Frank's letter says. Their
relationship was never physically consummated; in fact, Frank never even
kissed her, but Camilla knew that he loved her. That the love was unful-
filled makes the ache of parting even more painful.

See index for other improvisations from this source.

Source: *City Hall,* a film by Harold Becker, screenplay by Ken Lipper, Nicholas Pileggi, Paul Schrader, and Bo Goldman

Characters
One male: A Brooklyn borough political boss

Place
The boss' parked car in New York City

Background
A little boy was accidentally killed in a drug bust; the subsequent investigation revealed ties between the mayor and the Mafia. The Brooklyn
borough boss worked with Mayor John Pappas, a veteran politician, and
was summoned to court to reveal what he knew about the scandal. (The
police knew that he had information, which he would reveal if he were
sent to jail.) Meanwhile, the Godfather went to the boss' home to give
him an order: either the boss kills himself or his wife and child will be
murdered.

Situation
The boss drives to a spot near the river, puts his favorite song in the tape deck, takes out a gun, and shoots himself.

Comments
A note to the actor: keep him human. He is not a hardened politician. There will be a moment's hesitation before he can bring himself to commit suicide. He loves musicals. His favorite song is "Walk Through the Storm" from *Carousel*. Take time to listen to the song. The actor can imagine the music or use an actual tape. The song must have special meaning to the character.

Source: *The Color Purple,* a novel by Alice Walker

Characters
One female: Celie, an African American woman

Place
A bedroom in Celie's house in Atlanta, Georgia; late-nineteenth century to early-twentieth century

Background
Celie and her sister Nettie were as close as two sisters could be. Their father having had incestuous relations with Celie, Nettie was sent away from home to escape the same fate. She lived with Celie and her husband, until he tried to rape Nettie. She hit him and ran away. He was so angry with her that he threw her out of the house.

Eventually, Nettie was hired by a clergyman and his wife to take care of their children. Nettie knew that both children were Celie's—the products of incest—and that the girls' father had given them to the clergyman and his wife.

The clergyman's family moved to Africa, taking Nettie with them. Over a period of years, Nettie wrote many letters to Celie. Celie never received them, because she was not allowed to approach the letter box; the mail always arrived when her husband was at home. One day, Celie's friend picked up Celie's mail for her, and they discovered a letter from Nettie. The two women searched through Celie's husband's belongings and found, hidden in a box, all of Nettie's letters.

Situation
Celie is reading the letters—all the news about Nettie's life in Africa and about Celie's children. Celie has feared that Nettie might be dead, since she has never heard from her.

Comments

The actor should have a sense of what she is reading in these letters. They are full of discoveries, both sad and happy. There are many letters to read, and Celie relishes them all. Nettie is the only person in Celie's life who ever loved her, and she never gave up hoping that her letters would reach Celie. Celie has had a wretched life with her abusive husband, who was cruel enough to confiscate these letters that would have meant so much to her.

See index for other improvisations from this source.

Source: *A Dark-Adapted Eye,* a novel by Barbara Vine

Characters
One female: Faith, a young girl

Place
A public park

Background
Faith lives with her aunt, Vera. She often takes a neighbor's baby out for a stroll in his carriage. Today, she went on a picnic with a girlfriend. They spread a blanket on the ground for the picnic and parked the baby carriage a few feet away.

Situation
The girls have just finished lunch. Faith's friend leaves. Faith puts away the picnic things, folds the blanket, and approaches the baby carriage. To her horror, the baby has disappeared! There is no sign of him anywhere, nor is there anyone in sight. Alone with an empty baby carriage, Faith is now faced with having to report this catastrophe to the baby's parents.

Comments
The actor playing Faith should have no premonition of the baby's disappearance. The contrast of atmospheres here—from a pleasant day in the park with a friend to a moment of terrified alarm—is significant. For the actor, this is also an exercise in discovery. Faith's relationship with her friend and the child should be established; the park should also be clearly visualized. This is a situation in which the actor might talk to herself out loud.

The baby is never found, and there is no logical explanation for its disappearance—until years later. Faith then happens to learn that, over a period of time, many babies had disappeared, kidnapped by a mentally disturbed man.

Source: *Dead Poets Society*, a film by Peter Weir, screenplay by Tom Schulman

Characters
One male: Neil's father

Place
The living room of his home

Background
Neil's father worked hard all his life to send Neil to a prestigious prep school. He wanted his son to become a doctor and warned him to devote all his energy to his studies. Neil, however, auditioned for a school production of *A Midsummer Night's Dream* and was cast in the role of Puck. His father discovered what Neil was up to on the opening night of the play. After the performance, he dragged Neil home and told him that he was to be withdrawn from the prep school and enrolled in a military academy. Later that night, Neil's father was awakened by a loud noise and went downstairs to investigate.

Situation
Neil's father finds his son dead on the living room floor. He has committed suicide with his father's gun.

Comments
The improvisation should begin with the father hearing the gunshot. This moment is a major discovery for the father—not just the death of his son, but the realization of the impact his behavior has had on his son. Up until this moment, he thought he was doing what was best for Neil. His son's suicide is too harsh a lesson.

See index for other improvisations from this source.

Source: "Desiree's Baby," a short story by Kate Chopin in *The Awakening and Selected Stories*, edited by Sandra M. Gilbert

Characters
One male: Armand Aubigny

Place
Armand's home in New Orleans, Louisiana; shortly before the Civil War

Background
Armand and Desiree were happily married, until Desiree realized that their three-month-old baby is black. Assuming that it was Desiree who had "black blood," Armand sent her away with their baby.

Situation
Some weeks after Desiree left, Armand is sorting through a bundle of letters that she had written to him. He finds one old letter, not from Desiree but from his mother to his father. In it, his mother wrote that she was thankful that Armand would never know that she—his mother—"belongs to the race that is cursed with the brand of slavery."

Comments
Here we find quite an irony. Having sent his wife away in disgrace, Armand turns out to be the one who is black. If he believes that blacks are inferior, the consensus among whites at this point in time, then he must think of himself as inferior.

See index for other improvisations from this source.

Source: *The Diary of Anne Frank,* a dramatization by Frances Goodrich and Albert Hackett of the book, *Anne Frank: Diary of a Young Girl*

Characters
One female: Anne Frank, a teen-aged girl

Place
Amsterdam, Holland; during World War II (1939–1945)

Background
With the help of friends, the Frank family and the Van Daan family went into hiding in the building in which Mr. Frank once operated his business. Their hope is to live out the rest of the war by concealing themselves from the persecution of the Nazis and the horrors of the concentration camps.

Situation
In this scene, Anne speaks aloud as she writes in her diary. She describes what it feels like to go into hiding, what she has had to give up and leave behind, and the burden of fear she feels constantly.

Comments
More than the reflections of a single entry, this scene should be a collage
of experiences that Anne has recorded in her diary during her many
months in hiding. It will be helpful if the actor is given some historical
background, although she should use her own experiences with loss and
fear to guide her remarks. It is the reality of the actor's emotions and
thoughts that will allow the character of Anne to come to life. Since Anne
is writing as she speaks, the pace of the scene can be set by the act of writ
ing and thinking, which should allow another aspect of reality to influence
the situation.

See index for other improvisations from this source.

Source: *Dinner Theatre* (an original improvisation written by UCLA student Ryan Cadiz)

Characters
One male: David, a young adult

Place
A front-row table in a crowded dinner theatre

Background
David's sister, Lucy, announced that she had auditioned for and won the
role of Mama Rose in a local dinner theater's production of the musical
Gypsy. The entire family was impressed and proud; Lucy had had three years
of vocal training prior to getting the part, and the family has seen several
excellent musicals performed at the theater. They were all excited about
Lucy's triumph and agreed to be at the front table on opening night.

Situation
David has just sat through a terrible opening night performance. He
must now watch Mama Rose's closing number. Lucy, along with the rest
of the cast, has been embarrassingly bad throughout the entire show. After Lucy's final number, David must applaud with the rest of the audience, while the house lights come up and reveal to Lucy his reaction to
the play.

Comments
The actor playing David should decide what his reaction will be to Lucy's
last song, particularly in juxtaposition to her performance in the first por-
tion of the musical. This improvisation can also be done with the entire
family sitting at the table, reacting not only to the actors before them, but

also to each other. It could even be extended to a scene in which David congratulates Lucy after the curtain calls.

Source: *Escape From Slavery: The Boyhood of Frederick Douglass in His Own Words,* memoirs by Frederick Douglass, edited by Michael McCurdy

Characters
One male: Frederick Douglass, a fifteen-year-old black slave

Place
The woods; the mid-nineteenth century

Background
Frederick's master found the young man's work unsatisfactory and sent him to Edward Corey, a man who had earned a well-deserved reputation for breaking in young slaves. Although big for his age, Frederick had never worked as a field hand and was frightened of large animals. Soon after Frederick's arrival, Corey sent him in a cart drawn by a team of oxen to get wood. Twice, Frederick lost control of the oxen, which succeeded in up-setting the cart and its load of wood—and almost killing Frederick.

Frederick returned to Mr. Corey to report what had happened with the oxen. Corey ordered Frederick to follow him back to the woods. Corey cut three switches from a tree with his ax, trimmed them with his pocket knife, and commanded Frederick to take off his clothes. When Frederick remained silent, not following directions, Corey attacked him, tearing his clothes and whipping him brutally.

Situation
Alone now in the woods, Frederick struggles with the aftermath of this monstrous assault on his body and spirit.

Comments
Frederick has never been treated with such disdain and violence; his despair overwhelms him as much as his physical pain. This is the beginning of a terribly low period for him.

Source: *First Dance* (an original improvisation written by UCLA student Rita Clay)

Characters
One female: Amy, a teen-ager

Place
Amy's bedroom

Background
Amy has had a crush on Jason since her first year in high school. Jason, a year older than Amy, is the class clown and a member of the football team. He also hangs out with the jock crowd. Amy is one of the prettiest girls in her high school, but she is very quiet and a serious student. She doesn't enjoy going to social events, but she wants to fit in and be liked. So, Amy has decided to ask Jason to a school-sponsored turn-around dance (girls ask the boys). She gains the courage to take this step when she finds out (through a classmate) that Jason thinks she is pretty—and that he doesn't have a date.

Situation
In this scene, Amy is practicing what she will say to Jason when she invites him to the dance. What form this rehearsal takes is up to the actor playing Amy; she might use a mirror or a teddy bear as the stand-in for Jason. Part one would be this solo moment for Amy, while part two would be the telephone conversation between Jason and Amy when she asks him out.

Comments
Amy has never talked to Jason on the phone, nor has she talked to him much in person. Keep in mind that Jason is one of the most popular boys in school and that Amy is basically a loner. So, it isn't easy for Amy to do this; it's possible that she may not be able to go through with it and that if she does, she may get rejected.

Source: *The Fisher King*, a film by Terry Gilliam, screenplay by Richard LaGravenese

Characters
One male: Nick Lucas, the host of a talk radio program

Place
Nick's living room

Background
Nick hosts a controversial radio program; people call in with problems and he gives them advice. His suggestions are usually scandalous or outrageous in some way. This particular evening, a caller asked Nick what he should do about a girl who was ignoring him. Nick told the caller that the girl was

clearly a snobbish yuppie, and the only way to deal with yuppies was to kill them all. Apparently, the caller took Nick at his word. He went to a bar and shot yuppies, killing many people. He then turned the gun on himself.

Situation
Nick has just been cast in his first television show, and he is rehearsing. He is excited about this role and experimenting with a variety of ways to deliver his lines. He turns on the television to watch the evening news. The yuppie massacre is reported, and Nick's name is mentioned in connection with his earlier conversation with the caller. As he listens to the graphic details of the killings, he realizes, to his horror, that he has caused the death of these innocent people.

Comments
There should be a contrast between Nick's good mood while he is preparing for his first television role and his reaction to the shocking information that he hears on the news. Nick is an obnoxious person who doesn't care about anyone else, and this is the first time in his life that his irresponsibility backfires. After this incident, Nick's life changes radically: he loses his job, becomes an alcoholic, and endures an impoverished and miserable existence for a number of years.

Source: "Geraldo No Last Name," an extract from the novel *The House on Mango Street,* by Sandra Cisneros

Characters
One female: Marin, a young Latina woman

Place
The emergency room of an urban hospital

Background
Marin met Geraldo, a young Latino man, at a dance. As they were walking home, Geraldo was hit by a car. The driver did not stop. Marin took Geraldo to the hospital. He had nothing in his pockets to indicate who he was or where he lived. All Marin knew was that his name is Geraldo.

Situation
Marin sits in the emergency room for hours waiting for news about this boy with whom she danced one dance. Many thoughts go through her mind. Who is he? Did he leave anyone behind in another country? What would his people think if they never heard from him again?

Comments
Geraldo loses a lot of blood, and he dies. This would not have happened
had he been attended to sooner. It was not, however, considered important to give him prompt treatment because he was assumed to be an illegal
alien. Many other thoughts may enter the actor's head—what did Geraldo
look like? What did they talk about while they danced? Marin also needs to
explore why she is waiting for a person whom she barely knows. To end the
moment, another actor may enter and inform Marin of Geraldo's death.

Source: *Going After Cacciato,* a novel by Tim O'Brien

Characters
One male: Paul Berlin, a soldier in the United States Army

Place
Vietnam; 1968

Background
Paul's army outfit recently installed a radio–telephone hook-up with the
States. Several soldiers have spoken to their mothers. It is now Paul's turn;
he has been waiting eagerly.

Situation
Paul has planned something meaningful to say. He has questions to ask
about his family. He clearly visualizes the kitchen in Minnesota where his
mother will answer the phone, but the phone keeps ringing, and no one
answers it. No one is at home.

Comments
Paul has listened to his buddies' conversations with their mothers. He has
had time to plan everything he will say. The excitement and emotion have
built up in him. The war is horrible, and this talk with his mother would
have raised his spirits. This is a lost opportunity—a terrible disappointment. The actor playing Paul should imagine the conditions of the war,
Paul's great distance from his family, his loneliness, and what the sound
of his mother's voice would have meant. Remember that this scene is taking place in 1968 in Vietnam—opportunities to communicate with loved
ones in the States are practically nonexistent. Paul may never get another
chance to talk with his mother.

See index for other improvisations from this source.

Source: *In the Cemetery,* an incident from the life of Margaret Sanger

Characters
One female: Margaret Sanger, thirteen years old; her father, a sculptor (optional)

Place
A cemetery; one night in 1892

Background
Margaret Sanger's little brother died of pneumonia at the age of four. The bereaved mother had no pictures of him.

Situation
One night, Margaret's father takes her to the cemetery, along with a wheelbarrow full of tools. He opens her brother's grave to make a cast of his head and shoulders, while Margaret stands by, holding a lantern. This is the moment when Margaret looks at the body of her dead brother.

Comments
It is night in a cemetery, which is scary in itself. Moreover, Margaret's father is digging up a grave, which is highly illegal. One can imagine how frightening this event must be to a little girl, not to mention the terror and grief she would experience upon seeing her dead brother. This scene can be done with the father present, but the actual moment—seeing her brother—is Margaret's.

Source: *The Journey of the Fifth Horse,* a play by Ronald Ribman

Characters
One male: Nikolai Alexevich Chulkaturin, in his twenties

Place
A garden outside the home of Elizaveta Kirilovna, Saint Petersburg, Russia; the late nineteenth century

Background
Nikolai Alexevich has always loved Elizaveta, but she rejected him in favor of a dashing cavalry officer. At the time, Nikolai challenged the officer

to a duel, risking his life for Elizaveta. However, recognizing how uneven the fight would be, the officer withdrew from the duel, a further humiliation for Nikolai.

Nikolai left Saint Petersburg for some time. When he returned, he learned from Elizaveta's father that she had been impregnated and then deserted by the officer. Nikolai, who still loves Elizaveta, tells her father that *he* will marry her and save her from disgrace. (Having a child out of wedlock would have been unthinkably scandalous.)

Situation
Nikolai goes into the garden to propose to Elizaveta. He sees a mutual friend, Bizmionkov, sitting with her on a garden bench. Nikolai hears Bizmionkov mention his name and watches Elizaveta react to it in disgust. Bizmionkov then proposes to her himself, and she accepts.

Comments
Nikolai was elated at the prospect of rescuing the woman of his dreams. He went into the garden with great expectations, assuming that she would be grateful for his offer. What he sees and hears comes as a shock. He has always believed that she really loved him and she was only temporarily infatuated with the officer because of his rank. Nikolai discovers not only that she never loved him, but also that she is contemptuous of him. Other actors may be used to play Elizaveta and Bizmionkov. However, in film, the actor might not have that luxury and would have to imagine the conversation that he overhears.

Source: *Kindred,* a novel by Octavia E. Butler

Characters
One female: Dana Franklin, an African American woman in her twenties

Place
The eastern shore of Maryland; 1815 and 1976

Background
Dana Franklin lives in California. She is married to Kevin, who is white. The time is 1976. However, Dana has been mysteriously and repeatedly returning in time to the Weylin plantation in Maryland, where her forebears lived as slaves over one hundred and fifty years ago.

Situation
This is one of Dana's first trips back in time. She finds herself hiding in the woods in the middle of the night, watching a group of white men on

horseback. These men are known as patrons, groups of young whites who "maintain order" among slaves through beatings and torture. Dana realizes that she is hiding because all blacks are assumed to be slaves unless they have papers to prove that they have been freed.

The white men enter a log cabin in the woods, breaking the door down. Three slaves are dragged out of the cabin: a man, his wife, and their child. The whites demand to see the family's passes, which they do not have. The husband is naked, having been dragged from his bed. The men tie him to a tree. His wife attempts to cover herself with a blanket, but one of the white men tears it away from her. They whip her husband until he screams, while the mother and child are forced to watch. Dana hears the child crying. The husband is then tied to a rope and dragged by horses through the woods. One white man stays behind and punches the woman in the face. When Dana overhears the child being called Alice, she realizes that these black people are her ancestors.

Comments
This scene is, of course, a kind of science fiction, in that Dana goes back in time. However, when she is thrust back into the past, she is fully involved in all of its dangers. Dana wears pants, like a modern woman; she is well educated and married to a white man. To be propelled backward into the time of slavery is a great shock.

See index for other improvisations from this source.

Source: *Life,* a screenplay by UCLA student Joke Fincioen

Characters
One female: Josie, fifteen years old

Place
Josie's bedroom; evening

Background
While Josie's parents were at work, she invited her boyfriend over to her house. They had sex for the first time and both lost their virginity. The condom ruptured. Four weeks later, Josie still has not menstruated. She is very worried. Her parents are downstairs in the living room.

Situation
Josie is on her bed, with the pregnancy test in her hand. When she finally opens it, the test result shows that she is pregnant.

Comments
Actors take note: Josie is an A student. Also, she really loves her boy-friend. She was not pressured into having sex, but she abused her par-ents' trust, and fears most of all that now she will lose their love and respect. She doesn't know what to do. Keeping the child would mean giving up her dreams of school—and disgracing her family. Aborting the child would mean much secrecy; besides, she is not old enough to drive or to go away for a day. There is no way around it—she will have to tell her parents.

Source: *Little Women,* a novel by Louisa May Alcott

Characters
One female: Jo March, in her early twenties

Place
The bedroom of Beth March, one of Jo's sisters; the mid-nineteenth century

Background
Jo has been earning her living in New York City as a writer. She recently received a telegram saying that her sister, Beth, was very ill. Jo got home just in time to see Beth before she died.

Situation
Jo is in Beth's bedroom, rummaging through an old trunk full of Beth's belongings, sorting out things such as old letters and dolls. Everything she touches conjures up a memory.

Comments
The actor should carefully select the particular objects for this exercise: each should have a definite history. The scene can also be done with space objects. Specificity is important.

See index for other improvisations from this source.

Source: "Masculine Protest," a short story by Frank O'Connor in *Collected Stories*

Characters
One male: Denis, a twelve-year-old boy

Place
Denis' bedroom in his home in a small town in Ireland; the early twentieth century

Background
Denis lives with his parents and his younger sister, Martha. Today is Denis' birthday, but his mother told him that she wouldn't be at home to share in the celebration. When he cried at the news, she accused him of being unmanly. Denis has decided to run away to Dublin (about twenty miles from this town). He will go on his bicycle.

Situation
Denis prepares to run away from home. He believes this to be the last time he will ever see his own bedroom, where he has spent so much of his life. He grabs two items to carry with him on his bike, then takes one last look around.

Comments
The actor should choose the two significant items that Denis takes with him. In the story, he brings a little holy picture and a favorite storybook. Denis is sad to leave his room, but he also feels the romance of running away. He is leaving home because he is angry—and to prove to his mother that he can be manly.

See index for other improvisations from this source.

Source: *The Miracle Worker,* a play by William Gibson

Characters
One female: Kate Keller, the mother of the infant, Helen Keller

Place
Helen's nursery in the Kellers' Tuscumbia, Alabama, home; the 1880s

Background
Helen has been ill with measles but has recovered. According to her doctor, Helen will be none the worse for the experience.

Situation
Kate, filled with joy and relief that her daughter will live, is playing with Helen. When she attempts to get the baby's attention, she realizes that Helen cannot see or hear.

Comments
There is a contrast here between two moods: great joy and shock. The actor needs to imagine the infant in a crib and then find ways to attempt to get its attention.

Source: *The Moon by Night,* a novel by Madeleine L'Engle

Characters
One female: Vicky Austin, fifteen years old

Place
The Grand Canyon

Background
Vicky is on a camping trip with her family. She has met a boy named Zachary, whom she likes.

Situation
Vicky is sitting on a little rock shelf on the canyon's side, feeling lonely, when she sees a skunk. She freezes: she does not want to startle the skunk into spraying her. The little animal comes so close that it nearly steps on her toes. As soon as it passes, Vicky runs back to her family's camp site.

Comments
Vicky's worst fear is smelling like a skunk when she sees Zachary. In the novel, there is also a night scene in which Vicky senses a bear nearby. Either animal could be used, since both scenes deal with fear. The actor should consider why Vicky is feeling lonely at this point in time.

See index for other improvisations from this source.

Source: *Mrs. 'Arris Goes to Paris,* a novel by Paul Gallico

Characters
One female: Ada Harris, in her sixties

Place
Ada's flat in London; the mid-1950s

Background
Ada Harris, a widow, works as a charwoman. She cleans house for a wealthy lady, who one day received an elegant gown from the Christian Dior de-

sign boutique in Paris. Ada thought that it was the most beautiful thing she had ever seen and decided that she, too, would own such a gown. It took her three years of pinching pence to be able to afford a trip to France in quest of this dream. She sacrificed many comforts (walking to work every day to save the bus fare, for example) to save money for her trip.

Overcoming many obstacles, Ada flew to Paris at last and went straight to the posh salon of Christian Dior. The manager was very snobbish about her dowdy appearance and made it difficult for her to negotiate the purchase of a gown. However, Ada persevered and managed to buy her cherished dream. She remained in Paris for a week, while her gown was being constructed just for her, having many adventures and encountering people with lives very different from her own.

Situation
Ada has returned to London, having spent the most exciting week of her life in Paris. She is now alone in her shabby London apartment with this beautiful, expensive, custom-made, Christian Dior gown, for the acquisition of which she sacrificed and saved her money all those years.

Comments
The actor needs to imagine for herself the specific adventures Ada had and the people Ada encountered in Paris. She must be able to visualize the dress in detail. An actual dress should be used and embellished with the actor's imagination. There are all sorts of ways in which the gown could be used; for example, the actor may bring in another actor to play her friend and fellow worker, so that she can show it off.

The actor will discover how she feels through the improvisation; she may be elated and full of beautiful memories of the past week, or the reality of returning to her everyday life may evoke a different reaction. Probably, the actor will experience both emotions.

Source: *The New Car* (an original improvisation written by UCLA student JulieAnna Laffner)

Characters
One male or female: Robin, sixteen years old

Place
The driver's seat of a new car

Background
It is Robin's sixteenth birthday. She has been waiting for this day all her life and has been practicing driving for six months, coaxing her relatives

and older friends to take her driving at least twice a day since getting her learner's permit. This morning, when she was leaving the house to take her driver's test, she discovered a beautiful blue car parked in the driveway: a sixteenth birthday present from her parents. Elated, Robin ran off to take the driver's test. She failed.

Situation
Robin is sitting in her new car, devastated. She doesn't know how to tell her parents, and she can't understand why it seems everyone else in the world can pass a driver's test. Now she won't be allowed to drive her new car by herself.

Comments
Getting a driver's license is a milestone in a teen-ager's life. Recognize the independence and pride a person feels when able to drive. It is also important for the actor to acknowledge that today is a special day, and that he or she has received a special gift, but that the capacity to use it has been taken away, at least temporarily.

Source: "The New Dress," a short story by Virginia Woolf in *That Kind of Woman*, edited by B. Adams and T. Tate

Characters
One female: Mabel Waring, a young woman

Place
A party

Background
Mabel comes from a large, poor family. She has been invited to a party, but all she has to wear is an old, out-of-style, bright yellow dress.

Situation
The moment Mabel arrives at the party, she realizes that her dress is all wrong. The following is a simile describing how she perceives herself: "I feel like some dowdy, decrepit, horribly dingy old fly." Mabel's self-consciousness affects her physical behavior. The situation begins with Mabel arriving at the party and removing her coat. It ends with her putting on her coat and leaving the party.

Comments
The actor should imagine the other guests at the party—how they are

dressed, their conversations, how they interact and move about the room. In her short story, Woolf makes frequent use of mirrors in the room to emphasize and distort Mabel's view of herself. Obviously hypersensitive and self-conscious, Mabel doesn't feel that she belongs; her attitude has been shaped by a lifelong sense of inadequacy. The dress simply triggers a renewed awareness of this perception. She arrives at the party thinking that people will make fun of her and her dress; then she fulfills the prophecy.

Source: *Nightjohn*, a novella by Gary Paulsen

Characters
One female: Sarny, African American, twelve years old

Place
The slaves' quarters on a Southern plantation; shortly before the Civil War

Background
NightJohn is a free man who voluntarily returned to slavery to teach others how to read and write. At this time, literate slaves were severely punished. NightJohn has been secretly teaching the alphabet to Sarny. They meet late at night and draw the letters in the dirt with their fingers.

Situation
Sarny has learned the alphabet and writes her name, for the first time, in the dirt on the ground.

Comments
Seeing her name written out gives Sarny a real identity. It is a thrilling moment. But, because reading and writing are forbidden and the consequences (if the whites discover her secret) are so severe, she will have to wipe out her name.

See index for other improvisations from this source.

Source: *Péllèas and Mélisande*, a play by Maurice Maeterlinck, translated by Richard Hovey

Characters
One male, one female: Péllèas, in his late teens or early twenties; Mélisande, in her early teens

Place
Under Mélisande's window, outside a castle in France; 1892, late at night

Background
Mélisande and Péllèas are in love. However, because Mélisande is married to Péllèas's older brother, Golaud, the lovers must remain separated.

Situation
Mélisande is sitting at her window, brushing her long hair, which cascades to the ground. Péllèas, standing below, wraps himself in her hair; this is the closest he can get to Mélisande at this moment. They must be very quiet, so as not to wake the household.

Comments
This is a sensuous scene about forbidden love, similar to the balcony scene in *Romeo and Juliet*. The environment is important, because the lovers must be listening constantly for sounds of stirring in the castle. Péllèas risks death if he is caught. Later in the play, he is, in fact, killed by Golaud. This situation involves two actors, but it is basically a solo moment for Péllèas.

To indicate Mélisande's long hair, the actors can use fabric, ribbon, or imaginary hair.

See index for other improvisations from this source.

Source: *Rebecca,* a novel by Daphne Du Maurier

Characters
One female: Mrs. de Winter, in her early twenties. (Because Daphne Du Maurier never gave the main character in her novel a first name, she will be referred to here as Mrs. de Winter.)

Place
Rebecca's room in the west wing of Manderley in Cornwall, England; the 1930s

Background
Mrs. de Winter's parents are dead. She was working as a lady's companion when, through her employer, she met Maxim de Winter, a wealthy man twice her age. Although she was young enough to be his daughter, he married her.

Max took his new bride to his home, Manderley, a stately English mansion complete with a large staff of servants. Mrs. Danvers was the housekeeper in charge. All the staff were devoted to Rebecca, Max's previous wife, and they—Mrs. Danvers in particular—resent the new Mrs. de Winter. Rebecca drowned at sea a year ago, and Max appears still to be grieving her loss.

The new Mrs. de Winter pales in comparison with the grandeur and beauty of Rebecca, who fit this social milieu like a glove and who ran the household in an orderly manner. Mrs. de Winter is a simple girl—plain, even—and this world of mansions and servants is completely foreign to her.

Max and Rebecca's bedroom was in Manderley's west wing, overlooking the sea in which Rebecca drowned. This wing has been closed off. Max and Mrs. de Winter reside in the east wing, which does *not* overlook the sea.

Situation

One day, Mrs. de Winter finds her way to the forbidden west wing. There, lying on the bed, is Rebecca's nightgown. Mrs. de Winter picks it up and holds it.

Comments

Everything in this mansion is indelibly stamped with Rebecca's personality. It is as if she were still alive. Why was her nightgown left on the bed? The actor playing Mrs. de Winter might experience a number of emotions in handling the garment. This is the first time she has ventured into the famous west wing and into the bedroom where this beautiful, perfect, and irreproachable creature slept with the second Mrs. de Winter's husband.

See also the following improvisation.

Source: *Rebecca,* a novel by Daphne Du Maurier

Characters

One female: Mrs. de Winter, a young woman

Place

The grand staircase at Manderley in Cornwall, England; the 1930s

Background

Maxim de Winter lost his first wife, Rebecca, in a drowning accident near their home. He remarried and brought his bride to live at Manderley. The mansion is staffed with servants, all of whom resent the second Mrs. de Winter because, in their eyes, no one could replace Rebecca. Mrs. Danvers, the head housekeeper, especially dislikes the new Mrs. de Winter.

A large portrait of Rebecca, wearing an elegant gown, hangs above the grand staircase. Mrs. Danvers encourages Mrs. de Winter to wear this gown at a formal party to be held at Manderley, insisting that it would please Maxim greatly to see her in this dress.

Situation
The party has begun, and Mrs. de Winter makes her entrance, descending the grand staircase in Rebecca's gown. All of the guests gasp in horror. Max orders Mrs. de Winter to return immediately to her room to remove the dress.

Comments
The actor can imagine that she is wearing a magnificent gown or she may costume herself in something appropriate. It is also possible to have another actor contribute Maxim's voice to the scene. Mrs. de Winter loves Max and wants more than anything to make him happy. His disapproval is devastating to her.

The situation can be extended to the scene between Max and his wife in their bedroom after the guests have departed. Mrs. de Winter accuses Max of cherishing an obsession with Rebecca, which he does not dispute.

See also the preceding improvisation.

Source: *Scorpions,* a novel by Walter Dean Myers

Characters
One male: Jamal Hicks, twelve years old, African American

Place
A bodega (a small Hispanic grocery store) in the Harlem section of New York City

Background
Jamal's older brother, Randy, was the leader of a gang called the Scorpions. Randy is now in jail and, until his release, wants Jamal to take his place as the leader of the Scorpions. Some of the gang members are opposed to Jamal's leadership and have been threatening him.

Jamal needs money to pay for an appeal that might get Randy out of jail. He has just gotten a job as a delivery boy at a bodega. His boss, Mr. Gonzalez, has told him that no gang members are to come near the store. However, some of the Scorpions come into the bodega to threaten Jamal, causing Mr. Gonzalez to fire him. Even though the gang members steal some items on their way out, Mr. Gonzalez pays Jamal the twenty-one dollars owed him for wages.

Situation
Jamal leaves the store with the twenty-one dollars in his hand. It is the first time he has ever been paid for a job, and now the job is gone.

Comments
Jamal needs this money, not only to get Randy out of jail, but also to help his mother, who is struggling to take care of him and his younger sister. Jamal doesn't really want to be the leader of this gang; after all, he's only twelve years old. This job could have been his way out.

See index for other improvisations from this source.

Source: *Shunkan,* a scene from *Heike Nyogo No Shima* a play written by Monzaemon Chikamatsu

Characters
One male: Shunkan, a political exile

Place
A shack on Devil's Island, Kikaigshia, Japan; the seventeenth century

Background
Shunkan, along with Naristsune, led an abortive plot against the tyrant, Kiyomori, leader of the powerful Heike clan. The plotters were banished to a desert island, and they have lived there for three years. Shunkan misses his wife and child, who are still in Kyoto. His friend, Naristsune, fell in love with Chidori, an island girl, and took her as his wife.

One day, a ship docked at the island. An envoy came ashore and announced that Naristsune and one other exile had been granted special amnesty—but not Shunkan. The envoy reported that Kiyomori bears him a particular grudge.

As they boarded the vessel, Chidori, Naristsune's island wife, was denied passage. Naristsune pleaded on her behalf, but his pleas were denied. He then refused to leave the island without her. He told Shunkan to board the ship in his place. As Shunkan was preparing to depart, the envoy told him that his wife had been killed. Devastated, Shunkan chose to remain on the island in continued exile. He insisted that Chidori go in his place, and he pushed her aboard the departing ship.

Situation
Shunkan waves farewell to his beloved friends (who have become his family and his only connection with civilization). He follows the ship with his eyes, waving farewell. As the vessel draws farther away, he changes his mind and calls it back. But it is too late. He is alone.

Comments

The actor playing this role has probably felt the pangs of parting from his family. This sorrow will be magnified when he realizes that he will never see the people he loves again and compounded by the awareness that he will be without human companionship for the rest of his life. A ship will not come to this forsaken place again. In the play, the tide comes in and Shunkan climbs to the top of a cliff in a futile attempt to call back the departing vessel. The actor can use whatever furniture is available to create this effect.

See index for other improvisations from this source.

Source: "Sire," an extract from the novel *The House on Mango Street* by Sandra Cisneros

Characters

One female: Esperanza, a teen-aged girl

Place

A street in Esperanza's neighborhood

Background

The boy next door looked at Esperanza, and she stared back. Her parents told her he was a "punk" and instructed her not to talk to him.

Situation

Esperanza sees the boy's girlfriend come by to visit him. She is wearing lots of makeup. Esperanza hears them laughing. She sees them drinking beer and riding on his bike. They walk together and hold hands. She wonders where they go together; she imagines them kissing. Esperanza yearns for him, or a boy like him, to hold her.

Comments

This scene is about longing and loneliness. The actor may imagine almost anything about these two people. Esperanza may fantasize about having a boyfriend, or she may believe that she will never find anybody to love her. The task for the actor is to clearly picture this boy and his girlfriend.

Source: *The Stationmaster's Wife,* a film by Rainer Werner Fassbinder based on the novel by Oskar Maria Graf

Characters

One male: Bolweiser, the stationmaster

Place
A small town in Bavaria; shortly before the rise of Adolf Hitler

Background
Bolweiser is sexually enslaved by his beautiful wife, Hanni. She has had affairs with other men, which torments him. She has taken his money to give to other men for their businesses. Meanwhile, Bolweiser was sent to prison for perjury. (He lied to protect Hanni.) He has been in prison for months, in solitary confinement, and is beaten down physically and mentally.

Situation
Bolweiser is called from his cell to meet with a lawyer. The lawyer has a document from Bolweiser's wife, granting her a divorce. The lawyer persuades Bolweiser to sign it, telling the prisoner that he looks bad and wouldn't want to appear in court that way. Bolweiser submits; he is a broken man.

Comments
The solo moment is the reading of the divorce decree, the decision to sign it, and the signing. The actor, however, may choose not to sign it. The actor needs to be very clear in his own mind about Bolweiser's relationship with Hanni. (This improvisation can be done with another actor to portray the lawyer.)

Source: "The Story of an Hour," a short story by Kate Chopin, in *The Awakening and Selected Stories,* edited by Sandra M. Gilbert

Characters
One female: Mrs. Mallard, a young woman

Place
Her bedroom; the late nineteenth century

Background
Mrs. Mallard just learned that her husband, Brently, was killed in a railroad accident. Since she heard the news, she has been crying in her bedroom.

Situation
Suddenly, the word *free* escapes from Mrs. Mallard's lips. She realizes that, for the first time in her life, there is no one to tend to anymore, that she will now be living only for herself. She finds herself whispering, "Free! Body and soul, free!" Her sister, Josephine, is outside the door, imploring

her to open it, but Mrs. Mallard refuses, assuring her sister that all is well. Sitting in her chair in her room, Mrs. Mallard dies of happiness—literally.

Comments

Mrs. Mallard's grief for the loss of her husband is genuine; she does love him. However, she is intoxicated by the thought of freedom. Later, when the doctor arrives, his diagnosis is that she died of "heart disease of joy that kills."

The actor should take into account what life was like for women in the late nineteenth century. A woman was expected to devote her life to her husband and children; self-fulfillment was unthinkable.

As it turns out, Mr. Mallard was not killed in the accident. He came home to learn of his wife's strange death.

Source: "A Sunrise on the Veld," a short story by Doris Lessing in *The Doris Lessing Reader*

Characters
One male: A fifteen-year-old boy

Place
The South African veld

Background
The boy awoke in the early morning before it was light, got dressed, took his gun, tiptoed past his parents' room, gathered his dogs, and went out onto the veld. He was excited about being fifteen years old and going out to hunt on his own. He shouted with joy and sang out loud because he felt so courageous.

Situation
The boy hears a strange sound among the trees. He sees a small buck making gasping sounds and leaping about. He realizes that the buck is wounded and sees that it is being consumed by swarms of carnivorous ants. There is nothing he can do to stop it. He watches the carcass of the buck being picked clean by the ants.

Comments
This is a story about coming of age. The boy discovers that he is helpless, unable to save this tortured buck. He learns "the knowledge of fatality, of what has to be." Just the moment before, he was overflowing with energy and youthful confidence: now he is "unable to make any movement of brain or body except to say, 'Yes, yes. That is what living is.'" He realizes that

there is nothing he can do to stop the cycle of nature. The actor should begin this improvisation with the boy's exuberance and shouts of joy, and then experience the change in emotions after he comes upon the buck.

Source: *Tous les Matins du Monde (All the Mornings of the World)*, a film by Alain Corneau, story and screenplay by Pascal Quignard

Characters
One female: A middle-aged woman; her former lover (optional)

Place
The woman's bedroom in her father's country house in France; the baroque period

Background
The woman's father, a great baroque cellist, became a recluse after his wife's death, playing only for the purpose of reaching her beyond the grave. He taught his two daughters to play; later they became a famous trio. When they were invited to perform regularly at the king's court, the father refused; he believed that doing so would destroy their music.

One day, a young man came to learn to play the cello from the master. The maestro refused to help him. One of the daughters (the one presently on her deathbed) sneaked the young man under the house to listen while her father played. Day after day, they listened to the father's chords and technique, and the young man memorized them. The woman taught him all that she had learned from her father about the cello, and, eventually, the young man became the premiere musician of the court. He forgot her—the woman who taught him about music—and ended up marrying her younger sister.

Over the years, the woman pined away for her lost love. When they were together, he had composed a melody especially for her. Now on her deathbed, she has requested that he come with his cello and play this piece for her.

Situation
The man, no longer young, arrives to find an emaciated woman on her deathbed. She requests that he play the melody for her, and he does.

Comments
Another actor may be used to play the (imaginary) cello. However, what is important is the desire of the actor, playing the woman, to hear the music one more time. This piece means more to her than anything in the world.

Source: *The Tragedy of the 1996 Mount Everest Expedition* (an original improvisation, based on an actual event, written by UCLA student Adam de la Pena)

Characters
One male: Rob Hall, one of two leaders of a mountaineering expedition

Place
A blinding snowstorm on top of Mount Everest

Background
In 1996, two teams, one headed by Rob Hall of New Zealand and the other by Scott Fischer of the United States, set out to climb Mount Everest. As they moved out from base camp, three thousand feet below the summit, the situation began to deteriorate. Fatigued, the teams began to move too slowly and fell behind their timetables. As the group finally began its descent, a massive storm hit, plunging the temperature to seventy degrees below zero. The teams were separated as the storm raged on and visibility dropped to four feet. When the storm finally passed, eight people, including both team leaders, lay dead on the mountain (the most lost in any twenty-four-hour period on Mount Everest).

Situation
This is Rob Hall's last satellite telephone call, made to his pregnant wife in New Zealand. Hall made the call just before he died, trapped in a snow hole on the mountain.

Comments
The actor playing Hall should know he is going to die on the mountain. Hall is suffering from oxygen deprivation, which induces hypoxia, a condition causing brain and body processes to slow and finally shut down.

Source: *The Wedding,* a novel by Dorothy West

Characters
One female: Miss Josephine, twenty-seven years old, white

Place
The sidewalk outside a post office in the South; the early twentieth century

Background
When Miss Josephine was growing up, she and her mother lived in poverty. A kind neighbor, a black woman who cooked for white people, sent food to

Miss Josephine and her mother. Twice a week, the woman's son, Hannibal, would take them for an outing. He fell in love with Miss Josephine.

When Hannibal went up North, he and Miss Josephine were separated for a few years. He wrote letters to his mother about his adventures. Unable to read, his mother brought the letters to Miss Josephine's house, along with her food, to have them read aloud. Miss Josephine was thrilled with Hannibal's adventures; they consumed her thoughts. But, when Hannibal's mother died, the letters stopped.

Now middle-aged and not wanting to live alone, Hannibal wrote a letter to Miss Josephine, proposing marriage.

Situation
Miss Josephine has just received this unexpected letter from Hannibal. She stands outside the post office reading it. Hannibal claims that he has money to provide for her. Feeling hungry and old-maidish, Miss Josephine decides to grasp at what she believes is her last chance. Although she realizes that the union may cause a scandal and make her mother unhappy, she decides to accept Hannibal's proposal. She writes a note at the bottom of his letter and mails it back to him.

Comments
In the early 1900s, interracial marriages were generally unacceptable. Also at this time, a woman who was not married by the age of twenty-seven would be branded an old maid. Born into poverty, Miss Josephine might not have another opportunity to marry. This situation resembles a theme of the movie *Driving Miss Daisy,* in that Josephine has feelings for Hannibal, but, until this moment, the thought of marrying a black man has never even entered her mind.

The actor should bear in mind how profoundly the mores of this period shaped the relationships and attitudes of the characters.

See index for other improvisations from this source.

Source: *A Yellow Raft in Blue Water,* a novel by Michael Dorris

Characters
One female: Rayona, fifteen years old

Place
Rayona's bedroom in her grandmother's house on an Indian reservation in Montana

Background
Several months ago, Rayona's mother, distraught over her upcoming divorce, left Rayona to live with her grandmother, known as Aunt Ida. Her mother's high school yearbook, which Rayona had found, became a prized possession to Rayona because it was the only memento of her mother. One day, a package addressed to her mother arrived at the house. Rayona was excited; she believed that she would see her mother again when she came to pick up the package. The box remained on the table for two weeks.

Situation
Rayona discovers that the package is gone. She realizes that her mother must have been there to pick it up. She looks for a note from her mother but finds nothing. She notices that her mother's high school yearbook is also gone. Her mother has obviously searched through Rayona's belongings—so it must have been clear to her that Rayona was still living there—but she didn't want to see her daughter.

Comments
Rayona is faced with the realization that the package is more important to her mother than is Rayona herself. She misses her mother. This is a great disappointment; for these last two weeks Rayona has lived in hope that she would see her mother.

See index for other improvisations from this source.

6

Special Problems: Physical/Psychological

Uta Hagen, in *A Challenge for the Actor,* discusses the importance of a character's obstacle to fulfilling his wishes. She writes, "Anything worthy of presentation reflects a human struggle to overcome problems posed by fate, the world or society, the particular circumstances and the other people in the life of an individual" (Hagen 1991, 283). Unquestionably, unusual physical features will influence the answer to one of the most fundamental questions an actor can pose: What is in the way of what I want? The selections in this chapter challenge the actor to portray characters who are faced with special obstacles. While there are obstacles for every character in every scene, these characters have even bigger odds to overcome.

Whether a character is deaf or blind, communicates with difficulty, operates with restricted mental or physical capacity, or (in the case of A. R. Gurney's *Sylvia*) is not a human being, but a dog, the actor is advised to do research before tackling these situations. Even playing a character such as George Washington in Jean Fritz's *The Cabin Faced West* requires research into the particular attributes of this man. Most are impossible to do without some knowledge of and respect for the particular obstacle involved. An uninformed actor risks coming across as false and, perhaps, somewhat ridiculous.

While it is important to understand the external differences that make these characters tick, the actor should not get lost in research. In Stanislavski's *Building a Character* (1949), the director Tortsov discusses how external distortion impinges on the character's personality. He suggests that one's inner life may remain the same, but external physical features will have a bearing on one's feelings and on how one relates to other people. Examples of characters influenced by unusual physical features are Shakespeare's Richard III and Helen Keller in *The Miracle Worker*. Tortsov states: "Each person evolves an external characterization out of himself, from others, takes it from real or imaginary life, according to his intuition, his observation of himself and others. He draws it from his own experience of life or that of his friends, from pictures, engravings, drawings, books, stories, novels, or from some simple incident—it makes no difference. The only proviso is that while he is making this external research he must not lose his inner self" (Stanislavski 1977, 7).

SPECIAL PROBLEMS: PHYSICAL/PSYCHOLOGICAL SITUATIONS

One male
"A Crush"

One male, one female
Awakenings
The Cabin Faced West
Epiphany
The Kentucky Cycle—Part One
The Killer
The Report Card
Richard III
The Tumbleweeds

Two females
The Tumbleweeds

Two males
Birdy
The Foreigner
Going After Cacciato
Of Mice and Men
Péllèas and Mélisande
Sling Blade
Winter Sun

Ensemble
"Immigration Blues"

Jane Eyre
Sylvia

Source: *Awakenings,* a film by Penny Marshall based on the book by Dr. Oliver Sacks, screenplay by Steve Zaillian

Characters
One male, one female: Leonard, forty-one years old; a woman in her late twenties or early thirties

Place
The chronic disease ward of a large metropolitan hospital

Background
Leonard contracted encephalitis when he was eleven years old, leaving him in a coma-like state for thirty years. Dr. Sayers, recently hired by the hospital to work in its chronic diseases ward, discovered that a new "miracle" drug being used to treat Parkinson's disease, L-Dopa, revived Leonard and other patients. Since he regained consciousness, Leonard has developed a relationship with a young woman whom he met during one of her visits to her hospitalized father.

Situation
It has been several weeks since Leonard emerged from his coma, and he has started to experience severe twitches and spasms. He has become grotesque. The young woman sits at his bedside, because he is no longer allowed to leave the ward. Leonard must tell her that this is the last time he'll be able to see her; his condition is deteriorating rapidly. His facial grimaces and twitching make it very difficult for him to communicate.

Comments
The drug has failed; in a few days Leonard will again lapse into unconsciousness. He and the young woman love each other, but this is a hopeless situation. The actors will discover what happens between Leonard and the young woman in their last few moments together. Remember that they are surrounded by the bustle of the hospital ward; whatever they say will be overheard by other patients and medical staff.

This situation is based on an actual case, conducted in 1969 by Dr. Oliver Sacks. His patients revived for a short time and then, when the drug failed, they regressed to an unconscious state, in which they remained for the rest of their lives.

See index for other improvisations from this source.

Source: *Birdy,* a novel by William Wharton

Characters

Two males: Al; Birdy—both are in their late teens or early twenties

Place

A military hospital; just after World War II

Background

When they were boys, Birdy and Al were great friends. It always seemed that Birdy should have been a bird: he was a keen amateur ornithologist and had a large collection of birds in his bedroom. He even broke his arm jumping off a tower because he believed he could fly.

Birdy and Al were both drafted into the army during World War II. After witnessing the destruction of his entire company, Birdy suffered a mental breakdown and was hospitalized on a special ward for difficult mental cases. He has been acting like a bird. Dr. Weiss, the army psychiatrist, has summoned Al to help break through to the real Birdy by jogging his childhood memories. Al has also been through a trauma; badly damaged by an exploding bomb, half of his face is covered in bandages. He doesn't know what he will look like when the dressings are removed.

Situation

Al enters Birdy's room and finds him perched in the corner like a bird. Al attempts to reach Birdy by reminiscing about childhood pranks. Birdy continues to act like a bird; Al can't tell if Birdy is responding to him or not. He also is not sure whether Birdy has really had a mental breakdown or if, for some reason, he's faking it.

Comments

Birdy *is* pretending to be a bird as a means of dealing with his trauma. Although that is a form of madness, itself, he is consciously engaged in it. However, he must never give himself away, even to Al. Birdy has found life far too hazardous; it's much safer to be a bird. Al is frustrated by his inability to connect with Birdy, his only real friend.

In the novel, the characters relive Al's reminiscences of their childhood through flashbacks. It would be a good exercise for the actors to shift back and forth between past and present.

Source: *The Cabin Faced West,* a novel by Jean Fritz

Characters

One female, one male: Ann Hamilton, a young girl; George Washington, the first president of the United States

Place
A house on Hamilton Hill (now known as Ginger Hill) in Washington County; September 18, 1784

Background
Ann had been feeling out of sorts all day, and she didn't know why. Her mother finally sent her out to pick some grapes.

Situation
When Ann's pail is almost full of grapes, she hears horses and riders coming along the road. Afraid that they are thieves, she hides in the grass. One man on a horse stops right in front of her. The man asks what her mother is making for dinner that night. Something about the man's voice puts Ann at ease, and she answers his question. Eventually, the man reveals that he is George Washington. He would like to have dinner with her family that evening.

Comments
It is exciting for anyone to meet the president of the United States in person, and even more so to have him as a dinner guest. Until this day, there has been very little excitement in Ann's life. There is a big difference in her attitude before and after she encounters the president.

The actor playing George Washington is faced with a special challenge: Washington was a powerful figure. The actor playing Washington should research the physical attributes and manner of speech of this man. (Apparently, he was quite impressive and charismatic.) Both actors may find it helpful to investigate the history of this period. Consider, also, that Washington is riding a horse: perhaps he could dismount.

The actors may also choose to improvise the scene in which Washington dines with the Hamilton family. What would they discuss?

N.B.: George Washington recorded in his diary that he took supper with the Hamiltons on September 18, 1784. Ann Hamilton was a real person.

Source: "A Crush," a short story by Cynthia Rylant

Characters
One male: Ernie, between twelve and twenty years old

Place
Ernie's bedroom in a group home

Background
Ernie's mind has not developed at the normal rate. He lived at home with

his mother until her death. After her death he stayed in a dark room, watching television with a bag of cookies.

One day, a parcel of Burpee seeds was mistakenly delivered to his house. Ernie was fascinated by the pictures of flowers on the packages. When his mother died, he was sent to live in a group home, and he carefully brought the seed packets along with him.

Situation
This is Ernie's first day in the group home. He is alone in his room.

Comments
The seed packets are Ernie's only connection with anything familiar; they are central to this improvisation. He knows that his mother is gone, and the loss overwhelms him. He is mentally retarded, but his depth of feeling is great.

Source: *Epiphany,* a play by Lucy Cores

Characters
One female, one male: Karen, twenty-one years old; Peter, twenty-three years old

Place
The terrace of an institution for the physically disabled; a spring afternoon

Background
Karen was once a ballet dancer but is now confined to a wheelchair. Her parents used to have terrible fights about paying for her ballet lessons; she now feels that she has let them down. She believes that they sent her to the institution so that they wouldn't have to look at her. Karen is bitter about her situation and is withdrawn from the rest of the group most of the time.

Peter suffered a stroke, which robbed him of his power of speech. Now he can express himself verbally with only one syllable: "gah."

Situation
Overhearing Karen's complaints about her condition, Peter attempts to make contact with her. She does not want to relate to him. He takes out a pack of cards to play a game with her, but she will have none of it. She tells him that she wants to be left alone, and she mocks his inability to talk. To get back at her, Peter attacks her physically.

The second part of this improvisation occurs a little later on the same day. A concert, comprising a medley of Chopin études, is performed for the patients. Peter stands next to Karen as both listen to the music.

Karen imagines that she rises from her wheelchair, takes Peter's hand, and dances with him. When the music ends, Peter conducts Karen back to her wheelchair. The actors can live out this fantasy. (In the play, Karen *does* reach out her hand to Peter.)

Comments
Peter really struggles to bring Karen around. The actor can find any number of ways to make this happen, but his only dialogue is "gah." In the play, Peter grabs Karen by the shoulders and shakes her violently; the actors can let the fight develop any way it can happen—or it may not happen. What the actors should realize is that this is fundamentally a love scene.

Both actors should fill in the background as to how and when the characters' disabilities began and what these two people were like before their accidents.

At the beginning of this chapter, the importance of obstacles is discussed. In this situation, both characters need to overcome great obstacles in order to connect with each other. For Peter, the challenge is his lack of speech. For Karen, her bitterness is even more an impediment than her physical disability.

Source: *The Foreigner*, a play by Larry Shue

Characters
Two males: Charlie Baker; Ellard Simms, mentally disabled

Place
Betty Meek's Fishing Lodge resort, Tilghman County, rural Georgia; 1980s

Background
Froggy Lesueur is a British demolition expert who runs training sessions at a nearby army base. He often visits the fishing lodge. This time he brings along a friend, Charlie, who is pathologically shy. Charlie tells Froggy that he is terrified of making conversation with strangers; to protect him, Froggy tells the family, at the fishing lodge, that Charlie cannot speak English. The joke has gone so far now that Charlie is stuck with the lie and cannot reveal that he understands everything. Ellard, who is also staying at the lodge, has always been treated like the dummy, and now discovers someone who (he thinks) knows less than he does.

Situation
Ellard proceeds to "help" Charlie learn English by placing different objects in front of him and teaching him the names for them. Ellard is ex-

cited by this. For the first time in his life, he is the smarter one; he is the teacher and someone needs *his* help. Charlie begins to realize the effect this is having on Ellard and plays the game to the fullest.

Comments

This game can be heartwarming for both the actors as well as for the characters. Each has found a way to help another human being for the first time in their lives. Charlie has always thought of himself as too boring to help anybody, while Ellard thought himself too stupid.

Source: *Going After Cacciato,* a novel by Tim O'Brien

Characters

Two males: Cacciato, a seventeen-year-old soldier in the United States Army; Paul Berlin, a comrade

Place

A hotel room in Paris, France; 1968, during the Vietnam War

Background

Paul Berlin and a group of other solders have spent months chasing Cacciato, a deserter from the Vietnam War. Cacciato is described by all of them as having a "boyish simplicity." He is always chewing gum, whistling, and smiling; they refer to him as "Dummy." One day, Cacciato had located Paris in an atlas and decided that Paris was where he wanted to go. And he went. Knowing the serious consequences of desertion, the men followed him. (Actually, the men were deserters themselves. It was *their* dream to go to Paris; their rationale was that they were going to find Cacciato.)

Situation

After a long, tortuous journey, the solders arrive in Paris and begin searching for Cacciato. Paul Berlin walks the halls until he recognizes a humming sound coming from one of the rooms. He knocks on the door. There is no answer, but the door is unlocked, so he goes in. Berlin finds Cacciato sitting on a cot in his underwear, peeling carrots with a knife. Berlin asks him to explain his desertion, but Cacciato says nothing. He just smiles.

Comments

Cacciato's smile is characterized as "beguiling and meaningless." Berlin later refers to him as "a big dumb baby." These men risked their lives to track down a retarded man who never belonged in the army in the first place. He didn't run away because he was scared. He was just a simple boy who wanted to go to Paris.

Cacciato was actually dead before his comrades found him. However, Berlin imagined a long chase, which took them all to Paris—their dream. The scene in the hotel room is imagined, but totally real for Berlin and the two actors. The actor playing Berlin is trying to justify for himself why they have spent so much energy trying to catch this innocent boy. Cacciato is unable to communicate well, and no one really knows what goes on in his mind. Is he smarter than the others in trying to escape from this horrible war, or is he totally innocent? Does he know that Berlin is there to turn him in? It is a challenge for the actor to play Cacciato as he is described. Although he does not speak in the scene in O'Brien's novel, the actor playing Cacciato may choose to behave differently, or he may just make sounds.

See index for other improvisations from this source.

Source: "Immigration Blues," a short story by Bienvenido N. Santos in *Scent of Apples: A Collection of Stories*

Characters
One male, two females: Alipio Palma, in his sixties; Antonieta Zafra, a middle-aged woman; Monica, Antonieta's older sister—all are immigrants to the United States from the Philippines

Place
Alipio Palma's apartment in San Francisco, California; the 1940s

Background
Alipio Palma's wife, Seniang, died over a year ago. Shortly after her death, he was in a car accident that left him hospitalized for almost a year. He has no retirement benefits and is now trying to make ends meet on Social Security checks and a small pension. He is hard of hearing and walks with a pronounced limp.

Six years ago, Antonieta Zafra married Carlito, a friend of Alipio's, to gain United States citizenship and thus avoid deportation. She and Carlito live on a farm, raising chickens and hogs. When possible, she works as a seamstress in town. Neither Antonieta nor Alipio has children. Antonieta does have an unmarried sister in the Philippines whose health has been getting worse and worse. At last, Antonieta has saved enough money to pay her sister's way to the United States.

Situation

Antonieta and her sister, Monica, pay an unexpected visit to Alipio. They help him prepare lunch with the small amount of food he has available. Antonieta tells Alipio the long story behind her decision to marry Carlito. Alipio then tells the sisters that he married his wife to rescue her from deportation, too. The marriage turned out very well. After this exchange, Antonieta can contain herself no longer. She blurts out that Monica is in trouble: she came to the United States on a tourist visa and must return to the Philippines within two days. Both sisters are ashamed of their hidden agenda in visiting Alipio, but explain that they thought he might like to have another wife.

Comments

The actor playing Alipio can decide whether to accept this proposal. It is important that all three actors have a clear understanding of their personal histories, with facts gathered from the background information and supplied by their imaginations. The sisters do not promote their scheme aggressively; they are proud people. They also hope that sharing their own histories will persuade Alipio to spontaneously suggest the proposed arrangement. Therefore, Antonieta must "sell" the story about her own marriage. The actor portraying Alipio must remember that he has two physical disabilities to contend with: a severe limp and a hearing problem.

A Brief History of Filipino Immigrants. The history of Filipino immigrants is one of displacement. For four hundred years, the Spanish ruled the Philippines; then, for half a century, the Philippines were under the control of the United States. Despite an uncertain national image—the result of generations of colonial rule—the Filipino family unit and sense of community are very strong. Due to a scarcity of opportunities in their own country, many Filipino professionals moved to the United States and Canada and sent money home to their families in the Philippines. Traditionally, it has been Filipino men who make the journey first, leaving their wives and sweethearts behind.

See also improvisations from the following sources: "Manila House" and "Footnote to a Laundry List."

Source: *Jane Eyre*, a novel by Charlotte Brontë

Characters

Two females, three males, ensemble: Jane Eyre; Edward Rochester; Richard Mason, Rochester's brother-in-law; Mrs. Rochester, Rochester's wife; a clergyman; servants

Place
A remote part of the Rochester mansion in the English countryside; the early nineteenth century

Background
Jane Eyre came to the Rochester mansion as a governess to Adele, Mr. Rochester's daughter. Rochester and Jane fell in love. They were in the chapel, about to be married, when Rochester's brother-in-law, Richard Mason, called a halt to the wedding. He announced that Rochester was already married to Mason's sister, who suffers from schizophrenia, a condition that has run in her family for three generations. Rather than send her to an institution, Rochester has kept her in his home under lock and key for all these years.

Situation
Rochester takes Jane to meet his wife. They go to a remote part of the mansion, where they find a half-crazed woman in the midst of a psychotic episode. Mrs. Rochester grabs Rochester by the throat and bites his cheek. Screaming fiercely, she lunges at Jane. With help from one of the servants, she is tied to a chair. Edward says to Richard Mason, the clergyman, and Jane, "That is my wife." He compares her to Jane and asks them if they truly expect him to be faithful to such a wife.

Comments
The actor playing Mrs. Rochester is encouraged to explore the nature of schizophrenia—to research the specific behavior of schizophrenics. Based on this research, the actor can find her own physical expression of her psychosis. Be careful about acting generalized madness. Although she is experiencing a psychotic episode, Mrs. Rochester obviously has feelings of jealousy and rage.

Rochester fears losing Jane, the only true love he has ever had. And Jane loves him more than ever. However, despite his pleas for her to stay, she leaves.

See index for other improvisations from this source.

Source: *The Kentucky Cycle—Part One*, a play by Robert Schenkkan

Characters
One male, one female: Michael Rowen; Morning Star, a Cherokee

Place
Michael Rowen's cabin in eastern Kentucky; the summer of 1776

Background
Michael Rowen needed a wife. It was difficult to find eligible women in the wilderness. The only solution he could find was to kidnap a Cherokee woman.

Situation
Michael and Morning Star, his kidnapped bride, arrive at his cabin. She does not speak English, nor does he speak much Cherokee. They cannot communicate verbally. Morning Star is furious and mortified to be in this situation. She refuses to cooperate and will not even eat.

Comments
The language barrier creates interesting problems for the actors. Alone in the cabin, these two people have to work out a modus vivendi. The actor playing Morning Star should find a way to externalize her feelings toward this man who has torn her away from her family and traditions. She is angry and powerless in this foreign world.

See index for other improvisations from this source.

Source: *The Killer,* a film by John Woo, screenplay by Barry Wong

Characters
One male, one female: Jeff, a man who kills for hire; Jennie, a nightclub singer

Place
Jennie's living room

Background
Jeff first saw Jennie at the nightclub where she works, and they were immediately attracted to each other. However, Jeff was there on business (to kill a drug lord); in the melee that accompanied Jeff's assassination attempt, he had to fire his pistol close to Jennie's face. The shot blinded her, but Jeff did not realize the extent of her injury at that time. Before he had hastily retreated, he tried to stop the bleeding by wrapping his white scarf around her eyes. Six months later, Jeff visited the nightclub again. He heard Jennie sing, and his old feelings for her were rekindled. When Jennie left to walk home, Jeff followed her and ended up rescuing her from two robbery attempts.

Situation
Jeff has just escorted Jennie to her home. She lives in a tiny, shabby apartment. At this point, Jeff does not know Jennie's history, and Jennie does not know that Jeff is the same man who caused her to lose her vision six months earlier. Jeff notices the bloodstained white scarf that he wrapped around her just as Jennie reveals the incident at the nightclub.

Comments
While Jeff is horrified and cannot forgive himself for the pain he has caused her, Jennie does not know that he was the one responsible for her loss of vision. She believes he is a noble and courageous man who saved her from violent treatment at the hands of the robbers. As the scene progresses, Jeff may feel compelled to reveal his identity, or Jennie may somehow sense who he is. The actor must deal with the special problems of blindness. She has only been blind for six months. Therefore, she would not be completely at ease in her apartment. She would have the memories of a sighted person.

Source: *Of Mice and Men,* a novel by John Steinbeck

Characters
Two males: George, a migrant worker; Lennie, his mentally retarded sidekick

Place
A sandy bank of the Salinas River in California; during the Great Depression of the 1930s

Background
George moves to wherever he can find work. Somewhere along the way, he befriended Lennie, who is retarded but a good worker. Lennie's retardation has caused George many problems. For example, Lennie loves to touch soft things, such as mice, but he clumsily squeezes them too hard, innocently killing them. He does not know his own strength.

George's boss, Curley, was married to a woman who persisted in flirting with Lennie. Lennie touched her hair, got carried away, and choked her to death. This tragedy finally convinced George that Lennie would never be able to live a normal life. He decided that he would have to kill Lennie himself, before the outraged townspeople did.

Situation
George finds Lennie on the river bank, burying a puppy he had accidentally killed. Lennie has a vague sense that he did something bad to Curley's

wife and tries to appease George. George tells Lennie to look across the river, and they talk about the place they're going to have one day—a place full of all different kinds of animals, especially rabbits—a subject Lennie loves. George stands behind him so that Lennie can't see the gun. When Lennie is completely entranced with their dream, George shoots him.

Comments

The actors must work out the timing of the shot so that it is clear exactly when Lennie is killed; that will end the improvisation. The subtext is very strong here for George. He loves Lennie; killing Lennie is like killing his own son. At the same time, George also wants his freedom from Lennie, who has become a burden. This is probably the first time George has killed anyone.

The actor playing Lennie needs to have an understanding of the character's mentality. Lennie's main goal is to please George. He knows George is the only one who cares for him, and he's totally dependent on George; he trusts him implicitly. Lennie should have no idea that he is about to be killed. There must be a strong relationship between the two characters, or the improvisation will be meaningless.

Source: *Péllèas and Mélisande*, a play by Maurice Maeterlinck

Characters

Two males: Golaud, husband of Mélisande, in his thirties; Yniold, Golaud's son from a previous marriage, ten to twelve years old

Place

The forest near Golaud's home in France; 1892

Background

Golaud met young Mélisande by the rock springs in the forest, fell in love with her, and married her. Golaud's brother, Péllèas, is Mélisande's age. It is often necessary for Golaud to take long trips away from home, thus Péllèas and Mélisande are often left together. Golaud has discovered that the two have fallen in love.

Situation

Golaud's son, Yniold, is somewhat mentally disturbed. Golaud questions him relentlessly about what he has seen and heard when Mélisande and Péllèas are together. He is obsessed with knowing about the relationship, and he pumps Yniold for details.

Comments
The actor playing Yniold should determine exactly what he has observed, although he may not understand the significance of what he has seen. He may be afraid to tell his father (who has a fierce temper), but he also may be afraid *not* to tell him. It is something of a dilemma for Yniold, who is very fond of his Uncle Pélléas and of Mélisande, who has now replaced his mother in his affections. Yniold does not function at full capacity, which makes communication difficult. The actors need not pay attention to the country or time period; this situation is played just as well in the present.

See index for other improvisations from this source.

Source: *The Report Card* (an original improvisation written by UCLA student Jonathan Sayres Rosenthal)

Characters
One male, one female: Frank, a sixteen year-old high school student; his heavily sedated mother (optional)

Place
The intensive care unit at New York University Hospital

Background
Eight days ago, Frank's mother had multiple seizures in front of him and his father. Frank was well aware of his mother's illness and susceptibility to seizures, and he had witnessed about a half dozen of her less serious seizures. This episode, however, was much more violent. His mother was rushed to the hospital, where she hovered between life and death for two days, her left side paralyzed.

Situation
Frank is visiting his mother in the hospital, in a room with three other patients. He has received five As and one B on his report card and wants to tell her the good news to cheer up both of them. Although his mother's life is not in danger, the full extent of her injury is unclear, and her left side remains paralyzed. She is conscious and coherent but extremely tired from all the medication, as well as from the respirator tube that had to be inserted down her throat. While she struggles to stay awake, Frank reads the grades to his mother. She congratulates him with a weak squeeze of the hand and by momentarily opening her eyes. Frank must repeat his grades to her over and over, because he sees that his mother keeps losing track.

Comments

Consider that there is more than one reason for Frank to tell his mother his grades. There is a strong need to share this information, not only to cheer her up, but because Frank needs his mother's support and excitement over the good news. Good grades are often strived for to please parents. Also, consider Frank's uncertainty about how his life will change in the future. The actor playing Frank should note that, of the three other patients in the room, none looks as ill as his mother.

Source: *Richard III,* a play by William Shakespeare

Characters

One male, one female: Richard III; Anne Neville

Place

A street in London, England; the fifteenth century

Background

Richard is aiming for the crown and killing anyone who stands in his way, including his own two brothers. Richard has a large hump on his back, a bad arm, a noticeable limp, and strange growths on his head. Because of his deformed body, he believes himself to be fit only for villainy. Marrying Lady Anne Neville, the daughter of the Earl of Warwick, will further his ambition to become king. He has murdered Anne's husband, Prince Edward, and the prince's father, King Henry VI.

Situation

Lady Anne is accompanying the blood-stained corpse of Henry VI to the monastery, cursing Richard for the murders of her husband and her father-in-law. Richard enters. Anne accuses him of murder; after a first denial, Richard admits to having killed both the prince and the king. He flatters Anne, telling her that he committed both deeds for her sake. He appeals to her sympathy, saying that his deformity has caused him to go through life without love. He finally persuades her to wear his ring and accept his attentions. Even Richard is surprised when Anne yields to his advances. Later, she does become his wife.

Comments

Here, Anne comes face to face with the man who murdered both her husband and her father-in-law. The actor playing Anne must find the reason or reasons for her sensual attraction to Richard, after the atrocities he has committed. She is in a state of grief and probably quite vulnerable. Under these circumstances, people often behave unpredictably.

The actor playing Richard has to deal with his deformity. He should be specific about each part of his body that is deformed and how it affects him physically and mentally.

Richard has had a loveless life. At that time in history, society (Richard included) believed that ugly people were evil. Richard's personality has become as twisted as his body. The actor should fully understand what has brought this man to commit these ruthless deeds. The actor should also find moments of compassion and humor in Richard.

Source: *Sling Blade,* a film by Billy Bob Thornton

Characters
Two males: Carl, a mentally disabled man; Jerry, a social worker

Place
A mental institution in the southern United States

Background
At the age of twelve, Carl found his mother in bed with a man. He killed both of them with a sling blade. For his crime, Carl was placed in an institution, where he lived for seventeen years. He has just been released. He has neither a job nor a place to live.

Situation
Carl returns to the institution and tells Jerry, his social worker, that he wants to come back; he is lost in the outside world. Jerry explains that there is nothing he can do. Carl was diagnosed as being well, and was, therefore, discharged.

Comments
The dilemma for Jerry is that he does not have the power to take Carl back. However, he is not hard-hearted, and he is very fond of Carl. Jerry wants to find a solution; he can't just turn Carl out onto the street. In the film, Jerry takes Carl home for the evening; the next morning he gets Carl a job in a garage, fixing small engines, work for which Carl has an aptitude. (The actors need not follow this scenario.)

Attention should be paid to the physicality and vocal quality of Carl's character. The actor playing Carl should study several people with mental disabilities. Using elements of their personalities, mixed with his own personal experience, he can develop his own character. Not only is Carl mentally disabled, he also hasn't been out in the "real" world for seventeen years. The events surrounding the murders must be clearly imagined; they are part of what makes Carl who he is.

See also the following improvisation.

Source: *Sling Blade,* a film by Billy Bob Thornton

Characters
Two males: Carl, a mentally disabled man; Frank, a twelve-year-old boy

Place
In the woods, somewhere in the southern United States

Background
At the age of twelve, Carl found his mother in bed with a man. Carl killed both of them with a sling blade. He was placed in a mental institution, where he lived for seventeen years. He has just been released.

Carl befriends Frank, a twelve-year-old boy, whose father is dead. Before he met Carl, Frank was nervous all the time. Having seen the calming effect that Carl has on her son—and also feeling compassion for Carl's plight—Frank's mother invites Carl to live with them.

Frank's mother is dating Dole, an abusive, hard-drinking man who taunts Frank and Carl behind her back, calling Frank a wimp and Carl a retard. Dole tells them that he is about to marry Frank's mother, and he orders Carl to get out of the house. Carl and Frank don't tell Frank's mother about Dole's pronouncement; they are trying to protect her. They know that if she confronts Dole when he is drunk, he will attack her— perhaps even kill her.

Situation
It has been decided that Carl will leave the house. He meets Frank in the woods and gives him his most precious belongings—five books, one of which is the *Bible*. This is a painful separation for both characters. Carl is Frank's only friend, and he does not want him to go.

Comments
In the film, a tender relationship has developed between these two characters. The actors are advised to improvise a series of scenes as background for this situation, such as their first meeting, the introduction of Frank's mother, her invitation for Carl to live with them, witnessing

Dole's abusive treatment of Frank's mother, and Dole's ordering Carl to leave.

A note to the actor playing Carl: Carl is mentally slow, which is reflected in his speech and physical demeanor, but his depth of feeling is profound. The challenge here is to find ways to communicate Carl's feelings for Frank within the mental limitations of the character. Carl's speech is not eloquent, but his love for the boy is genuine. The character of Carl is similar to Gelsimina in the Fellini film *La Strada*.)

At the age of twelve, Frank is more intellectually developed than Carl—a grown man—but Carl is more emotionally adjusted than Frank and is a comfort to the boy.

Additional subtext for the actor playing Carl: In the film, Carl plans to kill Dole in order to free Frank and his mother. He makes Frank promise to stay at a friend's house that evening and later makes arrangements for Frank's mother to also be out of the house. Carl then kills Dole. He turns himself in to the police, and he is returned to the institution.

See also the preceding improvisation.

Source: *Sylvia*, a play by A. R. Gurney

Characters
Ensemble; Two females, one male: Sylvia, a German shepherd dog; Greg, Sylvia's owner; Kate, Greg's wife

Place
Greg and Kate's apartment in Manhattan, a borough of New York City

Background
Bored with his job, Greg has been taking afternoon walks in the park. On one of his walks, he found a stray dog. He immediately took the dog under his wing and named her Sylvia. The two have already become inseparable.

Kate, Greg's wife, is devoted to her career. She is obsessed with bringing Shakespeare to inner-city schools.

Situation
Greg takes Sylvia home to the apartment, a small, but comfortable place. Kate takes one look at the dog and says, vehemently, "No!" She points out that, given the couple's heavy social schedule, the dog would have to be left alone a great deal of the time. Besides, Kate doesn't want dog hairs all over the furniture. Greg begs Kate to let Sylvia stay.

The play's clever conceit is that both Greg and Kate can understand everything Sylvia says, and they address her as though she were another human being. And Sylvia comprehends and responds to everything Greg and Kate say to and about her.

Comments

This is a challenging role for the actor playing Sylvia. She should carefully study the physical behavior of a dog and figure out how she, personally, can achieve it. It will entail some muscle control; she'll need to change her own walk, rhythm, behavior, and attitude. The actor should ask herself: What are all the things that I would do in an apartment? What are my needs and limitations as a dog in this environment? What is my attitude toward these people? Here, the actor is concerned not only with physical characteristics, but also with the dog's emotions. This dog has one extraordinary quality: she talks. We can hear her subtext, as well as her conversation with her owners.

The actors playing Greg and Kate should accept that Sylvia is a dog, even though she talks with them. Greg is obsessed with her, and Kate is threatened by her. The fight over Sylvia begins to affect other issues in the couple's marriage. Compromises will have to be made.

Source: *The Tumbleweeds,* a play by UCLA student Christina Ham

Characters

Two females: Vivian, a beautiful young woman in her teens or early twenties, mute; Bessie, the owner of a bar

Place

Bessie's bar

Background

Vivian stopped speaking when her father poured scalding hot water on her ear several years ago. As a result, she is not only mute, but also mentally backward. Bessie rescued Vivian from her abusive family situation and gave her a job in the bar. She has tied Vivian to a long rope to keep her under control. Bessie is obsessive about Vivian. She makes Vivian do most of the work, including fixing her (Bessie's) hair every night.

Caleb is a wealthy landowner; Bertrand has just returned to town after a long absence. They are brothers, feuding over land and both romantically interested in Vivian. They untie her each evening, and she dates Bertrand one night, and Caleb the next.

Situation
Vivian is helping Bessie count the money at the bar. Bessie takes her to task for going out with two feuding brothers at the same time. Bessie tells Vivian that people will call her a hussy, and she warns her that there is animosity between the brothers and that they are using her as a pawn. Because Vivian cannot speak, she must respond to Bessie physically by using the rope. At the end of the scene, Vivian discovers that she can untie the rope herself and be free.

Comments
This is a very interesting task for the actor playing Vivian: she needs to communicate her feelings to Bessie without using words. Vivian does not want to give up her romantic involvement with the two men. Although Vivian loves Bessie, she receives a different kind of attention from the two brothers. Bessie is sad and jealous that Vivian is finding companionship elsewhere. There is a lot of tension between the two women. The rope is a symbol of Bessie's need to control Vivian and is an important element of the scene; the improvisation should be done with Vivian tied to a solid object by a long rope. The scene is like a tug of war between the two. Vivian is constrained, and she feels it physically as well as psychologically. She is a tool and the object of everybody's affections, veering from one abusive relationship to another. She wants love from all of them, but she doesn't know how to get it.

See also the following improvisation.

Source: *The Tumbleweeds,* a play by UCLA student Christina Ham

Characters
One male, one female; Bertrand, a young man; Vivian, a beautiful young women in her late teens or early twenties, mute

Place
A park

Background
Vivian stopped speaking when her father poured scalding hot water on her ear several years ago. As a result, she is not only mute, but also mentally backward. Bessie rescued Vivian from her abusive family situation and gave her a job in the bar. She keeps Vivian tied to a long rope to keep her under control.

Caleb is a wealthy land owner; Bertrand has just returned to town after a long absence. They are brothers, feuding over land and both romantically interested in Vivian. They untie her each evening, and she dates Bertrand one night, Caleb the next.

Bessie recently told Vivian that she must stop dating both brothers at the same time and that they were only using her as a pawn in their battle over land; besides, people would call Vivian a hussy. At the end of this confrontation, Vivian discovered that she could untie the rope and set herself free.

This scene follows the fight with Bessie about seeing the two brothers. Vivian has decided to sacrifice her job and her friendship with Bessie for her love affair with Bertrand.

Situation
Vivian meets Bertrand to convey to him what she has decided. Bertrand tells Vivian that he has figured out a way to get the land, adding that he can't see her until after the feud with his brother is settled. Essentially, he is rejecting Vivian's love. The shock to Vivian is so great that it impels her to speak for the first time in years.

Comments
A trauma brought on Vivian's loss of speech, and a trauma restores it. The actor playing Vivian should have no idea what these new words might be; they come as a total surprise to both parties. The brothers, in their cycle of feuding, have come to believe that the land is more important than their love for each other. Completely obsessed with his quest for the land, Bertrand has no room in his heart for Vivian's love. Her ability to speak again, however, will clearly affect him in some way.

See also the preceding improvisation.

Source: *Winter Sun,* a screenplay by UCLA student William H. Grignon

Characters
Two males: Willy Benson, six years old, blind; Grandpa

Place
The kitchen of Grandpa's home

Background
Willy was orphaned at the age of six and was sent to live with his grandfather, a retired United States Army career officer. Willy has recently lost his

mother. He has led an overprotected life, while his grandfather is accustomed to a vigorous military regimen.

Situation

This is Willy's first day living with Grandpa. He doesn't understand where his mother has gone, and Grandpa must explain her death to him. The two of them have quite a few adjustments to make to each other. For example, Grandpa is upset when he discovers that Willy eats with his hands.

Comments

The daunting task for the young actor playing Willy: he is blind and in a totally new environment. He investigates Grandpa's house using only his sense of touch. With his fingers, he explores Grandpa's face to know his expressions. Grandpa, too, has suddenly had his whole life turned around. He is totally unprepared for this blind, undisciplined, six-year-old boy who has come along and disrupted his routine.

7

Subtext

Subtext is a name we give to the unexpressed feelings and thoughts that constantly circulate in our heads. This inner dialogue, whether it arises from past experiences or hoped-for futures, goes on within every character in every situation, no matter how dramatic or how mundane. To create a believable role, actors must probe the recesses of their characters, learn how they operate and what motivates them, and locate their inner dialogue. When Milton Katselas, in his acting class, says, "the character must know and feel more than he says" he is referring to the submerged dialogue known as a character's subtext.

Characters may reveal their subtext—by accident or by design. They may also do all that they can to conceal their inner thoughts and emotions. In either case, the actor consults his character's inner dialogue as a road map to his behavior, reactions, and beliefs. The influence of subtext on a character's words and actions is always profound.

Identifying a character's central obstacle is one key to unlocking his subtext. *Improvisation* is another. It is a method frequently used by actors working to understand their characters, especially when they are having difficulty making a connection with other characters while rehearsing a scripted play. When using her own words through improvisation, the actor creates her own subtext; she composes the unspoken dialogue underneath the playwright's lines. *Beneath the words* is, in fact, the literal meaning of the term *subtext*.

The situations in this chapter provide opportunities for subtext to influence the content and direction of a scene. Of course, any scene will be strengthened and any performance enriched when the actor listens to the secrets of his character's inner dialogue.

SUBTEXT SITUATIONS

One male, one female
Camilla
Dead Man Walking
The Diary of Anne Frank
Jane Eyre
Little Women
Much Ado About Nothing
The Remains of the Day
The Shop Around the Corner
To Play the King
Twelfth Night

Two females
The Autobiography of My Mother
Changes of Heart
Emma
Kindred
Recess
Stage Door
The Wedding

Two males
"The Beauty of Passage"
Sleepers

Ensemble
Anne of Green Gables
The Awful Truth
The Color Purple
A Masked Ball

Source: *Anne of Green Gables,* a novel by L. M. Montgomery

Characters
Four females: Mrs. Spencer; Marilla Cuthbert; Mrs. Blewett; Anne, a young orphan

Place
Mrs. Blewett's home on Prince Edward Island

Background
Marilla and Matthew Cuthbert, a sister and brother, had asked the orphanage in Halifax, Nova Scotia, to send a young boy to help out around the farm in exchange for his room and board. Instead, the orphanage sent a girl, Anne. While Matthew has taken a liking to Anne and wants her to stay, Marilla is uncomfortable with Anne's flair for the dramatic and believes that she will be of no use. Rather than send Anne back to Halifax, Mrs. Spencer (who brought Anne from the orphanage) thinks she may be able to place Anne with Mrs. Blewett, who has expressed an interest in having an orphan work for her.

Situation
Mrs. Spencer takes Marilla and Anne to meet Mrs. Blewett. Mrs. Blewett begins to interview Anne to see if she would be a suitable helper. Anne makes up fantastic stories about her life, despite protestations from Mrs. Spencer and Marilla. Finally, Mrs. Spencer reads from the official report the facts about Anne's life—back and forth between foster care settings and orphanages—since her parents died when she was three months old.

Comments
Anne has developed a fantastic imagination as a way of dealing with the harsh realities of her life. The actor playing Anne needs to be willing to behave in an outrageous manner, while remembering that her behavior is a cover for her true feelings. All of the adults will have their own reactions to Anne and to the facts that her outrageous words and actions are covering up.

See index for other improvisations from this source.

Source: *The Autobiography of My Mother*, a novel by Jamaica Kincaid

Characters
Two females: Xuela, fifteen years old; Madame LaBatte, a middle-aged woman

Place
Madame LaBatte's home on the West Indian island of Dominica

Background
Xuela is the daughter of a Carib woman and a Scottish African man. Her mother died the moment Xuela was born. Her father entrusted the infant

Xuela to the care of his laundress; she had six children of her own, and they all seemed to be a burden. Xuela did not like the laundress and did not speak until she was four years old.

Xuela was sent to live and work in the home of Madame and Monsieur LaBatte. Madame LaBatte has lost her youth. She has always wanted to have a child but is unable to conceive. Soon, Xuela began sleeping with Monsieur LaBatte because Madame wanted her to, although the arrangement has never been discussed.

Situation
Madame LaBatte has just finished washing Xuela's hair and is combing it out. The two have a conversation without words. Xuela knows that Madame hears her making love with Monsieur LaBatte at night; she realizes that Madame wants her to have the child Madame could never have, but Xuela does not want this.

Comments
Here is an interesting exercise for two women, because it is all subtext. Even though they are not related by blood, they are so close that they know each other's thoughts. The activity of combing out Xuela's hair can reflect a lot of inner dialogue. This is an unusual relationship; it is not one of jealousy, but of love.

See index for other improvisations from this source.

Source: *The Awful Truth*, a film by Leo McCarey and Vina Delmar based on a play by Arthur Richman

Characters
Two males, two females: Jerry Warriner; Lucy Warriner, Jerry's former wife; Daniel Lesson, Lucy's new boyfriend; a girl singer, Jerry's date for the evening

Place
A restaurant with a floor show

Background
Lucy divorced Jerry because he told her he was in California, but the oranges he sent her were from Florida, where he was having a fling. This restaurant was a favorite hang-out for Jerry and Lucy when they were still married. Lucy has come here this evening with her new boyfriend, Daniel. By coincidence, Jerry brings his first- (and last-) time date to the same restaurant. As a mat-

ter of fact, she is part of the floor show. Daniel is something of a square and really no match for the sophisticated relationship between Lucy and Jerry. Although they may not realize it, Lucy and Jerry are still in love. Each is quite jealous of the other's date, although Lucy soon realizes she has little to worry about. Jerry's date turns out to be rather simple-minded.

Situation
The subtext is that Daniel wants to keep Lucy; Jerry wants Lucy back and wants Daniel out of the picture; Lucy wants to preserve her relationship with Daniel, although she has more rapport with Jerry, which infuriates her; and the girl singer wants to impress Jerry. These are the undercurrents in the scene, but the characters attempt to maintain the appearance of civility. At the beginning of the scene, Jerry is dancing with his date when he spots Lucy and Daniel at a table. He makes the decision to join them, welcome or not. At one point, Jerry's date excuses herself to perform in the floor show. She does a routine in which her dress blows upward on cue every time she sings the refrain to "Stormy Weather." Her act is an embarrassment to everyone at the table. Jerry keeps emphasizing that this is a first date.

Comments
The actors playing Lucy and Jerry should be clear about the distinctive nature of their previous relationship. They also need to establish the conditions that brought about the divorce. As hard as they try to find other partners, they are meant to be together. Each character in this situation is attempting to bond with the wrong person. Every once in a while, they will break through the subtext. The actors playing Daniel and the girl singer need to be concerned with their individual limitations: the girl doesn't have much more going for her than her act, and Daniel is just a conventional, decent guy, but no match for Lucy and Jerry.

This is essentially a humorous situation, but each character's need for a relationship must be intense. And the girl singer must go way out in her performance—she thinks that what she is doing is brilliant.

Source: "The Beauty of Passage," a short story by Nick Arens (improvisation written by UCLA student Nick Arens)

Characters
Two males: A Lutheran minister; a young man in his late teens

Place
The office of a Lutheran church

Background

The minister's wife recently left him, citing increased emotional distance as the primary reason for her dissatisfaction. The minister has also just been "called" to a new congregation. He has not yet left for the new church and has actually attempted to keep his situation a secret, since the rather conservative congregation would look down on the instatement of a minister with marital problems. The past months have been difficult for him; he has begun to question the value of his work and its effect on others.

The young man sought refuge within the church as a last-ditch effort to stave off the demons he fears are trying to invade his body and soul. Because he has come to believe that the nightmares that have plagued him are manifestations of satanic agents intent on gaining possession of his intellect, he has been keeping himself awake for some time. His background is unclear, but it is apparent that he has been living on the street for some time. Intellectually, he does not believe in God; however, he was brought up in the church and is familiar with its tenets and ideology.

The minister found the young man asleep behind one of the pews in the church. After having roused him and gotten him to shower and dress, the minister has invited the young man into his office to offer assistance.

Situation

When the young man initially explains his situation, the minister becomes invigorated at the prospect of doing some definite, uncomplicated good. However, as the conversation progresses, the minister begins to think that the roles of teacher and student are reversed, as the young man alludes to having some knowledge of the minister's personal situation and inner state. The minister feels increasingly drawn in by the young man's slow cadence and intensity, and eventually he fears that his excitement and attraction are less than noble. Possibilities of deception, even temptation by the devil himself, float through the minister's mind.

Comments

This situation should not be played as an exorcism or a seduction. The true motivations of the two characters should be allowed to manifest themselves within the scene and not be preimposed by the actors. The minister may question his sexual feelings or exhibit curiosity, but remember that he has never before engaged in even the mildest unconventional behavior, nor would he consider it ethical to do so. Likewise, the part of the boy should be played with an emphasis on the trust developed between the two and pushed forward by a genuine fear arising from his own state. One physical condition for the actor playing the young man to keep in mind is his state of utter exhaustion, against which he must fight.

Source: *Camilla,* a novel by Madeleine L'Engle

Characters
One female, one male: Camilla Dickinson, a fifteen-year-old girl; Rafferty Dickinson, an architect, Camilla's father

Place
An upscale New York City restaurant near Central Park

Background
Camilla's mother, Rose, is estranged from her husband and having an affair with a man named Jacques Nissen. Camilla is usually in her room doing homework during his visits. Recently, she came home from school and found her mother and Jacques relating in an intimate fashion. Her mother asked her not to mention it to Rafferty, Camilla's father, should he question her. Camilla dislikes Jacques; the only person with whom she discusses him is her close friend, Luisa.

Situation
Rafferty has taken Camilla out to dinner in a fancy restaurant for the first time, and he has even bought Camilla her very first drink. Though Camilla attempts to change the subject, he continually questions her about Jacques. Is she present when Jacques and Rose are visiting? How often does Jacques visit? Does Camilla like Jacques? Does he come to see her or to see Rose?

Comments
This is Camilla's first experience with alcohol. (In the novel, the drink makes Camilla sick and she has to go to the ladies room to throw up.) The actor playing Camilla can deal with it in any way she wants, but it *is* part of the situation. Her parents have put Camilla in a difficult position. On the one hand, Camilla wants to protect her mother, but, on the other hand, this means lying to her father.

When Camilla goes home after dinner, Rose pumps her about the content of her conversation with Rafferty. The actors could continue with this scene.

See index for other improvisations from this source.

Source: *Changes of Heart (Double Inconstancy),* a play by Pierre Carlet de Chamblain de Marivaux, translated and adapted by Stephen Wadsworth

Characters
Two females: Silvia; Flaminia—both are young women

Place
The drawing room of the prince's palace in France; the eighteenth century

Background
Silvia, a young subject of the prince, is betrothed to Harlequin; they have known each other since childhood. Meanwhile, unbeknownst to Silvia, the prince has fallen in love with her. He has confided in Flaminia, a member of the royal household, and she promised to help him win Silvia's affections. Flaminia has contrived a scheme whereby the prince poses as a guardsman; the idea is that without the trappings of his royalty, he will be able to stand on his own merits and woo Silvia as would an ordinary man. The scheme was a success, and Silvia fell in love with the guardsman. And in the midst of her machinations, Flaminia herself fell in love with Harlequin.

Situation
Flaminia is trying to find out how Silvia feels about the guardsman (the prince). She offers to take Harlequin off her hands so that Silvia will be free to marry the man she loves. Silvia, who has fallen for the guardsman, feels that she must honor her commitment to Harlequin, whom she has known since she was a child.

Comments
Flaminia does not want to reveal that she has fallen in love with Harlequin, so she is trying to make Silvia believe that she is doing her a favor. A class distinction is also at work here. Flaminia is part of the royal household and lives by a looser moral code. Silvia is from a different milieu, in which loyalty to one man is an unquestioned virtue.

See index for other improvisations from this source.

Source: *The Color Purple,* a novel by Alice Walker

Characters
Three females: Celie, fourteen years old; a clergyman's wife; Olivia, a small child—all are African American

Place
A dry goods market in Atlanta, Georgia; the turn of the twentieth century

Background
Several years ago, Celie, impregnated by her father, gave birth. When the baby was two months old, Celie's father gave it to the clergyman and his wife to raise.

Situation

Celie is sitting in a wagon outside the market and sees a woman with a little girl. Immediately, Celie knows that this is her daughter; she recognizes the child's eyes. She remembers, before the baby was born, embroidering the name "Olivia" on sets of diapers, which were given to the couple. She follows the woman and little girl into the market and asks the woman a number of questions. Celie learns that the child's father is a clergyman and that the little girl's name is Pauline. However, the woman tells Celie that she calls the child Olivia; the name was embroidered on the diapers that the baby wore when she first arrived in their home. Celie is now certain that this is her child.

Comments

In Walker's novel, Celie never reveals her identity to the clergyman's wife, but this improvisation may have another ending. The subtext for Celie is quite intense. The clergyman's wife might sense something by the way Celie relates to the child. Olivia may also be drawn, in some way, to Celie.

See index for other improvisations from this source.

Source: *Dead Man Walking,* a film by Tim Robbins based on the book by Sister Helen Prejean (improvisation written by UCLA student Kristin Hanggi)

Characters

One male, one female: Matthew Poncelet, a prisoner on death row; Sister Helen Prejean, a middle-aged nun who works with the poor

Place

A state penitentiary visiting room—the two are separated by a wall through which they can see and hear but not touch each other

Background

Poncelet and his three younger brothers were raised by their mother; theirs was a "white trash" Illinois family. He is in prison now for the rape and murder of a teen-aged girl, Hope Percy, and the murder of a teenaged boy, Leroy Delicrox, whom he and a friend found making out in the woods. Poncelot has one daughter by the woman who turned him in; he has never seen the little girl. Poncelet has been on death row for six years, awaiting execution by lethal injection.

Sister Helen is from an affluent family, but she works in a poor community. She has been a nun since her graduation from high school; she has never been intimate with a man.

Poncelot wrote to the church, looking for someone who could help him with his case. Sister Helen wrote back, and the two have been exchanging letters.

Situation
This is the first time Poncelot and Sister Helen have met face to face. Poncelet needs her to help him find a lawyer so that he can get a court hearing. He swears that he is not guilty. Sister Helen has felt the desperation in his letters and is visiting him in prison to see what he is like and what he wants from her. She is afraid to become involved in a death row case; she also is not sure whether she should trust Poncelot.

Comments
Remember, actors, that Sister Helen is a nun and has never been inside a prison, let alone talked to a criminal on death row. She is there to do her job, and, although she is scared, she wants to stay poised. Her major goal in life is to "save" everyone; she would like to help Poncelot find salvation through Jesus Christ. At the same time, she is being pressured by her order not to get involved with this case.

Poncelot has been in and out of jail his whole life; he is a racist, and has a foul mouth. He is not religious; he has never spoken with a nun, and he has not seen a woman in a very long time. His primary relationship with women had been sexual. He is repelled by authority and anything structured. Although he is uneducated, he has gathered together all the information pertaining to the case. Sister Helen is his last hope.

Sister Helen is not dressed in traditional nun's attire, but her clothing is plain. Poncelot is in handcuffs and chain-smokes through the entire scene. The actors do not need to incorporate the smoking.

Source: *The Diary of Anne Frank,* a dramatization by Frances Goodrich and Albert Hackett based on the book *Anne Frank: Diary of a Young Girl*

Characters
One female, one male: Anne Frank, a thirteen-year-old girl; Peter Van Daan, a sixteen-year-old boy

Place
Amsterdam, Holland; July 1942

Background
With the help of friends, the Frank family and the Van Daan family have

just gone into hiding in the building in which Mr. Frank once operated his business. Their hope is to live out the rest of World War II by concealing themselves from the persecution of the Nazis and the horrors of the concentration camps.

Situation
Anne and Peter have never met; this is their first conversation. They realize that they will be living together in close proximity for an indefinite amount of time. Anne, an extrovert, is full of energy and eager to get to know Peter. He is, however, self-conscious and shy. They discover that they attended the same school, where Peter was a self-described "lone wolf" and Anne was always at the center of a crowd. As they talk, Peter takes a knife and rips the Star of David (which the Nazis required Jews to wear) from his clothing, with the intention of burning it. Anne follows suit, but cannot bring herself to destroy it.

Comments
Underneath Peter and Anne's interaction is the harsh reality of the Nazi occupation and the continual fear of discovery. They have just moved into their hiding place, and the memory of all they have left behind is painfully fresh.

See index for other improvisations from this source.

Source: *Emma*, a novel by Jane Austen

Characters
Two females: Emma, an attractive young woman; Harriet, a plain young woman

Place
Emma's home in the English countryside; the early nineteenth century

Background
Emma is a matchmaker, obsessed with finding a husband for her friend, Harriet. Emma persuaded Harriet not to marry Mr. Martin, a farmer (who really was the right person for her), because she had higher hopes for her friend. So far, Emma has failed at two attempted matches for Harriet. One was with Mr. Elton, a minister. At a festive occasion, Emma asked Mr. Elton to dance with Harriet. When he openly refused, Harriet was humiliated. Knightley, an old friend of Emma's, rescued Harriet by dancing with her. Frank Churchill, the second suitor Emma chose for Harriet, is now preparing to marry another woman.

Emma's old friend, Knightley, frequently visits Emma and her father. Although Emma and Knightley have always been like brother and sister, Emma has recently discovered that she is in love with him.

Situation
Expecting to find Harriet heartbroken over Frank Churchill's impending marriage, Emma has come to console her. However, Harriet announces that she cares nothing for Frank Churchill; she is in love with Knightley. It happened when Knightley asked Harriet to dance with him.

Comments
Emma, having only recently concluded that *she* loves Knightley, must conceal her true feelings from Harriet. She also fears that Knightley may care for Harriet. With the best of intentions, Emma has created a mess through her meddling. The actors should adjust to the Victorian era in which this novel was written. Marrying well was an important consideration for young women. Their other occupations were playing the piano, sewing, and charity work. They were not allowed to have a profession. It is easy to see why they were preoccupied with making the right match.

See index for other improvisations from this source.

Source: *Jane Eyre,* a novel by Charlotte Brontë

Characters
One female, one male: Jane Eyre; Edward Rochester

Place
Edward Rochester's mansion in the English countryside; the early nineteenth century

Background
Jane Eyre was ten years old when her parents died and she was sent to live with her aunt and uncle, the Reeds. The Reeds did not love her and treated her badly. She was sent to a strict school for girls, where she lived until she was a young woman. Jane Eyre then accepted a position as governess to a little girl, Adele, Edward Rochester's daughter. Rochester was a man of mystery, who rarely visited the mansion. Eventually, he and Jane became good friends; in fact, without quite realizing it, they fell in love. But, Mr. Rochester was to be betrothed to Mary Ingram, a woman who shares his social class and milieu, which Jane does not.

Situation
Rochester announces that he is going to marry Mary Ingram and that he will be sending Adele off to school in Paris. He tells Jane that he will help her to get a position in Ireland as governess for a family with five daughters. Jane is astonished. Rochester at last confesses that he loves Jane and that his impending union with Mary Ingram is simply a marriage of convenience. He proposes to Jane. She accepts.

Comments
The subtext in this improvisation is that Rochester is in love with Jane when he announces that he is about to be married to another woman. Jane's heart is broken at the news that he will be sending her away. The improvisation then becomes a great climactic moment as they discover that they love one another—something that neither of them has expressed before. It is unusual for a man of Edward Rochester's social stature to marry his daughter's governess. Although she has always been treated as his equal, Jane probably never expected that he would propose to her.

See index for other improvisations from this source.

Source: *Kindred,* a novel by Octavia E. Butler

Characters
Two females: Dana Franklin, a black slave; Margaret Weylin, the mistress of the house, white

Place
The library of the Weylin home on the eastern shore of Maryland; 1815

Background
Dana Franklin lives in California with her husband, Kevin, who is a white man. The time is 1976. However, Dana has been experiencing strange episodes, in which she returns in time to the Weylin plantation in Maryland, where her ancestors lived as slaves over one hundred and fifty years ago.

Dana has returned to the past again but has taken Kevin with her for protection. (Kevin was able to accompany her because he and Dana were in physical contact at the moment when she was hurled back in time.) Because they are married, Kevin and Dana naturally sleep in the same bedroom. That is, in California in 1976. They are now in Maryland in 1815 and the Weylins believe that Kevin is Dana's owner. As a slave, she *has* to sleep with him if he wants her to.

Situation
Dana is sweeping the library. Margaret Weylin rushes in and asks her
where she slept last night. Dana replies that she slept in Mr. Franklin's
room. There was no point in lying; all the house servants knew about the
arrangement. (Probably one of them had alerted Mrs. Weylin.) Margaret
accuses Dana of being a whore and tells her that this is a Christian home.
She orders Dana never to sleep in Mr. Franklin's room again.

Comments
Although she is in the past, Dana is still a woman of the twentieth century, absolutely unaccustomed to being treated this way. But her reality
now is the reality of one hundred and fifty years ago. She doesn't want to
be separated from Kevin, so she must be careful not to offend Mrs.
Weylin, her owner and mistress. Dana's subtext and what she says are
quite opposite. The subtext for Margaret Weylin: she is jealous of Dana
because she wants to sleep with Kevin herself.

See index for other improvisations from this source.

Source: *Little Women,* a novel by Louisa May Alcott

Characters
One female, one male: Jo, in her early twenties; Frederick, in his late
twenties

Place
On the road outside the March residence in Concord, Massachusetts; the
mid-nineteenth century

Background
Shortly after Jo turned down a proposal of marriage from her good friend
Laurence, she moved to New York City to try her hand at getting her
writing published. In the boarding house in which she lived, she met
Frederick, a German philosopher. He encouraged her to write about subjects that were familiar to her.
     Jo suddenly had to return to Concord, because her sister, Beth, was
close to death. After Beth died, Jo, while rummaging through her sister's
belongings, began to reminisce about her family. She followed Frederick's
advice and wrote about these memories. On completion of the manuscript, she sent it to Frederick in New York City; he brought it to a friend
who was a publisher. When news arrived that it was to be published,
Frederick decided to hand-deliver the manuscript to Jo.

Frederick traveled to Concord. Not finding Jo at home, he left the manuscript with her aunt. The aunt told him that Miss March was across the street with Lawrence, her new husband. She was referring to Amy March, Jo's sister, but Frederick assumed that she meant Jo. He left to catch the next train. Jo came home shortly after he had departed and was given the published manuscript by her aunt, who told her that it was delivered by a man with a foreign name. Jo ran down the road to find Frederick.

Situation

Jo catches up with Frederick and the two stand beneath his umbrella in the rain. He insists that he must catch the next train; he is going out west to teach. Jo pleads with him to stay. She explains that an aunt of hers has died and left Jo her house. Jo plans to use the house to start a school; she wants Frederick to be one of the teachers. He attempts to leave, still believing that Jo has married another man. When Jo makes it clear that her sister Amy is married to Lawrence, Frederick proposes to Jo. She happily accepts.

Comments

This situation is replete with subtext: Jo wants Frederick to propose; he loves her but is sad because he thinks she's married to Lawrence. They almost lose each other because of this misunderstanding. They are a good match; Frederick understands and appreciates Jo, and vice versa. He loves her as an equal, which was unusual in this time period.

See index for other improvisations from this source.

Source: *A Masked Ball,* an opera by Giuseppe Verdi (music) and Antonio Somma (libretto) based on the play *Gustave III, ou Le Bal Masque,* by Eugene Scribe

Characters

Two males, one female: Gustavus III, King of Sweden; Captain Anckarstrom, the royal secretary and Gustavus' best friend; Madame Arvidson, a soothsayer

Place

Madame Arvidson's hut, Sweden; the late eighteenth century

Background

King Gustavus is in love with Amelia, the wife of Captain Anckarstrom, his best friend. Amelia and Gustavus never consummated the affair, but they meet secretly to profess their love for each other. In disguise,

Gustavus has gone to the hut of Madame Arvidson, a renowned sooth-sayer, to test her psychic ability.

Situation
Madame Arvidson tells Gustavus' fortune. She predicts that he will be murdered by the next man who shakes his hand. No sooner has she said this than Anckarstrom strides in and shakes the king's hand. Gustavus reveals his real identity to his best friend. Anckarstrom had been searching everywhere for Gustavus to warn him that his life is in danger.

Comments
King Gustavus isn't sure what Anckarstrom knows about the relationship with Amelia, but there are three possibilities. The first is that Anckarstrom knows nothing and is simply warning the king of the assassination plot. The second is that Anckarstrom may be part of the plot himself. The third is that Anckarstrom may not now suspect that his best friend and his wife are having an affair, but will kill Gustavus when he finds out. The more interesting choice would probably be for the actor playing Anckarstrom to be suspicious. The actors should accept the use of soothsayers in this time period. After all, millions of people rely on psychics today.

   This opera is based on an incident that took place in Stockholm, Sweden, in 1792. King Gustavus III was assassinated by his political enemies while attending a masked ball.

Source: *Much Ado About Nothing*, a play by William Shakespeare

Characters
One female, one male: Beatrice; Benedict

Place
A courtyard in the palace of Beatrice's uncle in Italy; the sixteenth century

Background
The men of the country are returning home after fighting in a war, and they stop at the palace of Beatrice's uncle for a celebration. Joviality and lust are in the air. Beatrice and Benedict, sworn enemies, have nothing but slanderous things to say about each other. Their friends decide to play a trick: the men within earshot of Benedict talk about Beatrice's great love for him, which she will never reveal, while the women ensure that Beatrice overhears their discussion about Benedict's secret love for her.

Situation
Benedict and Beatrice meet in the courtyard. They are adept at insulting each other, and they continue to hide their feelings behind taunts and gibes. But the false information they heard earlier has worked a strange magic—Beatrice and Benedict are falling in love.

Comments
The fun here is in pitting a misogynist (Benedict) against a sexist (Beatrice). They are evenly matched adversaries who never imagined that their relationship would end up this way. Likely, without the mischievous trickery of their friends, Beatrice and Benedict would have continued to feud until the end of their days.

Source: *Recess* (an original improvisation written by UCLA student Tyler Fereira)

Characters
Two females: Nicole; Tracy—both are sophomores in high school

Place
A high school quad; the lunch hour

Background
Nicole has always been an outgoing sort of person. She likes to keep those around her pleased and content. Her life has always been safe and sheltered; she lives in an upper middle class suburb and leads a very structured existence. Nicole has been skimming across the surface of life in a way that most small towns promote—until today. Tracy has been living life in much the same manner as Nicole. Her score on the latest test, Friday nights, and football games are what's most important to her. She is Nicole's best friend.

Situation
Last night, Nicole found out that her mother has breast cancer. It has been caught early and can be operated on, but the news has shattered the apparent safety of Nicole's world. She is having a hard time pretending to be her usual happy self, and she is sitting alone at lunch. Tracy, without noticing that anything is the matter, comes over to talk with Nicole.

Comments
Nicole desperately wants to discuss what has happened, but she doesn't know if anyone will really understand or care. She still feels it necessary to

say "okay" when asked how she's doing. What makes the situation even more difficult is that Tracy is still talking about things like test scores and the upcoming football game. The actor playing Nicole needs to try to break Tracy's current way of thinking. Nicole needs someone terribly, and if she doesn't reach out to her best friend now, she never will. The stakes are very high. There is no correct resolution to this situation, and the outcome will be different each time. Sometimes Nicole will tell Tracy, sometimes she won't.

Source: *The Remains of the Day,* a film by James Ivory based on the novel by Kazuo Ishiguro, screenplay by Ruth Prawer Jhabvala

Characters
One male, one female: Mr. Stevens, the head butler; Miss Keating, the head housekeeper

Place
The hallway outside Miss Keating's bedroom in Lord Bramford's country mansion, England; the 1930s

Background
Years ago, Mr. Stevens hired Miss Keating to be the housekeeper. One thing that he emphasized at the beginning was no romance among the staff. However, the two have worked together for years and have developed a mildly romantic relationship. They have never alluded to it, although Miss Keating is aware of her feelings of affection for Mr. Stevens.

Situation
Miss Keating has just returned from a date with a suitor who has proposed marriage. She announces this to Mr. Stevens, hoping that the news will finally force him to divulge his feelings for her, but it is not in his nature to do so. Whatever he may feel remains unsaid.

Comments
This scene takes place at a time in history when service in the household was an art, governed by strict tradition. The actors need to accept that these two people are not able to open up to each other. It has been established earlier that Mr. Stevens suppresses his feelings. Ever the loyal servant, on the day his father died (his father was also in service to Lord Bramford), Mr. Stevens continued serving guests before looking in on his dying father.

Source: *The Shop Around the Corner,* a film by Ernst Lubitsch based on the play *Parfumerie* by Nikolaus Laszlo, screenplay by Samson Raphaelson

Characters
One male, one female: Alfred Kralik; Klara Novak

Place
A restaurant in Budapest, Hungary; the 1930s

Background
Mr. Kralik works as a clerk in Mr. Matuschek's shop. Miss Novak has recently been employed there as a salesperson. Their personalities clash; they bicker constantly. Mr. Kralik finds fault with everything she does.

Miss Novak had put an advertisement in the newspaper: "Modern girl wishes to correspond with a man on cultural subjects." The correspondence is now underway. The letters are always addressed to "Dear Friend," so that names need not be revealed. The correspondents also agree not to discuss their mundane jobs. Through their writing, they have fallen in love with each other. They have made arrangements to meet each other this evening in a restaurant at 8:30 P.M.

Little does Miss Novak suspect that Mr. Kralik is the man with whom she has been corresponding. Both have built up their hopes for a perfect romance. They have arranged that Miss Novak will wait for Mr. Kralik in the restaurant, holding a copy of the novel *Anna Karenina*, with a rose tucked inside it.

Situation
Mr. Kralik arrives at the restaurant. He looks in the window and sees Miss Novak sitting at a table—with a book and a rose! He suddenly realizes that *she* is the woman with whom he has been corresponding. He goes in and sits at her table, without revealing that he is the man for whom she is waiting. She begs him not to sit there because she has a rendezvous with someone special. He asks her questions about this "special" man. While she attempts to describe him, she realizes that Mr. Kralik could not possibly understand the sensitivity of her romantic writing partner and begins to insult him.

Comments
The interesting aspect of this relationship is that, while these two people love each other through their correspondence, they detest each other in their everyday life at Matuschek and Company. Miss Novak, unwittingly, is cruel to Mr. Kralik, believing him to be incapable of tender feeling. Mr. Kralik does not let on for several days that he is the writer of the letters.

He eventually does tell Miss Novak and they end up together by the play's conclusion. The actor playing Mr. Kralik needs to decide why he doesn't reveal his identity right away. Perhaps he thinks the disappointment would be too great for Miss Novak; perhaps he is enjoying playing with her—after all, she has been horrid to him.

Source: *Sleepers,* a film by Barry Levinson based on the novel by Lorenzo Carcaterra

Characters
Two males: Mike, approximately twelve years old; Father Robert, a priest

Place
The visiting room at the Wilkinson Correctional School for Delinquent Boys, upstate New York; 1966

Background
Mike and a group of his friends (John, Tom, and Shakes) lived in the poor Hell's Kitchen neighborhood of New York City. They loved to play pranks, most of which were harmless and in good fun, but the last prank they pulled changed their lives forever. Mike stole a hot dog from a street vendor. While the vendor was chasing him, the other boys moved the hot dog cart down the street to the entrance of a subway station. There, they lost control of it and the cart went crashing down the stairs, severely injuring a male pedestrian. The boys were caught and sentenced to one year at the Wilkinson School.

Father Bobby, as they called him, was the boys' priest in the neighborhood parish. He was once a tough kid, and he had even spent time at Wilkinson himself. He was a good friend to the boys and they respected him. Mike's father beat his mother; he did not have a happy life at home. Father Bobby was more of a parent to him than his father was.

The boys have been at Wilkinson for a few months. The guards there are sadistic and humiliating; they regularly sexually abuse the youngsters. Mike can hear his friend, John, sobbing in his cubicle at night. Mike has asked his parents not to visit; he is too ashamed to face them. Father Bobby, however, has written to say that he is coming to visit. One of the guards, Nokes, has warned Mike that if any of the boys reveal anything about what is going on at Wilkinson, they will suffer unspeakable consequences.

Situation
Father Bobby has come to visit. Mike cannot look at him because he feels so humiliated. Father Bobby knows that something is wrong; he remem-

bers Mike as a lively, fun-loving boy. Mike is aching to unburden himself to the priest, but he does not, even though Father Bobby is his dearest friend.

Comments

The actor playing Mike must imagine the horrors that Mike has experienced. Mike is still a boy and overwhelmed by what is happening to him. He needs the love of Father Bobby at this moment, as he has never needed it before. But the guard, Nokes, is nearby, watching, and Mike, although crumbling inside, doesn't want Nokes to see him cry.

Father Bobby also spent time at Wilkinson, so he has some idea of what goes on behind its walls. He has probably been abused himself, although the nature and the extent of the abuse that he experienced are unspecified.

The novel and the film are based on actual events. To complete the story: The boys remained at Wilkinson for the rest of the year, and the abuse continued. In a coincidence worthy of ancient Greek drama, two of the boys, John Riley and Tom Marcano, who had become professional "hit men," saw the guard, Nokes, in a restaurant. Although many years had passed, the men had not forgotten the guards' treatment. They walked up to Nokes and coolly shot him.

Riley and Marcano were brought to trial, and Mike, now a district attorney, prosecuted their case. The men could afford only a down-and-out, alcoholic lawyer to represent them, but Mike met with the lawyer secretly and fed him all the questions he would ask them in court. The guards from Wilkinson were exposed, and Riley and Marcano were acquitted.

A few years later, the two hit men themselves were gunned down. Mike gave up the law, moved to Scotland, and became a carpenter. Too damaged to have a normal relationship, he was unable to marry the woman he loved. And Shakes, who is really Lorenzo Carcaterra, is the author of the book *Sleepers*.

Source: *Stage Door,* a play by Edna Ferber and George S. Kaufman

Characters
Two females: Terry Randall; Kay Hamilton

Place
A boarding house for actresses in New York City; the 1930s

Background
A theatrical producer was searching for the right actor to play the lead in his new Broadway show. Kay had her heart set on the role; she knew that

it was tailor-made for her. However, her friend, Terry, managed to finagle the role for herself. Terry was a terrible actor, whereas Kay would have been brilliant in the part.

Situation
It is opening night. Terry is getting ready to go to the theater, and Kay comes in to wish her good luck. Terry expresses her nervousness; she knows she's not up to the role. She also knows that Kay wanted this role. Kay has been ill ever since she found out that Terry was chosen over her.

Comments
This role meant everything to Kay, and her disappointment is overwhelming. After Terry leaves the residence for the theater, Kay, despondent, goes upstairs and jumps out of the window to her death. However, a word of warning to the actor: Kay's decision to commit suicide is made after Terry leaves. If the actor contemplates suicide beforehand, the scene becomes morose. The interesting part of this exercise is that Kay's suffering is all subtext. On the surface, she helps Terry and wishes her well. The actor must find her own reasons for behaving in this way.

The actor playing Terry must be very specific in her preparation for the theater. Also, an actual play and role should be chosen. Terry can solicit help on certain lines and attitudes; she is suffering from terrible stage fright and needs Kay's help. Kay is an artist; Terry is superficial.

Source: *To Play the King,* a BBC miniseries by Paul Seed based on the novel by Michael Dobbs

Characters
One male, one female: Francis Urquhart, prime minister of England; Sarah, his assistant

Place
The prime minister's office in London

Background
Francis Urquhart acquired the office of prime minister through his ruthless tactics. His wife aided him in trapping young women, who are in strategic positions, into becoming his assistants. He enticed them into romantic relationships to ensure their loyalty. Sarah, who was happily married, with children, was hired by Urquhart for her "great brain." She has been neglecting her family to be at his beck and call.

The last woman who worked for Urquhart was a young journalist named Mattie. When Mattie began to suspect that Urquhart was responsible for the murder of a man, she confronted him with the allegation. Urquhart killed her by pushing her off a balcony. However, Mattie had hidden a tape recorder on her person, which recorded her conversation with Urquhart and her death.

A disgruntled assistant of the prime minister recovered the tape and kept it in a safe until now. Since he has just learned that Urquhart has no intention of promoting him after years of loyal service, he gave a copy of the tape to Sarah. Urquhart knows that Sarah has become suspicious about Mattie's demise, but he does not know of the existence of the tape.

Situation

Sarah has been called to Urquhart's office to spend the night. She now fears that she is about to go the way of Mattie but must pretend that nothing is wrong. In the morning, the tape will be turned over to the police. In the meantime, Urquhart must not think that anything has changed.

Comments

No matter how good you might be at pretending to love someone whom you have discovered has used you as a pawn and destroyed your marriage, it is difficult to hide your true feelings. Sarah will be killed if she does not play out this love affair. She is both hurt and terrified, because she knows Urquhart will not hesitate to kill her. Urquhart would, however, feel a change in her.

Source: *Twelfth Night,* a play by William Shakespeare

Characters

One male, one female: Duke Orsino; Viola (masquerading as Cesario)

Place

Duke Orsino's chambers in his castle in Illyria, an ancient country on the eastern coast of the Adriatic

Background

Viola was shipwrecked in Illyria. Her twin brother, Sebastian, was traveling with her; Viola believes (mistakenly) that he went down with the ship. Viola has learned that Duke Orsino, an enemy of her family, governs Illyria. To conceal her identity from Orsino, Viola disguised herself as a young man named Cesario and was taken into the duke's service as his page.

Duke Orsino is in love with Olivia, who is grief-stricken over the death of her brother. She has gone into mourning for seven years and told the duke that she cannot accept his attentions until this time has elapsed. Viola, still mourning her own loss, feels drawn to Olivia.

Meanwhile, a quintessentially Shakespearean tangle of romantic complication has come to pass. Duke Orsino, greatly taken with Cesario (who is Viola in disguise), wants to send the page to Olivia as his envoy of love; Viola has fallen in love with the duke; and Olivia has fallen in love with Cesario!

Situation

Duke Orsino has called Cesario (Viola in disguise) to his chamber. As the duke paces the floor, he professes his love for Olivia and bemoans the shallow and capricious ways of women. What is he to do? He begs Cesario to advise him, man to man. Cesario (Viola), a woman herself, tells the duke that he is mistaken in his assessment of the gender and cites his sister (actually referring to herself, Viola) as an example. She is in love with a man who does not know that she loves him, Cesario says, but she has said nothing, waiting patiently for him to come around.

Comments

The actor portraying Cesario (Viola) has the challenge of being a female playing a female who is posing as a male. As Duke Orsino describes his lovesick state to Cesario, Viola empathizes only too well, but she must hold her tongue. Duke Orsino is taken with Cesario because Cesario understands him so well and has such insight into the female psyche. Duke Orsino is confused, because he finds himself strangely attracted to this young boy. He has, without realizing it, fallen in love with Viola. Later in the play, her true identity is revealed and they marry.

See index for other improvisations from this source.

Source: *The Wedding,* a novel by Dorothy West

Characters

Two females: Corrine Coles, mother of Shelby and wife of Dr. Clark Coles; Rachel, mistress of Dr. Clark Coles

Place

Two locations, on the telephone: the Coles' residence and the office of Dr. Coles in the Deep South; early twentieth century

Background

Corrine knows that her husband, Clark, is having an affair. She is not happy about it, but she can do nothing to prevent it. Clark and Corrine are the parents of two children, which holds their marriage together. Their little girl, Shelby, wandered away from home while playing in the back yard. Corrine has notified the police, but Shelby has not yet been found.

Situation

Corrine is faced with having to telephone her husband at work; she knows that his nurse, Rachel, who is also his mistress, will answer the phone. This is no time to leave a message, so Corrine must tell Rachel her terrible story. The two enemies are forced to speak to each other.

Comments

The hostility these two women feel toward each other is a powerful subtext. Rachel would like to marry Clark and raise her own family with him. And Corrine wants her husband back. But, right now, Corrine is frantic with worry. (Eventually, Shelby *is* found, but, at this point, nobody knows where she is.)

See index for other improvisations from this source.

$$\longrightarrow\!\!\!\!\blacklozenge\!\!\!\!\longleftarrow$$

8

Unusual Circumstances

The situations in this chapter may or may not be likely to occur in everyday life. Unlike fantasy, all of the situations are within the realm of possibility. Unusual circumstances may take actors to different places or periods in history with different social mores and styles. Actors will be required to deal with circumstances that may be real but new to them.

Many of the circumstances in this chapter will stretch the actors' imagination by challenging their ability to deal with the unexpected and the unfamiliar. The actors must act and react as honestly and naturally—in extraordinary circumstances—as they would in ordinary circumstances. It is the truth underneath the actors' actions and words that makes a scene work and acting believable. Regardless of how bizarre the situation or unusual the circumstance may seem, it is the actors' total devotion to the reality of a scene that allows the audience to suspend its disbelief. These situations will help actors gain the ability to create events and situations that can or might happen.

UNUSUAL CIRCUMSTANCES SITUATIONS

One male, one female
God Would Be Rich
Going After Cacciato
The Lark

The Pearl
Schindler's List
Uncle Tom's Cabin

Two females
Antigone
Kindred
Twelfth Night

Two males
Antigone
The Kentucky Cycle—Part One
The Pearl
The Shepherds of Saint Francis
To Beat a Tiger

Ensemble
Baby
Chronicle of a Death Foretold
A Doctor in Spite of Himself
Shlemiel the First
Shunkan

Source: *Antigone,* a play by Sophocles

Characters
Two females: Antigone; Ismene—sisters of Eteocles and Polynices

Place
Outside the palace of Creon, ruler of Thebes, an ancient city of Greece; the third century B.C., at dawn

Background
Eteocles and Polynices, sons of Oedipus, once the king of Thebes, were rivals for their father's throne. Eteocles enlisted the support of Creon, the present ruler of Thebes, who banished Polynices. In exile, Polynices built an army among the Argives, and stormed Thebes. At the gates of the city, the two brothers met, fought, and killed each other. Creon had Eteocles buried with full state honors. Polynices, however, considered an enemy of the state, was left unburied.

Situation
Ismene, grieving over the loss of her two brothers, does not yet know about the decree. It is left to Antigone to inform her that Creon gave Eteocles a soldier's funeral, while Polynices, who also fought bravely, has been left to rot in the fields.

Antigone has decided to bury Polynices in defiance of Creon's orders, and she wants Ismene to help. She tells Ismene that it is her duty as a sister to give her brother a decent burial; if Ismene refuses to help, she is a traitor to her family. Ismene thinks her sister has gone mad and warns her of the danger involved in burying Polynices: the law states that anyone who disturbs the body is to be stoned to death in the public square. Ismene says that they are only women—they cannot stand up to men with power and authority. Antigone, however, is determined to bury her brother—even if she must die for it.

Comments
Antigone and Ismene are two different personality types. Ismene is passive, refusing to challenge authority; Antigone is strong-willed and defies Creon. Ultimately, she does bury Polynices and is condemned to death. When Ismene begs to share her fate, Antigone rejects this sacrificial offer. In terms of Antigone's motivation, it is unthinkable not to have a proper burial for someone you love. The ancient Greeks believed that the soul of a person whose dead body was left to decay without burial was condemned to eternal unrest. Anyone who neglected a corpse brought down the wrath of the gods.

See also the following improvisation.

Source: *Antigone,* a play by Sophocles

Characters
Two males: Creon, ruler of Thebes; Haimon, husband of Antigone, son of Creon

Place
The palace of Creon in Thebes, an ancient city of Greece; the third century B.C.

Background
Creon rules in Thebes. Antigone's two brothers, Eteocles and Polynices, were bitter rivals; Eteocles allied himself with Creon, who banished

Polynices for plotting against the state. The brothers killed each other in a battle between the Thebans and the Argives, which had been precipitated by the exiled Polynices. Creon gave Eteocles a hero's burial, with full military honors, but decreed that Polynices, the "traitor," go unburied. Antigone is determined to defy Creon's decree and bury her brother. If she does, the law states that she will be stoned to death in a public square.

Situation

Antigone's husband, Haimon, has come to see his father, King Creon, to persuade him to reverse the decree. Haimon explains that it would be wisest to bury Polynices: the Thebans fear Creon's temper and only tell him what he wants to hear, but their sympathies are with Antigone. He pleads that Antigone's only crime is that she wants to cover her brother's body, that Creon must spare her life.

Creon's response is that Haimon has lost his head over Antigone. She holds the law in contempt, and he will not countenance that. Creon is unbending in his resolution: he does not want to appear weak before his subjects.

Comments

Haimon is caught in a conflict of loyalties between his father and his wife, while Creon's conflict is between his son and the state. Anarchy, Creon contends, is the greater evil, for it destroys cities. (He is also terrified of losing his power.) Creon views all women, including Antigone, as inferior to men. This confrontation is painful for both father and son because they love each other, but Haimon also loves Antigone and cannot bear to lose her. In the play, Creon eventually has Antigone locked up in a burial vault. Later, when he goes to free her, he finds that she has hanged herself.

See also the preceding improvisation.

Source: *Baby*, a novel by Patricia MacLachlan

Characters

Ensemble; Two females, one male: Larkin Byrd, twelve years old; Lily Byrd, Larkin's mother; Larkin's father

Place

The driveway of the Byrds' home on an island off the east coast of the United States

Background

Summer is over, and the tourists are leaving the island on which the Byrds are permanent residents. The Byrds are feeling restless and talk about needing some excitement. Six months ago, Lily had had a baby that lived for only one day. The infant was buried, and there has been no further mention of it.

Situation

The Byrds are returning to their house after seeing friends off at the ferry. To their amazement, they find a basket in the driveway with a baby sitting in it. There is a note, which reads, "This is Sophie. She is almost a year old and she is good . . . I love her: I will come back for her one day." The note goes on to explain that Sophie's mother cannot take care of her now but that she knows Sophie will be safe with this good family. She begs them to keep the baby for her. She will send money.

Lily begins to cry. Larkin's father insists that they call the police, but Lily scoops up the baby and refuses to let her go. The Byrds have a heated argument, but end up agreeing to keep the baby—for the time being.

Comments

Sophie has special meaning to the family because of their recent loss. It is a crime to keep a foundling without reporting it to the authorities, but Lily's feelings are so strong that her husband gives in. It is dangerous for the Byrds to become too attached to Sophie; her mother is coming back and they will have to part with the baby sooner or later.

Some object should be substituted for the baby; she is an integral part of the scene. Each person will find their own personal connection with Sophie; each will hold her in a distinctive way.

See index for other improvisations from this source.

Source: *Chronicle of a Death Foretold,* a novel by Gabriel García Márquez

Characters

Ensemble; Two females, two males: Angela Vicario, Bayardo's wife; Pura Vicario, Angela's mother; Bayardo San Roman, Angela's husband; Angela's brother

Place

Pura Vicario's home in a Latin American country; the early twentieth century, late at night

Background
It has been only a few hours since Bayardo and Angela's spectacular wedding.

Situation
Pura Vicario awakes to knocking at her door. Some members of her household are asleep; others are still out celebrating the wedding. She goes to answer the door and finds the newlyweds standing outside on the step. Angela's dress is in shreds, and there is a towel wrapped around her waist. Bayardo announces that he is returning Angela: he has just discovered that she was not a virgin when she married him. Angela's brother comes home, learns what has happened, and begins to cross-examine Angela as to the identity of her lover.

Comments
A note to the actors: Respect the morality that prevailed in Latin America during the twentieth century, the code of ethics that men imposed on women and that women imposed on themselves, and the curious notions of honor that may dominate an isolated community. Bayardo believes that he has been dishonored; Angela must be returned in disgrace to her parents. That is the custom. In García Márquez's novel, Pura Vicario beats Angela after Bayardo leaves. The actors may find their own ways of dealing with this situation. This improvisation might stimulate discussion about codes and morals and how they are subject to change over time.

Source: *A Doctor in Spite of Himself,* a play by Aurand Harris, freely adapted from Molière

Characters
Ensemble; Two males, one female: Sganarelle, a woodcutter; Geronte; Lucinde, Geronte's daughter

Place
Lucinde's bedroom in Geronte's house

Background
Sganarelle's wife, Martine, decided to pay her husband back for the beating he gave her by playing a trick on him. Soon thereafter, two of Geronte's servants came to her house. They asked Martine if she knew where they could find a doctor for Geronte's sick daughter, Lucinde. The poor man was beside himself to find somebody to cure her. Martine told them that she knew a woodcutter by the name of Sganarelle (her husband) who is a physician but who denies it. He will only admit to being a doctor when beaten with a stick.

The servants sought and found a man who claimed to be a wood-cutter (Sganarelle) and asked him if he were a doctor, which, of course, he denied. They proceeded to hit Sganarelle with a stick until he admitted to being a doctor. They then took him to Geronte to cure Lucinde.

Now, Lucinde's only problem is that her father will not let her see the man she loves, Leandre, because he is poor. Her father is forcing her instead to marry a wealthy man named Horace. To escape her fate, she is pretending to be ill and unable to speak.

Situation
Sganarelle is presented to Lucinde. Geronte is afraid that his daughter will die, so he entrusts her completely to the care of "the doctor." Everyone is depending on Sganarelle to cure Lucinde; he must keep up the pretense of being a doctor.

Comments
The task for the actor playing Sganarelle is to pretend to be a doctor when he knows nothing about medicine. The fear of being beaten, however, forces him to be inventive. In the play, Sganarelle resorts to diagnosing the patient in Latin, which (he discovers) nobody, including himself, understands. The actor may use this device, or he may find his own method to get out of this predicament. The actors should accept the farcical mood of this improvisation and find their own logic within these circumstances. They should also accept that there is no other doctor who can cure Lucinde and that Geronte is at his wits' end.

Source: *God Would Be Rich,* a play by Helen Maley based on a true story

Characters
One female, one male: Verinda Brown; Thomas Brown, her husband—both are African American

Place
The back porch of Father Sublime's house, Sayville, Long Island; 1936

Background
Verinda and Thomas Brown heard Father Sublime speak at a church and were very impressed. Thomas warned Verinda that the minister's following seemed like a cult, but she finally persuaded her husband to become a member of the congregation. Verinda met with Father Sublime; he explained how she could become an angel. According to him,

Verinda and Thomas could both have eternal life, but, Father Sublime said, she must not keep anything a secret. The minister told Verinda that she and Thomas were not to live together any longer; they were not to see each other at all. Father Sublime told her, "To attain the spiritual consciousness that leads us to eternal life, you must forget he ever was your man. You must look at him like he is a stranger to you." He tells Verinda that he, Father Sublime, will become the most important person in her life from now on. She will take a new name, and everything she has will now belong to him—she will not need it for her eternal life.

Situation

Verinda must explain the situation to Thomas. She announces that they must separate. Thomas reminds her that they promised each other they would always stick together. Verinda repeats what the minister told her: they can't be eternal angels unless they give up everyone and everything. Thomas protests; the *Bible* never said anything about a man and wife separating to become angels. Verinda repeats Father Sublime's arguments, trying to convince her husband.

Comments

Thomas and Verinda do end up separating, and Verinda gives all of her money to Father Sublime. Thomas and Verinda love each other, but they are swayed by the power of this charismatic, compelling man. They believe in angels and eternal life; they think that they are doing the right thing. Good souls themselves, they do not discern the evil in Father Sublime. Eventually, they come to realize that they have been duped and, with great difficulty, extricate themselves from his influence.

The character of Father Sublime was based on a real man, Father Divine, who became very powerful in the 1930s. He had many followers. The men and women were housed in separate dwellings; all possessions were relinquished to the minister. Since that time, we have had no lack of fanatical evangelists—Aimee Semple McPherson, Jim Jones, the Bakers, and David Koresh of the Branch Davidians, to name just a few.

See index for other improvisations from this source.

Source: *Going After Cacciato,* a novel by Tim O'Brien

Characters

One male, one female: Eddie, a soldier in the United States Army; his mother

Place
Two locations, on the telephone: Vietnam and the United States; during the Vietnam War, 1968

Background
An army outfit recently installed a radio–telephone hook-up with the United States, the Military Air Radio System. Eddie is the first soldier to use the device. He telephones his mother.

Situation
Eddie's mother receives an unexpected call from her son in Vietnam. They discuss the family and other news. Eddie can hear his mother's cuckoo clock clearly.

Comments
The actors will discover their own dialogue. They need to be clear beforehand about their family members and history, and they should establish how long Eddie has been away.
    The war is going badly, but Eddie doesn't want to worry his mother. This is a very difficult time for both of them, and this phone call is a major, and a happy, event.

    See index for other improvisations from this source.

Source: *The Kentucky Cycle—Part One*, a play by Robert Schenkkan

Characters
Two males: Earl Tod, a Scottish trapper; Michael Rowen, an indentured Irish servant

Place
A clearing in the forest in eastern Kentucky; the late eighteenth century, an hour before daybreak

Background
Cherokee Indians massacred the village in which Michael Rowen's family lived; Rowen's wife and children were among those killed. Distraught, Rowen had been wandering through the woods all night, when he saw the light of a fire and smelled the aroma of food cooking. He stumbled into the clearing and found Earl Tod, a trapper and unprincipled trader, holding a gun on him.

Situation

Rowen asks Tod if he can warm himself by his fire and have something to eat. He looks—and feels—cold and hungry. Tod is holding a gun on Rowen because he suspects that every stranger is a potential enemy. (He is unaware that Rowen recognizes him.) After much coaxing, Rowen finally persuades the trapper to share his fire and food.

Gradually, Rowen reveals that he knows Tod has been trading rifles for pelts with the Cherokee Indians. Those rifles were used to kill Rowen's family. Rowen must now decide what to do with this man, whose greed brought about the murder of Rowen's wife and children.

Comments

Initially, Michael Rowen may not recognize this man as the murderer of his family. It is possible that the realization comes to him after he has accepted Tod's hospitality. On the other hand, he may have known from the beginning; the actor can make this decision. Cold and hunger are important motivators in this scene: Rowen desperately needs warmth and nourishment. The actors should transport themselves back in time to the rugged and cruel pioneer days, when survival often meant committing unethical and immoral acts. In the play, the scene ends with Rowen killing Tod; the actors may explore other possible resolutions.

See index for other improvisations from this source.

Source: *Kindred,* a novel by Octavia E. Butler

Characters

Two females: Sarah, a black woman in her twenties; Margaret Weylin, a white woman in her twenties

Place

The kitchen of the Weylin home on the eastern shore of Maryland; 1815

Background

Dana Franklin lives in California with her husband, Kevin, who is white. The year is 1976. However, Dana has been experiencing strange episodes, during which she returns in time to the Weylin plantation in Maryland, where her ancestors lived as slaves one hundred and fifty years ago. She has witnessed or participated in a number of dramatic and dangerous situations; this is one of them.

Sarah is a slave in the Weylin household. Her husband was killed in an accident, leaving Sarah with four young children—three boys and a girl, Carrie, who is mute.

Situation
Margaret Weylin informs Sarah that her three male babies will be taken from her and sold. However, Sarah can keep Carrie; the little girl is mute and her sale would not bring much money. Margaret Weylin is sending her husband to fetch the babies.

Comments
Sarah is a slave and has no power in the situation. She could run away, but her chances of survival are slim to none. Although she cannot prevent this terrible thing from happening, she will not stand by silently without protesting.

    This improvisation can be done with Margaret Weylin present; it can then become a solo moment for Sarah. Sarah's behavior in Margaret's presence will be quite different from her behavior when she is alone. Profound sorrow and anger are present in Sarah, but do not forget that she is a slave. Sarah is not a sophisticated African American woman of the twentieth century; cultural restrictions of the time make it impossible for her to fight back.

See index for other improvisations from this source.

Source: *The Lark*, a play by Jean Anouilh, adapted by Lillian Hellman

Characters
One female, one male: Joan of Arc, in her early teens; Saint Michael, an angel

Place
A meadow near Joan's home in Domremy, France; the fifteenth century

Background
Joan is a simple, hard-working girl who loves her mother, father, and brother.

Situation
One day, while Joan is watching her sheep in the meadow, she is touched on the shoulder from behind—but no one is there. A voice speaks to her, the voice of an angel. Joan attempts to tell the angel that he is in the wrong place, talking to the wrong person. She is just a simple girl. The angel reveals himself as Saint Michael and tells Joan that she must save France from the English invaders. She begs to be relieved of this task, but the angel insists that *she* has been chosen for the mission.

Comments

It is for the actor playing Saint Michael to determine how to play an angel—physically and vocally. It will be difficult to convince Joan to fight this battle for her country. Remember: although she has never heard voices before, she is religious and does believe in angels.

See also the following improvisations.

Source: *The Lark*, a play by Jean Anouilh, adapted by Lillian Hellman

Characters

One female, one male: Joan of Arc, in her early teens; her father

Place

A meadow near Joan's home in Domremy, France; the fifteenth century

Background

Joan is late for dinner, and her father is furious. Joan's brother tells him that she is still in the field, staring straight ahead as if looking at something. Her father suspects that she is waiting to meet a lover. He goes out to the field to punish her.

Situation

Joan's father finds her and accuses her of meeting a lover. Joan tells him that she has been talking to Saint Michael and that he wants her to lead France against the English invaders. Her father threatens to beat her if she continues to lie about saints conversing with her, but she insists that she is not lying. She must save France.

Comments

Joan's father thinks that all she wants is an opportunity to run off and live with soldiers, and he threatens to kill her. He believes that she is either lying—or that she has gone crazy. His treatment of Joan is unjust and cruel. Anouilh's conception of this conversation portrays Joan's father as being like any father attempting to discipline his rebellious daughter. But, as we know from history, Joan of Arc had a strong will. Nothing was going to stand in her way.

Joan would save France by asking the Sire de Beaudricourt for an armed escort to the dauphin at Chinon. She would convince the dauphin to fight. Then she would take the army to Orleans and push the English back to the sea.

See also the preceding and the following improvisations.

Source: *The Lark,* a play by Jean Anouilh, adapted by Lillian Hellman

Characters
One female, one male: Joan of Arc; Charles, the dauphin, ruler of France, a young man

Place
The dauphin's court in France; the fifteenth century

Background
Joan was visited by a vision of Saint Michael, an angel. He ordered her to go to the dauphin to request an army with which to fight the English, who had invaded France. Despite ridicule and threats, Joan persisted. She has finally made her way to the dauphin.

Situation
Joan meets Charles, the dauphin. He is not quite what she had expected; he is a frightened man who does not want to be a king. He is afraid of his archbishop. Joan shares her experiences of fear with Charles. She tells him that one must anticipate and confront fear, so that, in the face of danger, one will have already experienced apprehension and will be able to proceed with courage. When Charles is as afraid as he can get, Joan says, she will call in the archbishop. She does, and, emboldened by Joan's "pep talk," Charles orders the army. The improvisation can end at the moment Charles gains courage, or continue and include the archbishop.

Comments
The actor portraying Charles should understand what makes the dauphin frightened of assuming his power. Joan enters expecting a king. What she finds instead is a man who is like a little boy, who seems to need her more than she needs him. By being very natural with him, she is able to achieve what she wants. They both face their dread together.

See also the two preceding improvisations.

Source: *The Pearl,* a novel by John Steinbeck

Characters
Two males: Kino, an Indian; a doctor

Place
The doctor's home in La Paz, Mexico; the 1930s

Background

Kino is a fisherman and pearl diver. He is married to Juana and they have a baby, Coyotito. One day, the baby is stung by a scorpion. As Kino is preparing to go get help from the local doctor, all his neighbors tell him that the doctor will not come because Kino is so poor. Juana, however, is determined that Kino will fetch medical assistance. Coyotito is her first baby; she does not want to lose him.

Situation

Kino makes his way to the doctor's house on the other side of town. The fisherman and the doctor are not of the same race; the doctor's race has dominated Kino's people for four hundred years. Kino is afraid to approach the doctor, but the remembrance of the baby's screams urges him on. Kino pleads with the doctor to come save Coyotito. On hearing that Kino has no money to pay for the treatment, the doctor refuses to help. Kino has some seed pearls, which he offers as payment, but the doctor deems them unacceptable. Kino does everything he can think of to persuade the doctor, but to no avail.

Comments

In Steinbeck's story, Kino never even gets a chance to speak to the doctor; a servant relays Kino's request and the doctor's response. Finally, the servant tells Kino that the doctor has been called on a serious case and must leave.

The actor playing Kino needs to accept the difference that exists between races; it will take courage to bridge that gap and relate to the doctor as one human being to another. Kino loves his family. He cannot imagine that the doctor would not be sympathetic and understanding.

Steinbeck describes the doctor as fat and lazy. He is well dressed, lives in a richly furnished home, and has no family. He says in reference to helping Kino, "I am a doctor, not a veterinarian," thus demonstrating his contempt for Kino's race. However, the actor playing the doctor should not demonize him. He should try to see the situation from the doctor's point of view. The doctor believes that he should not have to work for nothing. He says he is tired of it, which means he has done it before. He just may be at the end of his rope and feel justified in refusing to help Kino.

See also the following improvisation.

Source: *The Pearl,* a novel by John Steinbeck

Characters

One male, one female: Kino; Juana, his wife

Place
Their home in La Paz, Mexico; the 1930s

Background
Kino is a fisherman and pearl diver. When his baby was stung by a scorpion, Kino went to the local doctor for help. Because Kino was poor and unable to pay his fee, the doctor refused to provide medical treatment. So, Kino went diving for a pearl to get money to pay the doctor. To his amazement, he found the greatest pearl in the world—and Coyotito, his baby, got better: the poison receded and the swelling went down. However, as a result of Kino's discovery of the pearl, the town swelled with greed. Everyone wanted part of the money that the pearl would fetch. The doctor, for example, gave one medicine to Coyotito to make him sick again and then another medicine to cure him.

Situation
Kino's wife, Juana, begins to see signs of evil things happening since Kino found the pearl. She begs him to throw it away before it destroys them. Kino cannot understand her attitude. He wants to use the money for so many things, such as a church wedding, a harpoon and rifle, and school for Coyotito so that he can live as a free man. When Juana attempts to throw the pearl away, Kino beats her.

Comments
Juana does not leave Kino when he beats her; she understands what is happening to him, but that doesn't mean that she isn't upset. Kino loves his wife and has never raised his hand to her before, but the pearl has changed him. In Steinbeck's story, Kino kills a man who was after the pearl. Eventually, Coyotito is killed, too. In the end, Kino returns the pearl to the sea.

Kino became everyone's enemy because he had something they all wanted but couldn't get. Had he thrown away the pearl, as Juana suggested, he could have prevented the tragedy of their son's death. Both Juana and Kino are right. Kino wants to do worthwhile things with the money, but Juana sees the seeds of greed and evil long before he does.

See also the preceding improvisation.

Source: *The Shepherds of Saint Francis,* a play by Lowell Swortzell

Characters
Two males: Saint Francis, a famous friar in his early forties; Leone, nineteen years old

Place
A church in the small town of Greccio, Italy; December 1223

Background
Saint Francis, originally from Assisi, was the son of a cloth merchant. He traveled the countryside, never knowing where he was going to sleep or eat, but he had faith that he would find shelter and food. He owned nothing and worked hard. Everything that he received, he gave to the poor. He had a following of devoted shepherds who traveled with him and followed the same manner of living. He is preparing to reopen a church that had been in ruins for years.

Leone is a young boy who lives in the village with his parents. He is accustomed to a comfortable life. He works for Saint Francis at the church.

Situation
Saint Francis is sweeping the church in preparation for the next service. Leone insists that the friar should not be doing the sweeping himself and tries to take the broom, but Saint Francis will not relinquish it. Leone tells Saint Francis that it is very important that he talk with the friar before the congregation arrives. He tells Saint Francis that God has communicated with him, instructing Saint Francis to move on immediately after the service, taking Leone with him. Saint Francis replies that Leone is too young and too accustomed to a protected life. He points out that the boy is dressed in a fine suit and would be embarrassed to dress in a robe tied with a rope. Saint Francis explains that, often, he and his shepherds are pelted with rocks, locked up in asylums, and called crazy. Leone is not deterred. He convinces Saint Francis that God truly has spoken to him; Leone's destiny is to roam the countryside with the saint, helping the poor.

Comments
The actor needs to recognize that God speaks to Saint Francis, so this concept will seem normal to the friar. Saint Francis questions whether God actually spoke to Leone and whether Leone is worthy of being one of his followers; it is a rugged life.

Later, Leone and Saint Francis staged the first nativity scene on a hillside outside Greccio. People attended on Christmas Eve, with all their animals—sheep, donkeys, cows—and they witnessed the first Christmas pageant.

Source: *Schindler's List,* a film by Stephen Spielberg based on the book by Thomas Keneally, screenplay by Steven Zaillian

Characters
One male, one female: a young Nazi officer; an attractive young Jewish prisoner

Place
The kitchen in a Nazi concentration camp; during World War II

Background
The officer selected this girl to cook, clean, and sew for him. She is a good worker, and he is pleased with her. This position is keeping her alive, while other prisoners go to their death.

Situation
One evening, the officer realizes that he is in love with the girl. In his desire for her, he attempts to kiss her. He is confused because he has been taught that Jews are not human, that they are creatures beneath contempt. He cannot understand his feelings for her, and this inner conflict turns to violence.

Comments
The actor playing the Nazi must create some terrible deed connected with this girl to justify his feelings of contempt. It's almost as if the situation were reversed: if he were a Jew and fell in love with a Nazi, how would he feel about himself? To the actor playing the girl: remember, she is striving to survive. She probably finds the officer repulsive; however, she might also find him strangely attractive.

Source: *Shlemiel the First,* a play by Isaac Bashevis Singer

Characters
Two males, two females: Shlemiel; Tryna Rytza, his wife; Gittel, their young daughter; Mottel, their young son

Place
The living room of the Shlemiel home in Chelm, a small village in Eastern Europe; a long time ago

Background
A very wise rabbi has moved to the village of Chelm. The other rabbis chose Shlemiel to spread the word of this throughout the countryside; his travels would take him away from home for two years. Shlemiel and his wife loved each other very much, and this was a sad parting. After a short time on the road, Shlemiel finds himself in another village. When told that he is in Chelm, he assumes that he has found the second of two Chelms.

Situation
Shlemiel has actually returned to his own village. However, because he has

been traveling for a few hours, he believes that this is Chelm 2, while his real home is in Chelm 1. His wife and children are very happy to see him, but he tells them that they are not his wife and children, although there *is* an uncanny resemblance. Shlemiel is certain that he is in Chelm 2. He is pleased that this woman, who looks like his wife, treats him—a complete stranger— so well. He keeps insisting that Tryna Rytza never treated him like this.

Comments

This story is one of many drawn from legendary characters in Jewish folklore; they are based on people and events in Singer's mother's native village, where Singer spent most of his teen-aged years. It is difficult to place this tale in any specific time period, because Singer's mother, her mother, and her grandmother, all told these stories.

The actors can have fun with this situation. Tryna Rytza, Gittel, and Mottel treat Shlemiel just as they would ordinarily. For them, nothing has changed—except for Shlemiel's peculiar insistence that they are not related to him. Shlemiel is convinced that this is not his family, and he is shocked by their familiarity. He is more attracted to the woman in Chelm 2 than he is to Tryna Rytza. This makes him feel very guilty and determined to remain faithful to his beloved wife back in Chelm 1.

Shlemiel and Tryna Rytza go to the wise rabbi for advice, and they are told that they must not sleep in the same bed—that a screen must be placed between them in their bedroom. Eventually, the wise rabbi's wife investigates the mystery of the two Chelms and tells everyone that there is only one Chelm, and that the Shlemiels are living together legitimately as husband and wife.

Source: *Shunkan* a scene from *Heike Nyogo No Shima*, a play by Monzaemon Chikamatsu

Characters

Three males, one female: Shunkan, a political exile; Naristsune, a political exile; Sen-o, an envoy; Chidori, Naristsune's island wife

Place

The shore of Devil's Island at Kikaigashima, Japan; the seventeenth century

Background

Shunkan, along with Naristsune, led an abortive plot against the tyrant, Kiyomori, leader of the powerful Heike clan. The dissidents were banished to a distant island, and they have lived there for three years. Shunkan misses his wife and child, left behind in Kyoto. His friend, Naristsune, fell in love with an island girl, Chidori, and took her for his wife.

One day, a royal ship landed on the island. Sen-o, an envoy from the ship, read a proclamation from Kiyomori: Naristsune had been granted special amnesty, but not Shunkan because Kiyomori bears him a grudge.

Situation
As they all joyfully board the boat, Chidori, Naristsune's island wife, is refused passage. Naristsune entreats Sen-o for permission to take his bride with him. When he sees that his pleas are in vain, he cries out that he will not leave the island without her. He orders Shunkan to board the boat in his place. At this point, Sen-o reveals that Kiyomori has killed Shunkan's wife. Devastated by this news, Shunkan decides to remain on the island, persuading Chidori to take his place on the vessel.

Comments
These exiles have become a tight-knit family. Each desperately wants to leave, but not at the cost of leaving one of the others behind. The envoy is unbending, because that is his job (though he does seem to enjoy his power inordinately). The actors should acknowledge the customs of the time and accept the inevitable: one person must be left behind. And bear in mind what the island is called (the Devil's Island). It is not an exotic, tropical paradise—it is a barren wasteland.

See index for other improvisations from this source.

Source: *To Beat a Tiger, One Needs a Brother's Help* a novel by Elizabeth Foreman Lewis

Characters
Two males: Wang the Elder; Wang the Younger, his brother

Place
The Wang's home in Soochow, a village in China; the 1950s

Background
Wang the Younger's parents died ten years ago, the victims of a typhoid epidemic. His brother, who was ten years older, became the object of Wang's devotion. They worked together, tending the crops on their farm. Then the Japanese invaded China, attacking the brothers' village by airplane. A neighbor's house was destroyed, and all in it were killed. The farmers and villagers met to discuss what to do.

Situation

Wang the Elder wakes his younger brother at dawn and tells him that he is being sent to Shanghai for safety. He will be leaving immediately with a family named Soo. Wang the Younger does not want to go to live among strangers, to leave his only living relative and his home. His brother insists that there is no other way. He gives Wang all the money they have saved, assuring him that he will send word when it is safe to return home. Before Wang the Younger leaves, he takes a handful of soil from the field that his family has tilled for generations.

Comments

This is a painful parting and as difficult for the older brother as it is for the younger. Both know, in their hearts, that they probably will never see each other again. Their relationship is important. Before attempting this situation, it may be beneficial for the actors playing the brothers to improvise the scene following their parents' death, the incident that gave birth to the strong bond between the younger and elder Wangs.

Source: *Twelfth Night,* a play by William Shakespeare

Characters

Two females: Olivia; Viola (masquerading as Cesario, a young man)

Place

Olivia's chambers in a castle in Illyria, an ancient country on the east coast of the Adriatic Sea

Background

Viola was shipwrecked in a strange land. She believes (mistakenly) that her brother, Sebastian, was drowned at sea. Soon, she discovers that she is in Illyria, a land governed by Duke Orsino. The duke loves Olivia, who is grieving the loss of her brother. Viola, hearing of this, feels drawn to Olivia in her sorrow, but Olivia refuses to see anyone while she grieves.

    Disguised as a man named Cesario, Viola is taken into Duke Orsino's service as his page. The duke likes Cesario (Viola) at once and confides in his page the history of his love for the lady, Olivia. Meanwhile, Viola falls in love with the duke.

    A message arrives from Olivia that she will not see the duke for seven years while she mourns for her dead brother. Duke Orsino, convinced that Olivia will listen to Cesario, sends the page to confess his (the duke's) passion for Olivia. Olivia agrees to see Cesario, who pleads the duke's case as best he can (a difficult enough challenge given that Viola wants to marry the duke herself). Olivia listens. And, believing Cesario to be what he appears to be—a charming, well-spoken young man—she falls in love with him. Viola has begun to suspect that Olivia's looks and manner are an indication that she has fallen in love with Viola's alter ego, Cesario.

Situation
Cesario (Viola) has gone again to profess the duke's love to Olivia. Olivia tells him never to speak of the duke again, revealing to Cesario that she is in love with *him*.

Comments
Viola has no choice but to carry out the duke's commands, although it is painful for her to do so. Since women were not allowed to work as pages at this time in history, Viola must masquerade as a man. The actor portraying Cesario (Viola) has the challenge of being a female playing a female who is posing as a male.

See index for other improvisations from this source.

Source: *Uncle Tom's Cabin,* a novel by Harriet Beecher Stowe

Characters
One male, one female: Simon Lagree, a white man; Eliza, a black slave

Place
Simon's home in the Deep South; 1859, before the Civil War

Background
A slave owner and trader, Simon Lagree regarded his slaves as animals, buying and selling them according to their strength. He didn't care if he split up families. At this time in the Deep South it was not uncommon for slave owners to sleep with their female slaves. Eliza, an attractive young woman, was owned by the Shelbys, who treated her well. However, the Shelbys were in serious financial difficulties and stood to lose everything. Simon Lagree pressured Shelby into selling him ten of his slaves, including Eliza.

Situation
Simon Lagree tells Eliza that she is to be his mistress. He will clothe her, feed her, and allow her to live in his mansion in luxury. She tells him that

she is married and has a child and begs him not to divide her family. Lagree does not view a slave marriage as a serious union. He does not regard his slaves as human beings; they are there only to serve him. He refuses Eliza's request.

Comments

Simon Lagree has complete control over Eliza; as a slave, she has no rights. She knows that living with him will entail sexual favors. She adores her husband and child and could never become the mistress of Lagree. In the novel, Lagree attempts to seize Eliza's child, knowing that this would force her to come to him. However, Mrs. Shelby helps Eliza escape with the child. Later, Eliza is reunited with her husband. Abraham Lincoln cited *Uncle Tom's Cabin* as one of the factors contributing to the abolition of slavery.

———————→ ◆ ←———————

BIBLIOGRAPHY

Professional Resources

Chekhov, M. 1985. *Lessons for the Professional Actor*. New York: Performing Arts Journal Publications.

Hagen, U. 1991. *A Challenge for the Actor*. New York: Scribner.

Nachmanovitch, S. 1990. *Free Play: Improvisation in Life and Art*. Los Angeles: Tarcher.

Shurtleff, M. 1978. *Audition: Everything an Actor Needs to Know to Get the Part*. New York: Walker.

Stanislavski, C. 1936. *An Actor Prepares*. Trans. E. R. Hapgood. New York: Theatre Arts Books.

————.1949. *Building a Character*. Trans. E. R. Hapgood. New York: Theatre Arts Books.

Strasberg, L. 1965. *Strasberg at the Actors Studio*. R. H. Hethmon, ed. New York: Viking.

Thomas, J. 1993. "Empowering the Actor with Stanislavski's Method of Active Analysis." Paper presented at the SETC conference, Arlington, Virginia, March, 1993.

Zeder, S. 1988. *In a Room Somewhere*. New Orleans: Anchorage Press.

Literary Works

Alcott, L. M. 1965. *Little Women*. Racine, WI: Whitman.

Allen, J. P. 1969. *The Prime of Miss Jean Brodie, a Drama in Three Acts*. New York: Samuel French.

Andersen, H. C. 1949. *The Emperor's New Clothes*. New York: Houghton Mifflin.

Angelou, M. "The Reunion." In *Hot and Cool: Jazz Short Stories*. M. Breton, ed. New York: New American Library.

Anouilh, J. 1956. *The Lark*. Adapted by L. Hellman. New York: Random House.

Atiyeh, W. 1955. *Ali Baba and the Forty Thieves*. Anchorage, KY: Children's Theatre Press.

Atwater, F., and R. Atwater. 1938. *Mr. Popper's Penguins*. Boston: Little, Brown.

Austen, J. 1993. *Emma*. New York: Norton.

Avery, H. 1981. *The Secret Garden*. New Orleans: Anchorage Press.

Babbitt, N. 1975. *Tuck Everlasting*. New York: Farrar, Straus & Giroux.

Barrie, J. M. 1980. *Peter Pan*. New York: Scribner.

Baum, L. F. 1979. *The Wizard of Oz*. New York: Ballantine.

"Beautiful Brown Eyes." 1993. In *African-American Folktales for Young Readers*. Collected by R. Young and J. Dockrey Young. Little Rock: August House.

Blume, J. 1972. *Tales of a Fourth Grade Nothing*. New York: Dutton.

————. 1985. *Freckle Juice*. New York: Macmillan.

Boublil, A. and G. M. Shonberg. *Miss Saigon*

Bradley, A., and M. Bond. 1974. *The Adventures of a Bear Called Paddington*. London: Samuel French.

Brecht B. 1972. "He Who Says Yes." In *All the World's a Stage: Modern Plays for Young People*. L. Swortzell, ed. New York: Delacorte.

————. 1972. "He Who Says No." In *All the World's a Stage: Modern Plays for Young People*. L. Swortzell, ed. New York: Delacorte.

Brontë, C. 1987. *Jane Eyre*. New York: Bantam.

Brooks, M. 1993. "A Boy and His Dog." In *Who Do You Think You Are?: Stories of Friends and Enemies*. Selected by H. Rochman and D. Z. McCampbell. Boston: Little, Brown.

Burnett, F. H. 1962. *The Secret Garden*. New York: Dell.

————. 1985. *A Little Princess*. New York: Lippincott.

Butler, O. 1988. *Kindred*. Boston: Beacon Press.

Carcaterra, L. 1995. *Sleepers*. New York: Ballantine.

Carroll, L. 1977. *Alice's Adventures in Wonderland*. New York: St. Martin's Press.

Chekhov, A. 1986. *The Seagull: A Comedy in Four Acts*. Trans. M. Frayn. London: Methuen.

Chikamatsu, M. 1979. *Heike Nyogo No Shima*. In *The Art of Kabuki, Famous Plays in Performance*. Translated and with commentary by S. L. Leiter. Berkley: University of California Press.

Childress, A. 1986. *Wedding Band.* In *Nine Plays by Black Women.* M. B. Wilkerson, ed. New York: New American Library.

Chocolate, D. 1996. *A Very Special Kwanzaa.* New York: Scholastic.

Chopin, K. 1984. "Desiree's Baby" and "The Story of an Hour." In *The Awakening and Selected Stories.* S. M. Gilbert, ed. New York: Penguin.

Cisneros, S. 1991. "Geraldo No Last Name." In *The House on Mango Street.* New York: Vintage.

Clarke, J. H. 1993. "The Boy Who Painted Christ Black." In *Black American Short Stories: One Hundred Years of the Best.* J. H. Clarke, ed. New York: Hill and Wang.

Danziger, P. 1974. *The Cat Ate My Gymsuit.* New York: Dell.

de Brunhoff, J. 1985. *The Travels of Babar.* Trans. M. S. Haas. New York: Random House.

de Marivaux, P. 1723. *Changes in Heart* (Double Inconstancy). Translated by Steven Wadsworth. Paris: Flagault.

Dickens, C. 1987. *The Posthumous Papers of the Pickwick Club.* New York: Oxford University Press.

————. 1992. *Great Expectations.* New York: Knopf.

Dorfman, A. 1990. "The Rebellion of the Magical Rabbits." In *Where Angels Glide at Dawn: New Stories From Latin America.* L. M. Carlson and C. L. Ventura, eds. New York: Lippincott.

————. 1992. *Death and the Maiden.* New York: Penguin.

Dorris, M. 1987. *A Yellow Raft in Blue Water.* New York: Henry Holt.

Douglass, F. 1994. *Escape From Slavery: The Boyhood of Frederick Douglass in His Own Words.* M. McCurdy, ed. New York: Knopf.

Du Maurier, D. 1965. *Rebecca.* New York: Modern Library.

Engar, K. M. 1967. *Arthur and the Magic Sword.* In *Twenty Plays for Young People: A Collection of Plays for Children.* Compiled by W. M. Birner. Anchorage, KY: Anchorage Press.

Faulkner, W. 1979. "The Bear." In *Uncollected Stories of William Faulkner.* J. Blotner, ed. New York: Random House.

Feiffer, J. 1993. *The Man in the Ceiling.* New York: Michael DiCapua Books.

Ferber, E., and G. S. Kaufman. 1939. *Stage Door.* In *Twenty Best Plays of the Modern American Theatre.* J. Gassner, ed. New York: Crown.

Fielding, H. 1970. *The Tragedy of Tragedies, or The Life and Death of Tom Thumb the Great, with the Annotations of H. Scriblerus Secundus.* J. T. Hillhouse, ed. St. Clair Shores, MI: Scholarly Press.

Fisher, S. 1980. *The Tale of the Shining Princess.* From a translation of the story by D. Keene. New York: Metropolitan Museum of Art/Viking Press.

Fleischman, S. 1986. *The Whipping Boy.* New York: Greenwillow.

Fox, P. 1993. *Western Wind.* New York: Orchard.

Fritz, J. 1958. *The Cabin Faced West.* New York: Coward-McCann.

Fry, R. K. 1995. *The Secret of Roan Inish.* New York: Hyperion.

Fugard, A. 1996. *Valley Song.* New York: Theatre Communications Group.

Galati, F. 1991. *John Steinbeck's The Grapes of Wrath.* New York: Dramatists Play Service.

Gallico, P. 1958. *Mrs. 'Arris Goes to Paris.* Garden City, NY: Doubleday.

García Márquez, G. 1983. *Chronicle of a Death Foretold.* Trans. G. Rabassa. New York: Knopf.

Geiogamah, H. 1994. *Coon Cons Coyote.* In *Hanay Geiogamah: Teatro.* Trans. Annamaria Pinazzi. Rome: Castlevecchi.

Gibson, W. 1960. *The Miracle Worker: A Play in Three Acts.* New York: Samuel French.

Gonzalez, R. 1994. "The Boiler Room." In *Nuestro New York: An Anthology of Puerto Rican Plays.* J. V. Antush, ed. New York: Penguin.

Goodrich, F., and A. Hackett. 1956. *The Diary of Anne Frank.* A dramatization based on *Anne Frank: Diary of a Young Girl.* New York: Random House.

Grahame, K. 1983. *The Wind in the Willows.* New York: Scribner.

Gray, N. S. 1951. *The Tinder-Box, a Play for Children.* London: Dennis Dobson.

Gurney, A. R. 1996. *Sylvia.* New York: Dramatists Play Service.

Hall, R. 1973. "The Princess of the Sea." In *Three Tales from Japan: Three Dramatized Folk Tales for Children.* Anchorage, KY: Anchorage Press.

Hamilton, V. 1965. "Doc Rabbit, Bruh Fox, and Tar Baby" and "The Lion, Bruh Bear, and Bruh Rabbit." In *The People Could Fly: American Black Folktales Told by Virginia Hamilton.* New York: Knopf.

————. 1995. "The Mer-Woman Out of the Sea." In *Her Stories: African-American Folktales, Fairy Tales, and True Tales.* New York: Blue Sky Press.

Harling, R. 1988. *Steel Magnolias.* New York: Dramatists Play Service.

Harris, A. 1980. *The Arkansaw Bear.* New Orleans: Anchorage Press.

————. 1989. *The Pinballs.* New Orleans: Anchorage Press.

————. 1991. *A Doctor in Spite of Himself.* In *Short Plays of Theatre Classics.* A. Harris, ed. New Orleans: Anchorage Press.

Heinlein, M. V. 1954. *The Panda and the Spy.* Anchorage, KY: Children's Theatre Press.

Hellman, L. 1972. *The Children's Hour*. In *Collected Plays*. S. M. Gilbert, ed. Boston: Little, Brown.

Henkes, K. 1995. *Protecting Marie*. New York: Greenwillow.

Hijuelos, O. 1992. *The Mambo Kings Sing Songs of Love*. New York: Harper Perennial.

Homer. 1996. *The Odyssey*. Trans. R. Fagles. New York: Viking.

Houston, V. H. 1993. *The Matsuyama Mirror*. In *Short Plays for Young Actors*. C. Slaight and J. Sharrar, eds. Lyme, NH: Smith and Kraus.

Hrdlicková, V., and Z. Hrdlicka. 1993. *Japanese Folktale Stories About Judge Ooka*. Prague: Aventinum.

Hugo, V. 1887. *Les Misérables*. Trans. I. F. Hapgood. New York: Thomas Y. Crowell.

———. 1937. *Notre-Dame de Paris*, or *The Hunchback of Notre Dame*. New York: Book League of America.

Hwang, D. H. 1996. *M Butterfly*. In *The Harcourt Brace Anthology of Drama*. 2d ed. Compiled by W. B. Worthen. Fort Worth, TX: Harcourt Brace College.

Ishiguro, K. 1990. *The Remains of the Day*. New York: Vintage.

Jones, L. 1964. *Dutchman, and The Slave*. New York: Morrow Quill.

Kaestner, E. 1934. *Emil and the Detectives: A Children's Play in Three Acts*. Adapt. C. Brooke. London: Samuel French.

Kalidasa. 1967. *Shakuntala*. In *A Treasury of the Theatre*. J. Gassner, ed. New York: Simon and Schuster.

Keneally, T. 1982. *Schindler's List*. New York: Simon and Schuster.

Kincaid, J. 1996. *The Autobiography of My Mother*. New York: Farrar, Straus & Giroux.

Kingston, M. H. 1989. *The Woman Warrior: Memoirs of a Girlhood Among Ghosts*. New York: Vintage.

Kraus, J. H. 1963. *The Ice Wolf: A Tale of the Eskimos, A Play for Young People in Three Acts*. Rowayton, CT: New Plays for Children.

Lee, H. 1960. *To Kill a Mockingbird*. Philadelphia: Lippincott.

L'Engle, M. 1960. *Meet the Austins*. New York: Vanguard.

———. 1964. *The Moon by Night*. New York: Ariel Books.

———. 1965. *Camilla*. New York: Thomas Y. Crowell.

Lessing, D. 1988. "The Old Chief Mshlanga." In *Somehow Tenderness Survives: Stories of Southern Africa*. Compiled by H. Rochman. New York: Harper and Row.

———. 1988. "A Sunrise on the Veld." In *The Doris Lessing Reader*. New York: Alfred A. Knopf.

Lewis, C. S. 1970. *The Lion, the Witch, and the Wardrobe*. The *Chronicles of Narnia* Series. New York: Collier.

Lewis, E. F. 1953. *To Beat a Tiger, One Needs a Brother's Help*. New York: Holt, Rhinehart and Winston.

Lindgren, A. 1950. *Pippi Longstocking*. Trans. F. Lamborn. New York: Viking.

Lionni, L. 1967. *Frederick*. New York: Pantheon.

———. 1970. *Fish Is Fish*. New York: Pantheon.

———. 1993. *Swimmy*. New York: Scholastic.

Lowry, L. 1993. *The Giver*. Boston: Houghton Mifflin.

MacDonald, B. B. 1975. *Mrs. Piggle-Wiggle*. New York: Lippincott.

MacLachlan, P. 1985. *Sarah, Plain and Tall*. New York: Harper and Row.

———. 1991. *Journey*. New York: Delacorte.

———. 1993. *Baby*. New York: Delacorte.

Maeterlinck, M. 1912a. *Pélléas and Mélisande*. New York: Dodd, Mead.

———. 1912b. *The Blue Bird*. New York: Dodd, Mead.

Marshall, J. 1991. *Rats on the Roof*. New York: Dial.

Martin, R. 1992. *The Rough-Face Girl*. New York: Putnam.

Mason, B. A. 1985. *In Country*. New York: Harper and Row.

McCully, E. A. 1992. *Mirette on the High Wire*. New York: Putnam.

Miller, M. 1964. *The Unwicked Witch*. Anchorage, KY: Anchorage Press.

Miller, S. 1987. *Inventing the Abbotts and Other Stories*. New York: Harper and Row.

Milne, A. A. 1926. *Winnie-the-Pooh*. New York: E. P. Dutton.

Molnar, F. 1960. *Liliom*. In *A Treasury of the Theatre: From Henrik Ibsen to Eugene Ionesco*. J. Gassner, ed. New York: Simon and Schuster.

Montgomery, L. M. 1983. *Anne of Green Gables*. New York: Grosset and Dunlap.

Munsch, R. 1981. *The Paper Bag Princess*. Toronto: Annick Press.

Myers, W. D. 1988. *Scorpions*. New York: Harper and Row.

Naylor, P. R. 1991. *Shiloh*. New York: Macmillan.

Nightingale: A Participatory Play for Children. 1983. Adapted from H. C. Andersen's story by J. Urquhart, R. Grossberg, and Yellow Brick Road Shows. New Orleans: Anchorage Press.

Norris, J. 1968. *Aladdin and the Wonderful Lamp*. New Orleans: Anchorage Press.

O'Brien, T. 1984. *Going After Cacciato*. New York: Dell.

O'Connor, F. "Masculine Protest." In *Collected Stories*. New York: Alfred A. Knopf.

O'Neill, E. 1996. *Ah, Wilderness!* In *The Harcourt Brace Anthology of Drama.* Compiled by W. B. Worthen. Fort Worth, TX: Harcourt Brace College.

Ortiz-Cofer, J. 1993. "American History." In *Who Do You Think You Are? Stories of Friends and Enemies.* H. Rochman and D. Z. McCampbell, eds. Boston: Little, Brown.

Paterson, K. 1978. *The Great Gilly Hopkins.* New York: Thomas Y. Crowell.

Paulsen, G. 1993. *Nightjohn.* New York: Delacorte.

Payne, E. 1944. *Katy No-Pocket.* Boston: Houghton Mifflin.

Perry, R. 1969. *The Emperor's New Clothes.* Chicago: Dramatic Publishing.

Porter, C. 1993a. *Happy Birthday Addy!: A Springtime Story.* Middleton, WI: Pleasant Company.

———. 1993b. *Addy Learns a Lesson: A School Story.* Middleton, WI: Pleasant Company.

———. 1993c. *Addy's Surprise: A Christmas Story.* Middleton, WI: Pleasant Company.

———. 1993d. *Meet Addy: An American Girl.* Middleton, WI: Pleasant Company.

———. 1994a. *Addy Saves the Day: A Summer Story.* Middleton, WI: Pleasant Company.

———. 1994b. *Changes for Addy: A Winter Story.* Middleton, WI: Pleasant Company.

Potter, B. 1987. *The Tale of Peter Rabbit.* London: Frederick Warne.

———. 1991. *The Tale of Jemima Puddle-Duck.* London: Frederick Warne.

Prejean, H. 1993. *Dead Man Walking: An Eyewitness Account of the Death Penalty in the United States.* New York: Random House.

Raphaelson, S. 1983. *The Shop Around the Corner.* In *Three Screen Comedies.* Wisconsin Center for Film and Theater Research. Madison: University of Wisconsin Press.

Ribman, R. 1978. *The Journey of the Fifth Horse.* In *Five Plays.* New York: Avon.

Rylant, C. 1985. *A Blue-Eyed Daisy.* New York: Bradbury.

———. 1990. "A Crush." In *A Couple of Kooks, and Other Stories About Love.* New York: Orchard.

Sacks, O. W. 1983. *Awakenings.* New York: Dutton.

Salinger, J. D. 1980. *The Catcher in the Rye.* New York: Bantam.

Santos, B. 1979. "Immigration Blues," "Manilla House," and "Footnote to a Laundry List." In *Scent of Apples: A Collection of Stories.* Seattle: University of Washington Press.

Satchell, M. 1994. *Langston Hughes: Poet of the People.* In *The Big Book of*

Large-Cast Plays: Twenty-Seven One-Act Plays for Young Actors. S. E. Kamerman, ed. Boston: Plays, Inc.

Schenkkan, R. 1994. *The Kentucky Cycle.* New York: Dramatists Play Service.

Scieszka, J. 1989. *The True Story of the Three Little Pigs.* New York: Viking Kestrel.

———. 1991. *The Frog Prince Continued.* New York: Viking.

Scieszka, J., and L. Smith. 1992. *The Stinky Cheese Man and Other Fairly Stupid Tales.* New York: Viking.

Seeger, P. 1986. *Abiyoyo.* New York: Macmillan.

Shakespeare, W. 1966. *The Plays and Poems of William Shakespeare.* New York: AMS Press.

Shue, L. 1985. *The Foreigner.* New York: Dramatists Play Service.

Smalley, W. 1981. *The Boy Who Talked to Whales.* New Orleans: Anchorage Press.

Sophocles. 1990. *Antigone.* In *Classic Tragedy, Greek and Roman: Eight Plays in Authoritative Modern Translations.* R. W. Corrigan, ed. New York: Applause Theatre.

Soto, G. 1991. *A Summer Life.* New York: Dell.

Stehli, A. 1991. *The Sound of a Miracle: A Child's Triumph over Autism.* New York: Doubleday.

Steinbeck, J. 1939. *The Grapes of Wrath.* New York: Penguin.

———. 1965. *Of Mice and Men.* New York: Modern Library.

———. 1975. *The Pearl.* New York: Bantam.

Stowe, H. B. 1969. *Uncle Tom's Cabin.* Columbus, OH: Merrill.

Swift, G. 1983. *Waterland.* London: Heinemann.

Swortzell, L. 1994a. *Cinderella, The World's Favorite Fairy Tale.* Charlottesville, VA: New Plays.

———. 1994b. *The Mischief Makers.* Charlottesville, VA: New Plays.

———. 1995. *The Shepherds of Saint Francis.* Woodstock, IL: Dramatic Publishing.

Tale of the Shining Princess, The. 1980. A Japanese tale adapted by S. Fisher from a translation of the story by D. Keene. New York: Metropolitan Museum of Art/Viking Press.

Tan, A. 1989. *The Joy Luck Club.* New York: Putnam.

———. 1991. *The Kitchen God's Wife.* New York: Putnam.

Thomas, J. 1987. *Newcomer.* New Orleans: Anchorage Press.

Tolstoy, L. 1961. *Anna Karenina.* Trans. D. Magarshack. New York: New American Library.

Treadwell, S. 1949. *Machinal, Episode Three: Honeymoon.* In *Twenty-Five*

Best Plays of the Modern American Theatre: Early Series. J. Gassner, ed. New York: Crown.

Tripp, V. 1991. *Meet Felicity: An American Girl.* Middleton, WI: Pleasant Company.

Truman, M. 1995. "Christmas Eve with the Trumans." In *First Ladies.* A Fawcett Columbine Book. New York: Ballantine.

Twain, M. 1946. *Tom Sawyer.* Cleveland: World.

————. 1964. *The Prince and the Pauper.* New York: Heritage Press.

Uchida, Y. 1971. *Journey to Topaz: A Story of the Japanese-American Evacuation.* New York: Scribner.

————. 1978. *Journey Home.* New York: Atheneum.

Villanueva-Collado, A. 1990. "The Day We Went to See Snow." In *Where Angels Glide at Dawn: New Stories from Latin America.* L. M. Carlson and C. L. Ventura, eds. New York: J. B. Lippincott.

"Vilma Martinez." In *Notable Hispanic Women.* D. Felgen and J. Kamp, eds. Gale Research.

Vine, B. 1987. *A Dark-Adapted Eye.* New York: Bantam.

Viorst, J. 1972. *Alexander and the Terrible, Horrible, No Good, Very Bad Day.* New York: Atheneum.

Waber, B. 1972. *Ira Sleeps Over.* Boston: Houghton Mifflin.

Walker, A. 1983. *The Color Purple.* New York: Pocket Books.

Walter, M. P. 1986. *Justin and the Best Biscuits in the World.* New York: Lothrop, Lee and Shepard.

Ward, L. 1952. *The Biggest Bear.* Boston: Houghton Mifflin.

West, D. 1995. *The Wedding.* New York: Doubleday.

Wharton, W. 1979. *Birdy.* New York: Knopf.

White, E. B. 1945. *Stuart Little.* New York: Harper and Brothers.

————. 1952. *Charlotte's Web.* New York: Harper and Row.

————. 1970. *The Trumpet of the Swan.* New York: Harper and Row.

Wilder, T. 1941. *Our Town.* In *Sixteen Famous American Plays.* B. A. Cerf and V. H. Cartmell, eds. New York: Modern Library.

————. 1972. *Childhood.* In *All the World's a Stage: Modern Plays for Young People.* L. Swortzell, ed. New York: Delacorte.

Williams, M. B. 1985. *The Velveteen Rabbit.* New York: Knopf.

Woolf, V. 1992. "The New Dress." In *That Kind of Woman.* B. Adams and T. Tate, eds. New York: Carroll and Graf.

Zeder, S. L. 1990. *Doors* and *In a Room Somewhere.* In *Wish in One Hand, Spit in the Other: A Collection of Plays.* S. Pearson-Dans, ed. New Orleans: Anchorage Press.

Zubizarreta, R., H. Rohmer, and D. Schecter. 1991. *The Woman Who Outshone the Sun: The Legend of Lucia Zenteno*. From a poem by A. C. Martinez. New York: Scholastic.

Films, Unpublished Plays, and Screenplays

Ah, Wilderness! 1935. MGM. Clarence Brown (director); Frances Goodrich, Albert Hackett (screenwriters); Eugene O'Neill (playwright); Hunt Stromberg (producer).

Aladdin. 1992. Walt Disney Productions. Ron Clements, John Musker (directors, screenwriters, producers); Ted Elliott, Terry Rossio (screenwriters).

Alice in Wonderland. 1951. Walt Disney Productions. Clyde Geronimi, Wilfred Jackson, Hamilton Luske (directors); Lewis Carroll (novelist); Winston Hibler, Ted Sears, Bill Peet, Erdman Penner, Joe Rinaldi, Milt Banta, William Cottree, Dick Kelsey, Joe Grant, Dick Huemer, Del Connell, Tom Oreb, John Walbridge (screenwriters).

Anna Karenina. 1997. Warner Brothers/Icon Productions. Bernard Rose (director, screenwriter); Bruce Davey (producer); Jim Lemley (associate producer); Stephen McEveety (executive producer).

Anne of Green Gables. 1985. TV. TV-60 Film Produktion/Wonderworks/Canadian Broadcasting Corporation (CBC)/ City-TV/ Sullivan Entertainment, Inc. Kevin Sullivan (director, producer); Lucy Maud Montgomery (novelist); Ian McDougall (producer); Joe Wiesenfeld (screenwriter).

Awakenings. 1990. Columbia Pictures Corporation. Penny Marshall (director); Lawrence Lasker, Walter F. Parkes (producers); Amy Lemisch (associate producer); Steven Zaillean (screenwriter).

Awful Truth, The. 1937. Columbia Pictures Corporation. Leo McCarey, Vina Delmar (directors); W. Sidney Buchman (director, uncredited); Arthur Richman (playwright); Leo McCarey (producer); Everett Riskin (associate producer).

Beauty and the Beast. 1991. Walt Disney Productions. Gary Trousdale, Kirk Wise (directors); Linda Woolverton (screenwriter); Don Hahn (producer); Howard Ashman (executive producer); Sarah McArthur (associate producer).

"Beauty of Passage, The." Arens, N. Unpublished short story by UCLA School of Theater, Film and Television student.

Bionda, La (The Blonde). 1993. Sergio Rubini (director); W. Gian Filippo Ascianone, Umberto Marino, Sergio Rubini (screenwriters); Domanico Procacci, Fandango (producers).

Birdy. 1984. TriStar Pictures/A & M Films. Alan Parker (director); Jack

Behr, Sandy Kroopf (screenwriters); William Wharton (novelist); Ned Kopp (associate producer); David Manson (executive producer); Alan Marshall (producer).

Carousel. 1956. 20th Century Fox. Henry King (director); Ferenc Molnár (author of the play *Liliom*); Oscar Hammerstein II (book and lyrics); Benjamin F. Glazer (adaptation); Phoebe Ephron, Henry Ephron (screenwriters); Henry Ephron (producer).

Charlotte's Web. (E. B. White's *Charlotte's Web.*) 1973. Paramount Pictures. Charles A. Nichols, Iwao Takamoto (directors); Earl Hamner Jr. (screenwriter); E.B. White (novelist); Joseph Barbera, William Hanna (producers).

Children's Hour, The. 1961. United Artists/Mirisch Company. William Wyler (director, producer); John Michael Hayes (screenwriter); Lillian Hellman (playwright); Robert Wyler (producer).

City Hall. 1996. Columbia Pictures Corporation/Sony Pictures Classics. Harold Becker (director, producer); Bo Goldman, Nicholas Pileggi, Paul Schrader (screenwriters); Ken Lipper (screenwriter, producer); Charles Mulvehill, Edward R. Pressman (producers); Thomas J. Mack, Elizabeth Carroll (associate producers).

Climbing Fences. 1993. UCLA School of Theater, Film and Television student film by Mark Lawrence.

Color Purple, The. 1985. Warner Brothers/Amblin Entertainment/ Guber-Peters Company. Steven Spielberg (director, producer); Alice Walker (novelist); Menno Meyjes (screenwriter); Peter Guber, Jon Peters (executive producers); Carole Isenberg (associate producer); Quincy Jones, Kathleen Kennedy, Frank Marshall (producers).

Convicts. 1979. Unpublished play by H. Foote.

Cronaca di un Amore (Story of a Love Affair, The). 1950. Italy. Michelangelo Antonioni (director, screenwriter); Danielle D'Anza, Silvio Giovannetti, Francesco Maselli, Piéro Tellini (screenwriters); Villani Film, Stephano Caretta, Franco Villani (producers). (Based on *The Postman Always Rings Twice.*)

Dark-Adapted Eye, A. 1994. BBC. Tim Fywell (director); Ruth Rendell (novelist, as Barbara Vine); Sandy Welsh (screenwriter); Philipa Gates (producer).

Dead Man Walking. 1995. Working Title Films/Gramercy Pictures/ PolyGram Filmed Entertainment. Tim Robbins (director, screenwriter, producer); Sister Helen Prejean (author of the book); Tim Bevan, Eric Fellner (executive producers); Jon Kilik, Rudd Simmons (producers); Allan F. Nichols, Mark Seldis, Bob White (associate producers).

Dead Poets Society. 1989. Silver Screen Partners IV/Touchstone. Peter

Weir (director); Tom Schulman (screenwriter); Steven Haft, Paul Junger Witt, Tony Thomas (producers); Duncan Henderson (associate producer).

Death and the Maiden. 1994. Canal+ Productions/Channel Four Films (aka Film Four International) (aka Channel 4 TV [uk])/Fine Line/Flach Films/Kramer/Mount/TFI Films Productions (fr); Roman Polanski (director); Ariel Dorfman (screenwriter, co-producer); Rafael Yglesias (screenwriter); Jane Barclay, Sharon Marel (executive producers); Bonnie Timmermann (co-producer); Josh Kramer, Thom Mount (producers); Gladys Nederlander (associate producer).

"Dénouement." Rosenberg, J. Unpublished short story by UCLA School of Theater, Film and Television student.

Diary of Anne Frank, The. 1959. 20th Century Fox. George Stevens (director, producer); Anne Frank (author of the diary); Frances Goodrich, Albert Hackett (screenwriters).

Dollhouse. 1994. UCLA School of Theater, Film and Television student film by Nicole Halpin.

Dreaming of Rope Ladders. Long, J.S. Unpublished play by UCLA School of Theater, Film and Television student.

Eating with Jude. 1997. UCLA School of Theater, Film and Television student film by Anne Kelly.

Emil and the Detectives. 1964. Walt Disney Productions/Buena Vista Television. Peter Tewksbury (director); A.J. Carothers (screenwriter); Erich Kaestner (novelist).

Emma. 1996. Haft Entertainment/Matchmaker Films/Miramax Films. Douglas McGrath (director, screenwriter); Jane Austen (novelist); Patrick Cassavetti, Steven Haft (producers); Donna Gigliotti, Bob Weinstein, Harvey Weinstein (executive producers); Donna Grey (associate producer).

Epiphany. Cores, L. Unpublished play, 70 East 10th Street, NY, NY 10003.

Fatal Beatings. 1994. Tiger Aspect Productions Ltd. John Howard Davies, Sue Vertue, Peter Bennett-Jones (producers).

Fisher King, The. 1991. Columbia Pictures Corporation. Terry Gilliam (director); Richard LaGravenese (screenwriter); Debra Hills, Lynda Obst (producers); Tony Mark, Stacey Sher (associate producers).

Fly Away Home. 1996. Columbia Pictures Corporation. Carroll Ballard (director); Bill Lishman (author of the autobiography); Vince McKewin, Robert Rodat (screenwriters); Carol Baum, John Veitch (producers); John M. Eckert (associate producer); Sandy Gallin (executive producer).

Fools Rush In. 1997. Columbia Pictures Corporation. Andy Tennant (director); Joan Taylor (story); Katherine Reback (story, screenwriter); Anna Maria Davis (co-producer); Doug Draizin (producer); Michael McDonnell (executive producer); Steven P. Saeta (associate producer).

God Would Be Rich. Maley, Helen. 1996. Unpublished play. Box 185, West Tisbury, MA 02575.

Godfather III, The. 1990. Zoetrope Studios/Paramount Pictures. Francis Coppola (director, screenwriter, producer); Mario Puzo (screenwriter); Gray Frederickson, Charles Mulvehill, Fred Roos (co-producers); Fred Fuchs, Nicholas Gage (executive producers); Marina Gefter (associate producer).

Grapes of Wrath, The. 1940. 20th Century Fox. John Ford (director); Nunnally Johnson (screenwriter); John Steinbeck (novelist); Darryl F. Zanuck (producer).

Great Expectations. 1946. Cineguild. David Lean (director, screenwriter); Charles Dickens (novelist); Anthony Havelock-Allen (screenwriter, executive producer); Cecil McGivern, Kay Walsh (screenwriters); Ronald Neame (screenwriter, producer).

Henry IV, Parts I and II. 1979. TV. British Broadcasting Corporation (BBC)/Time-Life Television. David Giles (director); William Shakespeare (playwright); Cedric Messina (producer).

Hercules. 1997. Walt Disney Productions. Ron Clements, John Musker (directors, screenwriters, producers); John McEnery, Irene Mecchi, Bob Shaw (screenwriters); Barry Johnson (story); Alice Dewey (producer); Kendra Holland (associate producer).

Hunchback of Notre Dame, The. 1996. Walt Disney Productions. Gary Trousdale, Kirk Wise (directors); Victor Hugo (author of the novel *Notre Dame de Paris*); Irene Mecchi, Tab Murphy, Jonathan Roberts, Bob Tzudiker, Nona White (screenwriters); Roy Conli, Don Hahn (producers); Philip Lofaro (associate producer).

Hunger Waltz, The. Callaghan, S. Unpublished play by UCLA School of Theater, Film and Television student.

In Country. 1989. Warner Brothers/Yorktown Productions. Norman Jewison (director, producer); Bobbie Ann Mason (novelist); Cynthia Cidre, Frank Pierson (screenwriters); Richard Roth (producer); Michael Jewison (associate producer); Charles Mulvehill (executive producer).

In the Cemetary. 1994. Sandra Caruso (producer, director). From the one-woman dramatic presentation of *In Their Own Words: A Dramatic Series; Margaret Sanger: A Radiant Rebel*. Beverly Hills Television, Beverly Hills, CA 90212.

Inside. 1997. UCLA School of Theater, Film and Television student film by Mario Hernandez Jr.

Inventing the Abbotts. 1997. 20th Century Fox/Imagine Entertainment. Pat O'Connor (director); Sue Miller (novelist); Ken Hixon (story).

Jane Eyre. 1996. Miramax Films. Franco Zeffirelli (director, screenwriter); Charlotte Brontë (novelist); Hugh Whitemore (screenwriter); Guy East, Riccardo Tozzi (executive producers); Joyce Herlihy (associate producer); Jean Francois Lepetit, Giovannella Zannoni (co-producers); Dyson Lovell (producer); Bob Weinstein, Harvey Weinstein (co-executive producers).

Jesus of 148th Street. 1994. UCLA School of Theater, Film and Television student film by Timothy Martin Mills.

Joy Luck Club, The. 1993. Hollywood Pictures. Wayne Wang (director); Ronald Bass (screenwriter, producer); Amy Tan (screenwriter, novelist, producer); Patrick Markey (producer); Jessinta Liu Fung Ping (associate producer); Oliver Stone, Janet Yang (executive producers).

Kid, The. 1921. Chaplin—First National. Charles Chaplin (screenwriter, producer, director).

Killer, The. (*Die xue shuang xiong.*) 1989. Cantonese. Magnum Entertainment/Film Workshop Ltd./Golden Princess Film Production Limited. John Woo (director, screenwriter); Hark Tsui (producer).

Kiss Me Kate. 1953. MGM. George Sidney (director); Dorothy Kingsley, Sam Spewack, Bella Spewack (screenwriters); Cole Porter (playwright); Willam Shakespeare (playwright of *The Taming of the Shrew*); Jack Cummings (producer).

Lady Jane. 1986. Paramount Pictures. Trevor Nunn (director); Chris Bryant (story); David Edgar (screenwriter); Ted Lloyd (associate producer); Peter Snell (producer).

Language of Flowers, The. Villarreal, E. Unpublished play by UCLA School of Theater, Film and Television faculty member.

Life. Fincioen, Jake. Unpublished screenplay by UCLA School of Theater, Film and Television student.

Linda. 1997. UCLA School of Theater, Film and Television student film by Vivian Weisman.

Lion, the Witch, and the Wardrobe, The. (Aka *The Chronicles of Narnia: The Lion, the Witch, and the Wardrobe.*) Wonderworks/British Broadcasting Corporation. Marilyn Fox (director); C.S. Lewis (author of the novels); Alan Seymour (screenwriter); Colin Shindler (executive producer); Paul Stone (producer).

Little Princess, A. 1995. Warner Brothers/Baltimore Pictures. Alfonso

Cuarón (director); Frances Hodgson Burnett (novelist); Elizabeth Chandler, Richard LaGravenese (screenwriters); Alan C. Blomquist, Amy Ephron (executive producers); Dalisa Cohen (co-producer); Mark Johnson (producer).

Little Women. 1994. Columbia Pictures Corporation/DiNovi Pictures. Gillian Armstrong (director); Louisa May Alcott (novelist); Robin Swicord (screenwriter, co-producer); Warren Carr (associate producer); Denise DiNovi (producer).

Mambo Kings, The. 1992. Warner Brothers/Alcor Films/Le Studio Canal/ Regency Enterprises. Arne Glimcher (director, producer); Oscar Hijuelos (novelist); Cynthia Cidre (screenwriter); Jack B. Bernstein (co-producer); Arnon Milchan (producer); Anna Reinhardt (associate producer); Steven Reuther (executive producer).

Men, Myths and Dogs. 1993. UCLA School of Theater, Film and Television student film by Anthony Pringle.

Midsummer Night's Dream, A. 1968. Peter Hall (director); William Shakespeare (playwright); Michael Birkett (producer).

Miracle Worker, The. 1962. Playfilm Productions. Arthur Penn (director); William Gibson (screenwriter, playwright); Helen Keller (author of *The Story of My Life*); Fred Coe (producer).

Misérables, Les. 1952. 20th Century Fox. Lewis Milestone (director); Victor Hugo (novelist); Richard Murphy (screenwriter); Fred Kohlmar (producer).

Much Ado About Nothing. 1993. British Broadcasting Corporation/Renaissance Films/Samuel Goldwyn Company. Kenneth Branagh (director, screenwriter, producer); William Shakespeare (playwright); Stephen Evans, David Parfitt (producers).

Nine Armenians. Ayvazian, L. Unpublished play. William Craver (agent); Writers & Artists, 19 West 44th Street, NY, NY 10036.

Of Mice and Men. 1992. Metro-Goldwyn-Mayer. Gary Sinise (director, producer); Horton Foote (screenwriter); John Steinbeck (novelist); Alan C. Blomquist, Russ Smith (producers).

Our Town. 1940. United Artists. Sam Woods (director); Harry Chandler, Frank Craven (screenwriters); Thornton Wilder (screenwriter; playwright); Sol Lesser (producer).

Parenthood. 1989. Universal Pictures. Ron Howard (director, screenwriter); Lowell Ganz, Babaloo Mandel (screenwriters); Brian Grazer (producer); Joseph M. Caracciolo Jr. (executive producer); Louisa Velis (associate producer).

Peter Pan. 1953. Walt Disney Productions. Clyde Geronimi, Wilfred Jackson, Hamilton Luske (directors); Milt Banta, William Cottrell, Winston Hibler, Bill Peet, Erdman Pener, Joe Rinaldi, Ted Sears, Ralph Wright (screenwriters); J.M. Barrie (playwright).

Pickwick Papers, The. 1952. Noel Langley (director, screenwriter); Charles Dickens (novelist); Bob McNaught (producer).

Pink Cookies. Taccone, Jorma. Unpublished play by UCLA School of Theater, Film and Television student.

Pippi Longstocking. (*Pippi Långstrump.*) 1997. Swedish. Trickompany/Beta Film/Nelvana Limited/TFC Trickompany GmbH/Iduna Film Productiongesellschaft /Svensk Filmindustri CSF/Téléfilm Canada. Bill Giggie (director, animation); Michael Schaack, Clive A. Smith (directors); Astrid Lindgren (novelist); Frank Nissen, Ken Sobol (additional dialogue); Waldemar Bergendahl, Hasmi Giakoumis, Merle-Anne Ridley (producers); David Ferguson (co-executive producer); Michael Hirsh, Patrick Loubert, Clive A. Smith (executive producers).

Pocahontas. 1995. Walt Disney Productions. Mike Gabriel, Eric Goldberg (directors); Carl Binder, Susannah Grant, Philip LaZebnik (screenwriters); Baker Bloodworth (associate producer); James Pentecost (producer).

Por Quinly Christmas, A. Long, Q. 1996. Unpublished play. Tantleff Agency, 375 Greenwich Street, Ste. 700, NY, NY 10013.

Postman Always Rings Twice, The. 1946. Tay Garnet (director); Niven Busch, Harry Ruskin (screenwriters); James M. Cain (novelist); Carey Wilson (producer).

Prime of Miss Jean Brodie, The. 1969. 20th Century Fox. Ronald Neame (director); Jay Presson Allen (screenwriter, playwright); Muriel Spark (novelist); Robert Fryer (producer).

Prince and the Pauper, The. Walt Disney Productions. George Scriber (director); Mark Twain (novelist); Dan Rounds (producer).

Proposals. Unpublished play by N. Simon.

Rebecca. 1940. Alfred Hitchcock (director); Daphne Du Maurier (novelist); Joan Harrison, Michael Hogan, Philip MacDonald, Robert E. Sherwood (screenwriters); David O. Selznick (producer).

Remains of the Day, The. 1993. Columbia Pictures Corporation/Merchant Ivory Productions. James Ivory (director); Kazuo Ishiguro (novelist); Ruth Prawer Jhabvala (screenwriter); John Calley, Ismail Merchant, Mike Nichols (producers); Paul Bradley (executive producer); Donald Rosenfeld (associate producer).

Rest of My Life, The. 1996. UCLA School of Theater, Film and Television student film by Mark Lawrence.

Richard III. 1995. United Artists/Bayly/Pare. Richard Loncraine (director, screenwriter); Ian McKellen (screenwriter, executive producer);

William Shakespeare (playwright); Maria Apodiacos, Ellen Dinerman Little, Joe Simon (executive producers); Stephen Bayly (producer); David Lascelles (line producer); Mary Richards, Michele Tandy (associate producers).

Schindler's List. 1993. Universal Pictures. Steven Spielberg (director, producer); Thomas Keneally (novelist); Steve Zaillian (screenwriter); Branko Lustig, Gerald R. Molen (producers); Lew Rywin (co-producer); Kathleen Kennedy (executive producer); Irving Glovin, Robert Raymond (associate producers). .

Seagull, The. (*Chaika.*) 1970. Russian. Mosfilm. Yuli Karasik (director, screenwriter); Anton Chekhov (playwright).

Secret Garden, The. 1993. Warner Brothers/American Zoetrope. Agnieszka Holland (director); Frances Hodgson Burnett (novelist); Caroline Thompson (screenwriter, associate producer); Francis Coppola (executive producer); Fred Fuchs, Tom Luddy, Fred Roos (producers).

Secret of Roan Inish, The. 1994. Samuel Goldwyn/First Look Pictures. John Sayles (director, screenwriter); Rosalie K. Fry (novelist); Sarah Green, Maggie Renzi (producers); John Sloss, Peter Newman, Glenn R. Jones (executive producers); R. Paul Miller (associate producer).

Secret Santa. 1995. New York University Tisch School of the Arts student film by Matthew D. Huffman.

Shlemiel the First. Unpublished play. Adapted by R. Brustein from I. B. Singer's play.

Shiloh. 1997. Zeta Entertainment Ltd. Dale Rosenbloom (director, screenwriter, producer); Carl Borack (executive producer); Zane W. Levitt, Mark Yellen (producers).

Shop Around the Corner, The. 1940. MGM. Ernst Lubitsch (director, producer); Ben Hecht (screenwriter, uncredited); Nikolaus Laszlo (author of the play *Parfumerie*); Samson Raphaelson (screenwriter).

Sleepers. 1996. PolyGram Filmed Entertainment/Ascot Elite Entertainment Group/Warner Brothers. Barry Levinson (director, screenwriter, producer); Lorenzo Carcaterra (author of the book, co-producer); Steve Golin (producer); Peter Giuliano (executive producer); Gerrit Van der Meer (associate producer).

Sleepless in Seattle. 1993. TriStar. Nora Ephron (director, screenwriter); Jeff Arch, David S. Ward (screenwriters); Gary Foster (producer); Patrick Crowley, Lynda Obst (executive producers); Jane Bartelme, Delia Ephron, James W. Skotchdopole (associate producers).

Sling Blade. 1996. Shooting Gallery Films/Miramax. Billy Bob Thornton (director and screenwriter); David L. Bushell, Brandon Rosser (producers); Larry Meistrich (executive producer).

Slow Dance. 1997. UCLA School of Theater, Film and Television student film by Carl Pfirman.

Something Is Missing. Staab, J. Unpublished play by Wheelock College faculty member. 200 The Riverway, Boston, MA 02215.

Stage Door. 1937. RKO Radio Pictures. Gregory LaCava (director); Edna Ferber, George S. Kaufman (playwrights); Morrie Ryskind, Anthony Veiller (screenwriters); Pandro S. Berman (producer).

Stationmaster's Wife, The. (Bolweiser.) 1977. West German. Bavaria Atelier. Rainer Werner Fassbinder (director, screenwriter); Oskar Maria Graf (screenwriter); Herbert Knopp (producer).

Steel Magnolias. 1989. TriStar. Herbert Ross (director); Robert Harling (playwright); Ray Stark (producer); Andrew Stone (associate producer); Victoria White (executive producer).

Swingers. 1996. Alfred Shay Company, Inc./Miramax. Doug Liman (director); Jon Farreau (screenwriter, co-producer); Victor Simpkins (producer); Cary Woods (executive producer); Avram Ludwig, Bradford L. Schlei (associate producers); Nicole LaLoggia (line).

Taming of the Shrew, The. 1980. TV. British Broadcasting Corporation/Time-Life Television. Jonathan Miller (director, producer); William Shakespeare (playwright).

To Kill a Mockingbird. 1962. Universal International/Pakula-Mulligan, Brentwood Productions. Robert Mulligan (director); Harper Lee (novelist); Horton Foote (screenwriter); Alan J. Pakula (producer).

To Play the King. 1994. Miniseries. British Broadcasting Corporation. Paul Seed (director); Andrew Davies (screenwriter); Michael Dobbs (novelist); Ken Riddington (producer).

Tom Sawyer. 1995. Walt Disney Productions/Painted Fence Productions. Peter Hewitt (director); Ron Koslow, David Loughery, Stephen Sommers (screenwriters); Mark Twain (novelist); John Baldecchi, Laurence Mark (producers); Barry Bernardi (executive producer).

Tous les Matins du Monde. (All the Mornings of the World). 1991. France. Paravision Int. S.A./D.D. Productions. Alain Corneau (director, screenwriter); Pascal Quignard (screenwriter); Bernard Marescot (producer).

Tumbleweeds, The. Ham, C. Unpublished play by UCLA School of Theater, Film and Television student.

Twelfth Night, or What You Will. 1996. Renaissance Films/Summit Entertainment. Trevor Nunn (director, screenwriter); William Shakespeare (playwright); Mark Cooper (line producer); Stephen Evans, David Parfitt (producers); Ileen Maisel, Greg Smith, Ruth Vitale, Jonathan Weisgal (executive producers).

Uncle Tom's Cabin. 1927. Silent. Universal Pictures (aka MCA/Universal Pictures). Harry A. Pollard (director); Harriet Beecher Stowe (novelist).

Waterland. 1992. United Kingdom. Channel Four Films (aka Film Four International). Stephen Gyllenhaal (director); Graham Swift (novelist); Peter Prince (screenwriter); Patrick Cassavetti, Katy McGuinness (producers); Ira Deutchman, Nik Powell, Stephen Woolley (executive producers).

Wind in the Willows, The. (US video title *Mr. Toad's Wild Ride.*) 1996. Allied Filmmakers. Terry Jones (director, screenwriter); Kenneth Grahame (novelist); Jake Eberts, John Goldstone (producers).

Winnie-the-Pooh. (*The Many Adventures of Winnie The Pooh.*) 1977. Walt Disney Productions. John Lounsbery, Wolfgang Reitherman (directors); Ken Anderson, Xavier Arencio, Ted Berman, Larry Clemmons, Eric Cleworth, Vance Gerry, Winston Hibler, Julius Svendsen (screenwriters); Ralph Wright (story); A.A. Milne (author of the novels); Wolfgang Reitherman (producer).

Winter Sun. Grignon, W. Unpublished screenplay by UCLA School of Theater, Film and Television student.

Wizard of Oz, The. 1939. MGM. George Cukor (director, test scenes, uncredited); Victor Fleming (director); Richard Thorpe (director, original scenes, uncredited); King Vidor (director, Kansas scenes, uncredited); L. Frank Baum (novelist); Noel Langley, Florence Ryerson, Edgar Allan Woolf (screenwriters); Irving Brecher, William H. Cannon, Herbert Fields, Arthur Freed, Jack Haley, E.Y. Harburg, Samuel Hoffenstein, Bert Lahr, John Lee Mahin, Herman J. Mankiewicz, Jack Mintz, Ogden Nash, Sid Silvers (uncredited screenwriters); Mervyn LeRoy (producer).

All inquiries regarding unpublished manuscripts, unreleased films, and unpublished short stories by UCLA School of Theater, Film and Television faculty or students should be directed to: UCLA, School of Theater, Film and Television, 102 East Melnitz, 405 North Hilgard Avenue, Los Angeles, CA 90024-1622.

INDEX

acting technique, improvisation as, xvii
Ah, Wilderness! (O'Neill)
    situation 1: solo moment, 125
    situation 2: relationship, 83–84
Alcott, Louisa May, 24, 100, 142, 196
Allen, Jay Presson, 37
All the Mornings of the World (Quignard),
    155
"American History" (Ortiz-Cofer), 126
Angelou, Maya, 63
Anna Karenina (Tolstoy), 84–85
Anne of Green Gables (Montgomery)
    situation 1: confrontation/conflict, 44–45
    situation 2: subtext, 184–185
    situation 3: solo moment, 126–127
Anouilh, Jean, 219, 220, 221
Antigone (Sophocles)
    situation 1: unusual circumstances,
      210–211
    situation 2: unusual circumstances,
      211–212
Antonioni, Michelangelo, 93
Arc, Joan of, 219, 220, 221
Arch, Jeff, 115
Arens, Nick, 187
Armstrong, Stephanie, 40
Ascianone, W. Gian, 87
The Assignment (Monroy), 45–46
Atkinson, Rowan, 72
Aunt Gail (Sunde), 3–4
Austen, Jane, 96, 97, 193
The Autobiography of My Mother (Kincaid),
    185–186
Avital, Natalie, 87
Awakenings (Zaillian)
    situation 1: climactic moment/discov-
      ery, 4–5
    situation 2: physical/psychological, 161

The Award (Wales), 85–86
The Awful Truth (Delmar, McCarey),
    186–187
Ayvazian, Leslie, 60

Baby (MacLachlan)
    situation 1: unusual circumstances,
      212–213
    situation 2: solo moment, 127–128
    situation 3: relationship, 86
Bach, Trung, 57
background details, in relationship situa-
    tions, 81
Bass, Ronald, 57
"The Bear" (Faulkner), 128
"The Beauty of Passage" (Arens), 187–
    188
Bedside Care (Wales), 5–6
Bethel, Brian C., 115
The Big, Bad World (Avital), 87
La Bionda (The Blonde) (Ascianone,
    Marino, Rubini), 87–88
Birdy (Wharton), 162
The Boiler Room (Gonzalez), 6
Boublil, Alain, 59
Brontë, Charlotte, 19, 168, 194
Brustein, Robert, 225
Bryant, Chris, 98
Burnett, Frances Hodgson, 23
Bushman, Jason, 56
Butler, Octavia E., 140, 195, 218
Byars, Betsy, 108

The Cabin Faced West (Fritz), 162–163
Cadiz, Ryan, 46, 134
Callaghan, Sheila, 97
Camilla (L'Engle)
    situation 1: subtext, 189

situation 2: relationship, 88–89
situation 3: solo moment, 128–129
Carcaterra, Lorenzo, 202
casting practices, xvi
The Cat Ate My Gymsuit (Danziger), 46–47
The Catcher in the Rye (Salinger), 7
Changes of Heart (de Marivaux)
  situation 1: subtext, 189–190
  situation 2: climactic moment/discovery, 7–8
Chekov, Anton, 114
Chikamatsu, Monzaemon, 151–152, 226
Childhood (Wilder), 89–90
The Children's Hour (Hellman), 8–9
Childress, Alice, 69
Chopin, Kate, 10, 132, 153
Christmas Eve with the Trumans (Truman), 47–48
Chronicle of a Death Foretold (Márquez), 213–214
Cidre, Cynthia, 25, 24
Cisneros, Sandra, 137, 152
City Hall (Lipper, Pileggi, Schrader, Goldman), 129–130
Clay, Rita, 135
climactic moment/discovery, 1
  ensemble
    Fools Rush In, 14–15
    The Grapes of Wrath, 16–17
    Jane Eyre, 19–20
    "Manila House," 26–27
    The Matsuyama Mirror, 27–29
    The Moon by Night, 29–31
    Newcomer, 31–32
    Nightjohn, 32
  one male, one female
    Awakenings, 4–5
    The Boiler Room, 6
    The Catcher in the Rye, 7
    Changes of Heart, 7–8
    "Desiree's Baby," 10–11
    The Diary of Anne Frank, 11–12
    The First Kiss, 12–13
    First Possession, 13–14
    God Would Be Rich, 15–16
    Journey Home, 20–21
    The Kentucky Cycle-Part One, 21
    The Language of Flowers, 21–22
    A Little Princess, 23
    The Mambo Kings, 25–26

The Odyssey, 33–34
The Pickwick Papers, 35–36
Pink Cookies, 36–37
Rebecca, 38–39
The Rest of My Life, 39–40
Waterland, 41
two females
  Aunt Gail, 3–4
  Bedside Care, 5–6
  The Children's Hour, 8–9
  Little Women, 24
  Parenthood, 35
  The Prime of Miss Jean Brodie, 37–38
  The Story, 40
two males
  Great Expectations, 17–18
  Inventing the Abbotts, 18–19
  The Mambo Kings, 24–25
  The Odyssey, 33
Climbing Fences (Lawrence), 90–91
The Colonel and His Son, 10
The Color Purple (Walker)
  situation 1: subtext, 190–191
  situation 2: solo moment, 130–131
conflict, understanding, xviii
confrontation/conflict, 42
  ensemble
    Dead Poets Society, 48–49
    Death and the Maiden, 50–51
    Nine Armenians, 60–61
    Scorpions, 63–64
    The Slave, 64–65
    To Kill A Mockingbird, 66–67
  one male, one female
    Anne of Green Gables, 44–45
    Christmas Eve with the Trumans, 47–48
    "Dénouement," 52
    The Godfather Part III, 55–56
    Peer Pressure, 62
    The Wedding, 68–69
  two females
    The Assignment, 45–46
    The Cat Ate My Gymsuit, 46–47
    Eating with Jude, 53–54
    "Footnote to a Laundry List," 54–55
    The Joy Luck Club, 57–58
    Miss Saigon, 59–60
    "The Reunion," 63
    Steel Magnolias, 65–66
    Vilma Martinez, 67–68
    Wedding Band, 69–70

two males
  The Deadly Crush, 49–50
  Dreaming of Rope Ladders, 53
  Henry IV, 56–57
  Langston Hughes: Poet of the People,
    58–59
  "The Old Chief Mshlanga," 61
Convicts (Foote), 91–92
Coppola, Francis, 55
Cores, Lucy, 164
"A Couple of Kooks" (Rylant), 92–93
*Cronaca di un Amore (The Story of a Love
  Affair)* (Antonioni, D'Anza,
  Giovannetti, Maselli, Tellini), 93–94
"A Crush" (Rylant), 163–164
Curtis, Richard, 72

D'Anza, Daniele, 93
Danziger, Paula, 46
A Dark-Adapted Eye (Vine), 131
Davies, Andrew, 204
The Deadly Crush (Monroy), 49–50
Dead Man Walking (Robbins), 191–192
Dead Poets Society (Schulman)
  situation 1: relationship, 94–95
  situation 2: solo moment, 132
  situation 3: confrontation/conflict, 48–
    49
Death and the Maiden (Dorfman), 50–51
de la Pena, Adam, 72, 156
Delmar, Vina, 186
de Marivaux, Pierre Carlet de Chamblain,
  7, 189
"Dénouement" (Rosenberg), 52
"Desiree's Baby" (Chopin)
  situation 1: climactic moment/discovery,
    10–11
  situation 2: solo moment, 132–133
dialogue
  determining meaning of, ix
  inner, 183
The Diary of Anne Frank (Goodrich,
  Hackett)
  situation 1: subtext, 192–193
  situation 2: climactic moment/discov-
    ery, 11–12
  situation 3: solo moment, 133–134
Dickens, Charles, 17, 35
Dinner Theatre (Cadiz), 134–135
discovery. *See* climactic moment/discovery
Dobbs, Michael, 204

A Doctor in Spite of Himself (Harris), 214–
  215
Dorfman, Ariel, 50
Dorris, Michael, 120, 157
Douglass, Frederick, 135
Dreaming of Rope Ladders (Long)
  situation 1: relationship, 95–96
  situation 2: confrontation/conflict, 53
Du Maurier, Daphne, 38, 148, 149

Eating with Jude (Kelly), 53–54
Edgar, David, 98
Elerick, John, 84
Elton, Ben, 72
Emma (Austen)
  situation 1: subtext, 193–194
  situation 2: relationship, 96–97
  situation 3: relationship, 97
Ephron, Nora, 115
Epiphany (Cores), 164–165
*Escape From Slavery: The Boyhood of
  Frederick Douglass in His Own Words*
  (Douglass), 135

fantasy situations, 71–72
  ensemble, *A Midsummer Night's
    Dream,* 77–78
  one male, one female
    *The Infernal Interdimensional Experi-
      ments of Doctor McFee,* 75–76
    Liliom, 76–77
    Shakuntala, 78–79
    *The Tragedy of Tragedies, or The Life
      and Death of Tom Thumb the Great,* 79
  two females, *Fatal Beatings,* 72–73
  two males
    Fatal Beatings, 72–73
    The Giver, 73–74
Fassbinder, Rainer Werner, 152
Fatal Beatings (Curtis, Atkinson, Elton),
  72–73
Faulkner, William, 128
Feiffer, Jules, 102, 103
Ferber, Edna, 203
Fereira, Tyler, 199
Fielding, Henry, 79
Fincioen, Joke, 141
First Dance (Clay), 135–136
The First Kiss (Lopez), 12–13
First Possession (Vernon), 13–14
The Fisher King (LaGravenese), 136–137

Fools Rush In (Reback), 14–15
Foote, Horton, 91
"Footnote to a Laundry List" (Santos),
   54–55
The Foreigner (Shue), 165–166
Frank, Anne, 11, 133, 192–193
Fritz, Jean, 162
Fugard, Athol, 118

Galati, Frank, 16
Gallico, Paul, 144
Ganz, Lowell, 35
"Geraldo No Last Name" (Cisneros),
   137–138
Gibson, William, 143
Giovannetti, Sylvio, 93
The Giver (Lowry), 73–74
The Godfather Part III (Coppola, Puzo),
   55–56
God Would Be Rich (Maley)
   situation 1: unusual circumstances,
     215–216
   situation 2: climactic moment/discov-
     ery, 15–16
Going After Cacciato (O'Brien)
   situation 1: unusual circumstances,
     216–217
   situation 2: solo moment, 138
   situation 3: special problems, 166–167
Goldman, Bo, 129
Gonzalez, Reuben, 6
Goodrich, Frances, 11, 133, 192
Graf, Oskar Maria, 152
The Grapes of Wrath (Galati), 16–17
Great Expectations (Dickens), 17–18
Grignon, William H., 180
Gulmatico, Marie, 59
Gurney, A.R., 177
Gustave III, ou Le Bal Masque (Scribe),
   197–198

Hackett, Albert, 11, 133, 192
Ham, Christina, 178, 179
Hanggi, Kristin, 191
Harling, Robert, 65
Harris, Aurand, 108, 214
Hellman, Lillian, 8, 219, 220, 221
Henry IV (Shakespeare), 56–57
Hixon, Ken, 18
Homer, 33
The House on Mango Street (Cisneros),
   137–138, 152–153

Houston, Velina Hasu, 27, 28
Howard, Ron, 35
Hughes, Langston, 58-59
Hugo, Victor, 106
The Hunger Waltz (Callaghan), 97–98

imaginary circumstances, xvii
imagination, fantasy situations and, 71
"Immigration Blues" (Santos), 167–168
improvisation
   as acting technique, xvii
   background, xvii
   definitions of, ix–xi
   history of, xv
   physical actions and, xviii
   psychology of, xviii
*The Infernal Interdimensional Experiments
   of Doctor McFee* (Tornado), 75–76
inner dialogue, 183
intergenerational theatre, xvi
In the Cemetary (Sanger), 139
Inventing the Abbotts (Hixon), 18–19
Ishiguro, Kazuo, 200

Jane Eyre (Brontë)
   situation 1: subtext, 194–195
   situation 2: climactic moment/discov-
     ery, 19–20
   situation 3: special problems, 168–169
Jhabvala, Ruth Prawer, 200
Joan of Arc, 219, 220, 221
Jones, LeRoi, 64
Journey Home (Uchida), 20–21
The Journey of the Fifth Horse (Ribman),
   139–140
The Joy Luck Club (Bass, Tan), 57–58

Kalidasa, 78
Kaufman, George S., 203
Kelly, Anne, 53
Keneally, Thomas, 224
The Kentucky Cycle–Part One (Schenkkan)
   situation 1: unusual circumstances,
     217–218
   situation 2: special problems, 169–170
   situation 3: climactic moment/discov-
     ery, 21
The Killer (Woo), 170–171
Kincaid, Jamaica, 185
Kindred (Butler)
   situation 1: solo moment, 140–141
   situation 2: subtext, 195–196

situation 3: unusual circumstances, 218–219
Kinsky, Nikolai, 7
Kosoff, Susan, 23

Lady Jane (Edgar, Bryant), 98–99
Laffner, JulieAnna, 145
LaGravenese, Richard, 136
Langston Hughes: Poet of the People (Satchell), 58–59
The Language of Flowers (Villarreal)
 situation 1: relationship, 99–100
 situation 2: climactic moment/discovery, 21–22
The Lark (Anouilh)
 situation 1: unusual circumstances, 219–220
 situation 2: unusual circumstances, 220
 situation 3: unusual circumstances, 221
Laszlo, Nikolaus, 201
Lawrence, Mark, 39, 90, 111
Lee, Harper, 66
L'Engle, Madeleine, 29, 30, 128, 144, 189
Les Misérables (Hugo), 106–107
Lessing, Doris, 61, 154
Levinson, Barry, 202
Lewis, Elizabeth Foreman, 227
Life (Fincioen), 141–142
Liliom (Molnar), 76–77
Lipper, Ken, 129
A Little Princess (Kosoff, Staab), 23
Little Women (Alcott)
 situation 1: climatic moment/discovery, 24
 situation 2: relationship, 100–101
 situation 3: solo moment, 142
 situation 4: subtext, 196–197
Long, Jason Sinclair, 53, 95
Lopez, Anel, 12
love, in relationship situations, 81
Lowry, Lois, 73
Lucas, Amy, 115

McCarey, Leo, 186
McCurdey, Michael, 135
Machinal, Episode Three: Honeymoon (Treadwell), 101–102
MacLachlan, Patricia, 86, 127, 212
Maeterlinck, Maurice, 147, 172
Maley, Helen, 15, 215
The Mambo Kings (Cidre)

situation 1: climactic moment/discovery, 24–25
situation 2: climactic moment/discovery, 25–26
"Manila House" (Santos), 26–27
The Man in the Ceiling (Feiffer)
 situation 1: relationship, 102–103
 situation 2: relationship, 103–104
Marino, Umberto, 87
Márquez, Gabriel García, 213
Martinez, Vilma, 67
"Masculine Protest" (O'Connor)
 situation 1: relationship, 104–105
 situation 2: solo moment, 142–143
 situation 3: relationship, 105
Maselli, Francesco, 93
A Masked Ball (Scribe), 197–198
Masters, Tess, 8
The Matsuyama Mirror (Houston)
 situation 1: climactic moment/discovery, 27–28
 situation 2: climactic moment/discovery, 28–29
Men, Myths, and Dogs (Pringle), 106
A Midsummer Night's Dream (Shakespeare), 77–78
Miller, Sue, 18
The Miracle Worker (Gibson), 143–144
Miss Saigon (Boublil, Schönberg), 59–60
Molière, 214
Molnar, Ferenc, 76
Monroy, Evangeline, 45, 49
Montgomery, L.M., 44, 126, 184
The Moon by Night (L'Engle)
 situation 1: climactic moment/discovery, 29–30
 situation 2: climactic moment/discovery, 30–31
 situation 3: solo moment, 144
Mrs. 'Arris Goes to Paris (Gallico), 144–145
Much Ado About Nothing (Shakespeare), 198–199
multicultural theatre, xvi
Myers, Walter Dean, 63, 113, 150

The New Car (Laffner), 145–146
Newcomer (Thomas), 31–32
"The New Dress" (Woolf), 146–147
Nightjohn (Paulsen)
 situation 1: climactic moment/discovery, 32

situation 2: solo moment, 147
Nine Armenians (Ayvazian), 60–61

O'Brien, Tim, 138, 166, 216
obstacles, overcoming, 159
O'Connor, Frank, 104, 105, 143, 142
The Odyssey (Homer)
   situation 1: climactic moment/discovery, 33
   situation 2: climactic moment/discovery, 33–34
Of Mice and Men (Steinbeck), 171–172
"The Old Chief Mshlanga" (Lessing), 61
O'Neill, Eugene, 83, 125
Ortiz-Cofer, Judith, 126
Our Town (Wilder), 107–108

Parenthood (Howard), 35
Paulsen, Gary, 32, 147
The Pearl (Steinbeck)
   situation 1: unusual circumstances, 221–222
   situation 2: unusual circumstances, 222–223
Peer Pressure (Thiel), 62
Péllèas and Mélisande (Maeterlinck)
   situation 1: special problems, 172–173
   situation 2: solo moment, 147–148
physical actions, understanding, xviii
physical/psychological situations, 159–160
   ensemble
      "Immigration Blues," 167–168
      Jane Eyre, 168–169
      Sylvia, 177–178
   one male, "A Crush," 163–164
   one male, one female
      Awakenings, 161
      The Cabin Faced West, 162–163
      Epiphany, 164–165
      The Kentucky Cycle–Part One, 169–170
      The Killer, 170–171
      The Report Card, 173–174
      Richard III, 174–175
      The Tumbleweeds, 179–180
   two females, *The Tumbleweeds,* 178–179
   two males
      Birdy, 162
      The Foreigner, 165–166
      Going After Cacciato, 166–167
      Of Mice and Men, 171–172

Péllèas and Mélisande, 172–173
Sling Blade, 175–176, 176–177
Winter Sun, 180–181
Pileggi, Nicholas, 129
The Pinballs (Harris), 108–109
Pink Cookies (Taccone), 36–37
Poeter, Damon, 75
The Posthumous Papers of the Pickwick Club (Dickens), 35–36
Prejean, Sister Helen, 191
preparation, x, 123
The Prime of Miss Jean Brodie (Allen), 37–38
Prince, Peter, 41
Pringle, Anthony, 106
problems, special. *See* physical/psychological situations
Proposals (Simon)
   situation 1: relationship, 109–110
   situation 2: relationship, 110
   situation 3: relationship, 110–111
Puzo, Mario, 55

Quignard, Pascal, 155

Raphaelson, Samson, 201
Reback, Katherine, 14
Rebecca (Du Maurier)
   situation 1: solo moment, 148–149
   situation 2: solo moment, 149–150
   situation 3: climactic moment/discovery, 38–39
Recess (Fereira), 199–200
relationship situations, 81–83
   ensemble
      Childhood, 89–90
      Climbing Fences, 90–91
      Dreaming of Rope Ladders, 95–96
      Scorpions, 113–114
      A Yellow Raft in Blue Water, 120–121
   one male, one female
      Ah, Wilderness!, 83–84
      Anna Karenina, 84–85
      The Big, Bad World, 87
      La Bionda (The Blonde), 87–88
      Camilla, 88–89
      "A Couple of Kooks," 92–93
      Cronaca di un Amore (The Story of a Love Affair), 93–94
      Emma, 96–97
      The Hunger Waltz, 97–98

Lady Jane, 98–99
The Language of Flowers, 99–100
Les Misérables, 106–107
Little Women, 100–101
Machinal, Episode Three: Honeymoon, 101–102
The Man in the Ceiling, 103–104
"Masculine Protest," 104–105
Our Town, 107–108
Proposals, 109–110, 110
Return Engagements, 112–113
The Seagull, 114
Sleepless in Seattle, 115
Starting Over, 115–116
The Taming of the Shrew, 117–118
Valley Song, 118–119
three females
   A Yellow Raft in Blue Water, 121
two females
   The Award, 85–86
   Baby, 86
   Emma, 97
   Proposals, 110–111
   The Rest of My Life, 111–112
   The Wedding, 119–120
   A Yellow Raft in Blue Water, 120
two males
   Convicts, 91–92
   Dead Poets Society, 94–95
   The Man in the Ceiling, 102–103
   "Masculine Protest," 105
   Men, Myths, and Dogs, 106
   The Pinballs, 108–109
   Swingers, 116–117
The Remains of the Day (Jhabvala), 200
The Report Card (Rosenthal), 173–174
research, of unusual characters, 159–160
The Rest of My Life (Lawrence)
   situation 1: climactic moment/discovery, 39–40
   situation 2: relationship, 111–112
Return Engagements (Slade), 112–113
"The Reunion" (Angelou), 63
Ribman, Ronald, 139
Richard III (Shakespeare), 174–175
Richman, Arthur, 186
Robbins, Tim, 191
Rosenberg, Jeff, 52
Rosenthal, Jonathan Sayres, 173
Rubini, Sergio, 87
Rylant, Cynthia, 92, 163

Sacks, Oliver, 4, 161
Salinger, J.D., 7
Sanger, Margaret, 139
Santos, Bienvenido N., 26, 54, 167
Satchell, Mary, 58
Schenkkan, Robert, 21, 169, 217
Schindler's List (Zaillian), 224–225
Schönberg, Claude-Michel, 59
Schrader, Paul, 129
Schulman, Tom, 48, 94, 132
Scorpions (Myers)
   situation 1: confrontation/conflict, 63–64
   situation 2: solo moment, 150–151
   situation 3: relationship, 113–114
Scribe, Eugene, 197
The Seagull (Chekov), 114
Shakespeare, William, 56, 76, 117, 174, 198, 205, 228
Shakuntala (Kalidasa), 78–79
The Shepherds of Saint Francis (Swortzell), 223–224
Shlemiel the First, 225–226
The Shop Around the Corner (Raphaelson), 201–202
Shue, Larry, 165
Shunkan Heike Nyogo No Shima (Chikamatsu)
   situation 1: unusual circumstances, 226–227
   situation 2: solo moment, 151–152
Simon, Neil, 109, 110
Singer, Isaac Bashevis, 225
"Sire" (Cisneros), 152
Slade, Bernard, 112
The Slave (Jones), 64–65
Sleepers (Levinson), 202–203
Sleepless in Seattle (Ephron, Ward, Arch), 115
Sling Blade (Thornton), 176–177
   situation 1: special problems, 175–176
   situation 2: special problems, 176–177
solo moment situations/soliloquies, 123–124
one female
   Anne of Green Gables, 126–127
   Baby, 127–128
   Camilla, 128–129
   The Color Purple, 130–131
   A Dark-Adapted Eye, 131
   The Diary of Anne Frank, 133–134

First Dance, 135–136
In the Cemetary, 139
Life, 141–142
Little Women, 142
The Miracle Worker, 143–144
The Moon by Night, 144
Mrs. 'Arris Goes to Paris, 144–145
The New Car, 145–146
"The New Dress," 146–147
Nightjohn, 147
Rebecca, 148–149, 149–150
"Sire," 152
"The Story of an Hour," 153–154
Tous les Matins du Monde (All the Mornings of the World), 155
The Wedding, 156–157
A Yellow Raft in Blue Water, 157–158
one male
Ah, Wilderness!, 125
"American History," 126
"The Bear," 128
City Hall, 129–130
Dead Poets Society, 132
"Desiree's Baby," 132–133
Dinner Theatre, 134–135
Escape From Slavery: The Boyhood of Frederick Douglass in His Own Words, 135
The Fisher King, 136–137
Going After Cacciato, 138
The Journey of the Fifth Horse, 139–140
"Masculine Protest," 142–143
The New Car, 145–146
Péllèas and Mélisande, 147–148
Scorpions, 150–151
Shunkan Heike Nyogo No Shima, 151–152
The Stationmaster's Wife, 152–153
"A Sunrise on the Veld," 154–155
The Tragedy of the 1996 Mount Everest Expedition, 156
Sophocles, 210, 211
Spark, Muriel, 37
Staab, Jane, 23
Stage Door (Ferber, Kaufman), 203–204
Starting Over (Lucas), 115–116
The Stationmaster's Wife (Fassbinder), 152–153
Steel Magnolias (Harling), 65–66
Steinbeck, John, 16, 171, 221, 222

The Story (Armstrong), 40
The Story of a Love Affair (Antonioni, D'Anza, Giovannetti, Maselli, Tellini), 93–94
"The Story of an Hour" (Chopin), 153–154
Stowe, Harriet Beecher, 229
subtext situations, 183
    ensemble
        Anne of Green Gables, 184–185
        The Awful Truth, 186–187
        The Color Purple, 190–191
        A Masked Ball, 197–198
    one male, one female
        Camilla, 189
        Dead Man Walking, 191–192
        The Diary of Anne Frank, 192–193
        Jane Eyre, 194–195
        Little Women, 196–197
        Much Ado About Nothing, 198–199
        The Remains of the Day, 200
        The Shop Around the Corner, 201–202
        To Play the King, 204–205
        Twelfth Night, 205–206
    two females
        The Autobiography of My Mother, 185–186
        Changes of Heart, 189–190
        Emma, 193–194
        Kindred, 195–196
        Little Women, 196–197
        Recess, 199–200
        Stage Door, 203–204
        The Wedding, 206–207
    two males
        "The Beauty of Passage," 187–188
        Sleepers, 202–203
Sunde, Sam, 3
"A Sunrise on the Veld" (Lessing), 154–155
Swift, Graham, 41
Swingers (Farreau), 116–117
Swortzell, Lowell, 223
Sylvia (Gurney), 177–178

Taccone, Jorma, 36
Tager, Kelli, 126
The Taming of the Shrew (Shakespeare), 117–118
Tan, Amy, 57